PROGRAMMING THE USER INTERFACE PRINCIPLES AND EXAMPLES

Judith R. Brown
The University of Iowa

Steve Cunningham
California State University, Stanislaus

WILEY

JOHN WILEY & SONS
New York • **Chichester** • **Brisbane** • **Toronto** • **Singapore**

Library of Congress Cataloging in Publication Data:

Brown, Judith R. (Judith Richmond)
  Programming the user interface.

  Bibliography: p.
  Includes index.
    1. Electronic digital computers—Programming.
  2. User interfaces-(Computer systems) I. Cunningham,
  Steve. II. Title.
  QA76.6.B763 1989   005.1   88-33941
  ISBN 0-471-63843-9

Printed in the United States of America

10 9 8 7 6 5 4 3 2 1

93   11912

To our children:

Randy and Deanne Brown
Rob and Rick Cunningham

Trademarks

This book uses a number of names which are trademarks of various corporations. In this section we give the appropriate credits.

Paradox is a trademark of Adapta Software, Inc.
PostScript and Display PostScript are registered trademarks of Adobe Systems.
Aldus PageMaker is a trademark of Aldus.
Apollo and Open Dialogue are trademarks of Apollo Computer.
Apple is a registered trademak of Apple Computer, Inc.
A/UX, HyperCard, HyperTalk, Lisa, MacApp, Macintosh, Macintosh Programmers
    Workshop, MPW, are trademarks of Apple Computer, Inc.
dBASE,dBASE II, dBASE III, dBASE III Plus, and dBASE IV are trademarks of Ashton-Tate
    Corporation.
Unix and Open Look are trademarks of AT&T.
AutoCAD is a trademark of AutoDesk.
Tell-a-Graf is a trademark of CA/ISSCO.
AppleWorks is a registered trademark of Apple Computer, Inc. licensed to Claris
    Corporation.
 MacDraw, and MacWrite are registered trademarks of Claris, Inc.
Amiga is a trademark of Commodore.
Algebra Drill and Practice I and Discovery Learning in Trigonometry are copyright by
    CONDUIT.
PLATO is a trademark of Control Data Corporation.
MPE and NewWave are trademarks of Hewlett-Packard Corp.
IBM, IBM PC, IBM PS/2, and IBM 3101 are trademarks of International Business Machines.
DataShow is a trademark of Kodak.
VoiceEM and VoiceRAD are trademarks of Kurzweil.
Lotus and 1-2-3 are registered trademarks of Lotus Development Corporation.
WordStar is a trademark of MicroPro.
Microsoft and MS-DOS are trademarks of Microsoft Corporation.
The X Window System is a trademark of MIT.
Writehander is a trademark of the NewO Company.
p-System is a trademark of Pecan Software Systems.
Headmaster and ScreenTyper are trademarks of Personics Corp.
PRIMOS is a trademark of Prime Computer.
NeWS and Sun are trademarks of Sun Microsystems.
MacPascal is a trademark of Symantec.
Versabraille II+ is a trademark of Telesensory Systems, Inc.
UTek and Tektronix 4010 are trademarks of Tektronix.
iCpak, Software-IC, and Objective-C are trademarks of The Stepstone Corp.
DataGlove and DataSuit are trademarks of VPL Research.
Lyon Large Print is a trademark of VTEK.
Mirage is a trademark of Zenographics.

TABLE OF CONTENTS

Preface

This book is an introduction to the issues and opportunities in user interface programming. It is intended to help programmers, especially programmers who work without strong user interface support, to get started in the area. Our orientation is practical. We are familiar with the research literature and studies in user interfaces and have used this literature in preparing this book, but we are addressing how to get actual user interface code written.

If the reader is a working programmer, the code sketches and working functions or procedures may be the most immediately interesting aspect of the book. These have either been tested directly in our own environments or have come from trusted sources in the computer industry. In all cases, our designs and code are starting points for developing your set of user interface tools for your own programming. Space limitations and the need for a general approach mean that our examples are far from industrial-strength code.

A user interface is much more than a collection of code objects. It is your way of ensuring that your user can work effectively with your software. Our description of user interface issues and statements of user interface principles come from our readings in the research literature and our observations as reviewers, consultants, teachers, and software consumers. The software environment is mature enough that software without careful interface design cannot be either useful or successful.

If the reader is a student, the book should be viewed as an introduction to what a software user interface does and how it can be constructed, from both the design and implementation viewpoints. We hope the examples show that there is no magic that dedicated programming cannot master in implementing a good user interface. This is especially true now that real user interface software support is becoming available. We introduce some of these user interface and window management tools in this book.

This book includes an appendix containing projects for most of the chapters. These projects are a way of extending the chapters' discussions in a very practical way. The programmer can use them as suggestions for further development or thinking, while they can be used as actual course work if the book is used as a text.

How did we come to write this book? At the 1986 ACM SIGGRAPH conference we were talking about educational software generally, and in particular about how awkwardly so much of it communicates with students. One of us said that someone should write a book to help these software authors do a better job, the other said that we could do that, and the conversation moved on to other things. About a month later, a short outline appeared with the comment, "What do you think of this?" This book project followed, thanks largely to the vision of our editor, Diane Cerra of Wiley & Sons Publishers.

This book bears a certain resemblance to that original outline but has changed as we got closer and closer to the subject. It has grown to include experimental interfaces and user interface management systems, both of which are important to the future of user interfaces and some of which were not yet announced when we began. It uses the C language for most of its coded examples because C, used simply, can express algorithms in a way that translates easily to other languages. It also seems that C is the most widely used language for major interactive software and interface work.

The authors owe a great deal of thanks to a number of people who have given us help and encouragement. Our thanks go to our families, for their support and encouragement; to Sara Bly (Xerox PARC), Jon Meads (Bell Northern Research), and David Sealey (The University of Iowa), for their encouragement, reading, and support; and our students Mike Elness, Jason Fox, and Chuck Quittmeyer at California State University, Stanislaus for their work on drafts of algorithms presented here. Many others contributed examples of their work for our inclusion, and their contributions are noted with their work; we are grateful for their support.

JUDITH R. BROWN
STEVE CUNNINGHAM

Iowa City, Iowa
Turlock, California
April 1989

## Chapter 1

INTRODUCTION

Today everyone seems to be using computers. Anyone engaged in any kind of information work, such as writing, printing, mailing, ordering, billing, budgeting, planning, or recording, will most likely use a computer regularly and may well have one on his or her desk. The days are gone when using a computer meant that you were a technical whiz. Everyone is a computer user or potential user, and average people have developed a fairly sophisticated outlook on what they want from computers.

Before personal computers, most programs were custom-built and required special training and skills to use. It was easier to train users than to do the extra work to build software that worked naturally with the user. User interface quality became an issue with the widespread use of personal computers. Beginning in the mid-1970's, the personal computer software market has grown to be billions of dollars annually. This generates revenue to support the cost of user interface development and also the competitive environment in which a program's user interface distinguishes it from other software for the same task.

The computer consumer is now very conscious of user interface quality and looks for it when evaluating software. To achieve any kind of acceptance, a program must help its user achieve a task. To have a major marketing success, a program must do this in a way that magnifies the user's skills and contributes to the user's success. A good user interface contributes a great deal to a program's acceptance and success.

As you write your programs with the user in mind, one of the most important things to remember is that nobody wants to use your program just for the sake of using it. They want to accomplish some task, and they may be willing (or be convinced) to use a computer to do so; but the task is what matters, not the computer and the program. Your job is to make the

1

computer and program as invisible as possible so the user can get on with the job.

This book is intended to help programmers implement good user interfaces. It is not really about the design of these interfaces, though we do talk about properties of good design. Rather, it is about making user interface techniques work to implement a good design.

1.1 An Example of an Interactive System

Our discussions of individual functions for the user interface in later chapters include a number of examples of software products. Here we look at one system, identify its various modes of operation, and talk about what each one means.

The system we describe is Lotus 1-2-3 (henceforth referred to as 1-2-3) from the Lotus Development Corporation, which runs on the IBM PC and other MS-DOS computers. Our discussion is limited to a selection of examples of different functions and how each is presented to and interacts with the user.

Lotus 1-2-3 is a financial modeling and budgeting program, commonly known as an electronic spreadsheet. Simply put, it presents a two-dimensional array of cells, each of which can hold text (a label), a number (a value), or an expression involving math functions and operations, constants, or the values in other cells (a formula). When a formula is written in a cell, the value of that formula is computed and displayed in the cell immediately; whenever a cell's value is changed, every cell that uses that value is also changed to reflect the changed value in the original cell. Figure 1.1 shows a 1-2-3 screen with a few cells filled in showing some simple calculations.

Note how this screen is laid out in several areas: command menu area, working cells, current cell address, and cell input area. In Chapters 5, 6, and 7 we discuss the function of special screen areas and show how to implement them.

The fundamental operation in 1-2-3 is moving around the spreadsheet and entering values in cells. This uses the cursor control keys to move horizontally or vertically among cells, highlighting the selected cells with inverse video or color, depending on the display present. This gives the user a direct manipulation access to the spreadsheet. When a value, label, or formula is entered, it is echoed in the input field above the cells. When the entry is completed, the cell's numeric value, text, or formula value is written immediately in the selected cell, and all other cells that depend on this value have their own values recomputed. Since this is done almost instantly, the user gets excellent feedback on his operation and has control of the spreadsheet at all times. We describe how to handle this kind of input and display in Chapter 5.

```
B7:
Worksheet Range Copy Move File Print Graph Data System Quit        MENU
Global, Insert, Delete, Column, Erase, Titles, Window, Status, Page
         A       B       C       D       E       F       G       H
 1
 2     First           125
 3     Second            8
 4
 5     Sum             133
 6
 7     Product        1000
 8
 9
10
11
12
13
14
15
16
17
18
19
20
```

Figure 1.1 *A routine 1-2-3 screen*

Copyright 1985, Lotus Development Corporation

There are a number of other operations that can be done on the spreadsheet besides entering things in cells. Rows or columns can be deleted or inserted. Portions of the spreadsheet can have their contents formatted (labels can be centered or left or right justified, values can be written with a specified number of decimal places or with a $ sign, and so on). Values or formulas can be copied within the spreadsheet. Spreadsheet files can be saved or loaded. This is all managed through the menu area at the top of the screen. In fact, 1-2-3 has a very good multilevel menu which allows novices to use cursor keys to choose an operation (using recognition memory) or experienced users to type command letters with type-ahead for greater speed (using recall memory). We describe how to write such menu systems in Chapter 3.

To show how the menu system works, the parts of Figure 1.2 show the use of a 1-2-3 menu in three steps to format a row of figures so as to have a $ sign and two decimal places. This same effect could have been achieved by simply typing /RFC as the command and then specifying the row as a range.

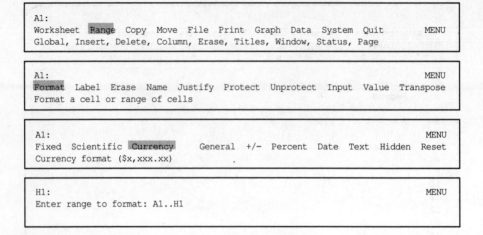

```
A1:
Worksheet  Range  Copy  Move  File  Print  Graph  Data  System  Quit        MENU
Global, Insert, Delete, Column, Erase, Titles, Window, Status, Page
```

```
A1:                                                                         MENU
Format  Label  Erase  Name  Justify  Protect  Unprotect  Input  Value  Transpose
Format a cell or range of cells
```

```
A1:                                                                         MENU
Fixed  Scientific  Currency      General  +/-  Percent  Date  Text  Hidden  Reset
Currency format ($x,xxx.xx)                      .
```

```
H1:                                                                         MENU
Enter range to format: A1..H1
```

Figure 1.2 *Formatting a row in 1-2-3*

Copyright 1985, Lotus Development Corporation

Lotus 1-2-3 has an extensive help system. At any point in the program, a user may ask for help by pressing the F1 function key, and the working cells are replaced by a text describing the effects of the currently-selected option in the menu line. Although the language is often quite spreadsheet-specific, the help information can even serve as a small tutorial on the program. Examples and a more complete discussion of help facilities are found in Chapter 12.

Errors are handled quite well in 1-2-3. File errors are handled by the operating system, but the program does not crash if a nonexistent file is requested; the system error message is simply passed to the user. Computation errors are well isolated. If an illegal function is entered or a computation cannot be completed, for example if a cell containing a label is used or if a division by zero is attempted, the cell containing the computation is given an error value and ERR is displayed in the cell. All cells that use this cell's value also get the error value and the ERR display. The program does not crash and error-free cells are not affected. When the cell is corrected (all cells can be edited) its value is shown and those cells using this value are recomputed. We discuss error handling in Chapter 13.

1.2 Interactive System Design

This book is not about the design of interactive systems, but about how to implement many of the standard features of interactive programs. This book is written for programmers and is intended to further their development in the areas of interactive techniques. Interface design itself is best given to user interface specialists, because it requires technical skills in dealing with people and understanding how they perceive and accomplish work. Programmers do not have a good track record on user interface design because their education is in how computers, not humans, accomplish work.

Ideally, perhaps, software design is accomplished by teams. Application and cognitive user specialists work on understanding the users' tasks and how users think about doing them. This is then translated into interaction and screen designs and specifications for what the user is to do and how the computer is to respond, and the programmer is asked to make it work. Occasionally a single individual will have the knowledge or intuition to understand how the user works with tasks and will have the programming skill to make it work, but this is very rare.

The overall design of a piece of software, then, has several components. The task itself must be defined and implemented up to the level of its input and output; this can often be done separately from the user interface. The user interface must be designed to provide inputs from the user to the task and interpret its output to the user; this may also be done separately. Of course, both task and interface must be done well and must be compatible, because a good user interface will not save poor task support just as a poor interface can make an otherwise good product unacceptable.

The user interface component of software usually takes a fairly standard path. The first phase is to learn how the user thinks of the task and how he or she expects the work to be done. In conjunction with application specialists, this may involve user interviews or any of a number of information-gathering or experiment techniques. The goal of this phase is a solid model of the user and how he or she works on the task as well as a metaphor for the task's function on the computer. This model is used to support the way the software implements the task internally as well as how the interface is built.

The second phase is to build prototypes of the user interface and have users work with these prototypes in an effort to find out what users respond to best. It is important to involve a graphic designer at this phase to make sure the interface implements sound graphic communication between the user and your software. Each prototype is built to support the user/task model, but each does so differently. These prototype tests are made with a variety of users in a variety of environments, and the most successful is chosen and refined to produce the final interface.

As we develop various parts of the user interface and techniques for communicating with users, we spend some time talking about what makes an interface useful as well as how to implement these techniques. If you want to get into the design aspect more deeply you should read in the literature of user interface design; we give some examples of this literature at the end of this chapter. Our goal in describing good interfaces and in presenting principles of interface design is to make it easier for the programmer (presumably you) and the designer (the person who is asking you to make the computer do impossible things) to work together. Bruce Tognazzini of Apple Computer has been quoted as saying that an interface designer spends 87% of his time fighting off programmers; we want to reduce this figure.

If you are a programmer working on software without the support of a designer or interface design team, remember that your own intuition is probably not a good basis for your user interface. Read the principles in this book, and try to assimilate as many as possible into your thinking. Write several alternate drafts of interface styles to try out ideas. Get some good friends in your software application area—the kind who can give you constructive criticism without worrying about your taking it personally—to give you a critical evaluation and some more alternatives. Finally, get evaluations from people who are prospective users and who have experience with similar applications to give you comparisons with things they now use. In other words, try to get the kind of evaluation you would have from a team approach. The results will be worth the effort.

1.3   Principles That Underlie User Interfaces

A number of principles seem to be consistent across all good user interfaces. We state them here as general principles and will run across them again in specifics when we deal with input, output, and other aspects of the interface.

The user interface handles all input and output. It must convey to the user all the instructions on the program's use, must allow the user to control the program as naturally as possible, and must provide the program's results to the user so they can be used. If the interface gives unclear instructions, or the user cannot control the task from his or her input as easily as if the computer were not involved, or the program's output is confusing, then the communication, the interface, and ultimately the software are unsuccessful.

PRINCIPLE: The main function of the user interface is communication.

The program must carry out the functions of giving instructions, allowing control, and presenting results without intruding on the task process. This takes some thought and planning, but among other things it means that all input should be free-format or natural choice, output should be very clean and have no clutter, confusing displays, or grammatical glitches, and all available tools should be used to make display screens quickly readable. These do not happen trivially, but they make the program work *with* the user and keep the computer from intruding on the task.

> PRINCIPLE: The interface must keep the computer from coming between the user and the work.

The interface must support a single model of the problem and its solution, allowing the user to develop a single way to think about the task on the computer and keeping him or her from wondering "Which way does the computer expect me to do this?" This lets the task become habitual and reinforces the previous theme of the invisibility of the computer.

> PRINCIPLE: The interface must be consistent throughout the program.

The program's users will range from symbol-oriented to word-oriented persons, from people who like numbers to people who like letters, from people who want to use the program without remembering anything to people who want to become "experts" on the program, and from people who like menus to people who insist on commands. To be fully successful, it should offer each group the option of working in the way that is most comfortable to it.

> PRINCIPLE: The interface must be flexible to work with a wide range of users.

Users get interrupted in their computing work, just as you do in every aspect of your own work. A quick telephone call may turn into an emergency, and the user may get back to the task at hand (working with your program) hours later. A good assistant would help him or her remember what was happening; so can the program by keeping a bit of current activity information easily available.

> PRINCIPLE: The interface must keep the user aware of what is going on in the task.

It is not reasonable to assume that only experts will use a program, and even experts do not remember everything all the time. The user must be able to get some kind of assistance, and that assistance is best if it is online and is specifically directed to the user's current activity. This is a challenging communication task, but it can be achieved with effort, thought, and planning.

> PRINCIPLE: The interface must include access to help.

All users hate to have their work interrupted (and lost) when a program fails. This is probably not so much an interface problem as it is a system problem, but we include it because of the effect of a crash, and the loss of work it usually means, on the user. 1-2-3 shows that it is possible to avoid most user-caused crashes, and this is an important goal well worth the effort.

> PRINCIPLE: The program must not crash.

The essence of these themes for the programmer is summed up quite simply:

> PRINCIPLE: The program should work hard so the user does not have to.

Each of the principles above involves considerable programmer effort to avoid common program (mis-)behaviors. Free-format input, carefully organized and presented output, readable screens, status and help information, and crashproofing take a great deal of work. However, the work pays off in user response, acceptance, and ability to perform work comfortably.

Consistency and Flexibility

The dual, and apparently contradictory, principles of consistency and flexibility need some elaboration. Consistency has two aspects—consistency in the mental model a user has of an application, and consistency in the way the user controls the application.

Consistency in the user's mental model is the job of the application specialist as described earlier in this chapter. As long as the user has a good grasp of the application and how it is controlled, there is room for some flexibility in how that control is managed. Thus a program can be controlled by commands or by menus; so long as the nature of the control and the effects of the control primitives are the same, the mental model is preserved. Users may even be allowed to choose the interface style they prefer.

Sometimes the application model needs to have a broader kind of consistency: consistency with other programs for the same application. Unless a program is in a brand-new field, its designer must pay close attention to the techniques used in the most successful program for a similar application, and must respect the users' habits in using these programs. If users are asked to unlearn their habits to use a new program, they must be provided with a very strong reason to do so. The experience of the commercial market shows us, for example, that every spreadsheet program fundamentally operates like VisiCalc, and that most screen painting programs have their basics in common with MacPaint. These similarities are not accidental; the user—the customer—has decided that ease of learning is important in choosing new software.

PRINCIPLE: Make your program work like others similar to it.

Consistency is also important in a program's internal controls. These controls should use a consistent mechanism throughout the program. In a system having full-screen editing, for example, if a user deletes the character *on* the cursor in one part of the program, he or she will not expect to delete the character *before* the cursor in another part of the program. If the program uses commands, the commands should use a consistent syntax and structure. If the program uses menus, each menu should allow selections to be made the same way and should react the same way to a user's choice. This can be done by allowing several options in menu selection at all times, as we show in a menu example in Chapter 3, or it can be done by configuring the program to use a single technique from a choice of possible techniques. The program can create a configuration file and allow the user to set it up with the desired choices for the program. However it is handled, this internal consistency is important in making users comfortable and productive with your program.

PRINCIPLE: Make all parts of your program work alike.

The idea of control consistency goes beyond a single program. One of the key factors in the success of the Macintosh is the consistency of programs' operation across many different vendors and applications. Systems such as Microsoft Windows and many user interface management systems, discussed in Chapter 10, are designed to provide a similar common look to all the applications that use them.

1.4   A User Interface Toolkit

Programming user interfaces is a lot of work, and, as we mentioned above, most programs need quite a lot of interface experiments before the final interface design is reached. This makes it impractical or impossible for every interface to be coded from scratch. Instead, a programmer working on interfaces needs what we will call a user interface toolkit.

A user interface toolkit contains general tools for accomplishing most of the tasks of an interface, including possibly

- presenting menus,
- parsing commands,
- reading free-format numeric input,
- handling text input with editing and wraparound,
- presenting information in formatted screens,
- presenting alerts and dialog boxes,
- using windows,
- presenting help, and
- dealing with errors.

This is a lot to ask a toolkit to do, but any missing piece means either a lot of repeated coding or the omission of some techniques from the design.

This book presents some pieces of such a toolkit, since each chapter on a specific interface technique includes examples of designs and code that accomplish it. We have made many of these examples quite general so you can use them in your own toolkits, although the emphasis in these examples is on clear and understandable code more than efficiency. A number of companies, often quite small ones, sell pieces of user interface toolkits. Usually these are menu or window-handling systems. Some vendors, however, sell complete user interface management systems (UIMS); Chapter 10 contains more information on some of these.

1.5   The Organization of This Book

Overall, the book is intended to give a programmer the tools with which to implement most widely used user interface techniques. It is divided into three sections: INPUT, OUTPUT, and HELP/ERRORS. In addition, there is a separate chapter dealing with special user interface issues for people with disabilities. Each section discusses several aspects of its topic in some detail.

The INPUT section covers menu, command, and data inputs. *Menus* (Chapter 3) describes both text and graphic menus with examples and describes the role and function of direct manipulation for user interfaces. *Commands* (Chapter 4) covers text input that is to be used for program control and introduces the idea of commands with parameters and user-defined commands. *Data Input* (Chapter 5) includes text input with editing and word wrap, free-format numeric input, and fill-in-the-blank techniques.

The OUTPUT section includes information on screen techniques, windowing, and color. *Screen Techniques* (Chapter 7) includes dividing the screen into special information areas, special display techniques, and an introduction to windows, and *Color* (Chapter 8) includes general principles and techniques for using color in programs.

Two further chapters discuss aspects of interface programming that cover both input and output. *Direct Manipulation Systems and Special Environments* (Chapter 9) discusses direct manipulation and object-oriented programming and gives some examples of exciting software using direct manipulation techniques. *Windows and User Interface Management Systems* (Chapter 10) discusses various systems and techniques for presenting windows and several available windowing systems and User Interface Management Systems. These two chapters point the way to the future of user interfaces.

We discuss in Chapters 11 through 13 some aspects of user interfaces that are sometimes overlooked. This HELP/ERRORS section includes techniques for help and for error handling. *Help* (Chapter 12) describes how to implement help systems and make them work, while *Error Handling* (Chapter 13) describes techniques for controlling file errors and computation errors; gives suggestions on device handling; and makes suggestions for recovery techniques if a crash, either of your program or the whole computer, should occur.

Finally, the chapter on users with disabilities (Chapter 14) focuses on the special user interface needs of these people. It should help interface implementors be aware of some of the problems and make more software accessible to these users.

1.6   Readings

The *Bibliography* at the end of this book lists a number of books on user interface design and implementation, but a few stand out. Since user interfaces are a special case of both design and communication, we especially recommend two books on design and one on communication. *Designing for People* by Dreyfuss is an excellent book on the design process written by one of the outstanding industrial designers of the 20th century and offers useful insights into the experimentation process and principles of design. *The Psychology of Everyday Things* by Norman takes this idea into a user-oriented discussion of applied design. *The Visual Display of Quantitative Data* by Tufte is really about visual communication and will help you develop a sense of what good communication is all about.

Among books actually about software user interface design, *The Elements of Friendly Software Design* by Heckel stands out. This book predates but foretells the Macintosh, is presented at a very general level, and remains very germane. It is deceptively simple, but points out a number of design issues. For programmers, Heckel points out several reasons why the thinking processes of programming get in the way of user interface design. We refer you to the book itself for more elaboration.

Another general book on interface design is *The Human Factor* by Rubenstein & Hersh. Again, this book offers a wide variety of helpful guidelines but few implementation details, and is a good reference. Much closer to the research literature is *Designing the User Interface* by Shneiderman, one of the leading researchers in the field. It offers a detailed look at some interface design issues and is often used as a text in interface design courses. Brown's book, *Human-Computer Interface Design Guidelines* provides an extensive set of guidelines for designing the user interface. This is based on his experience at Xerox and complements the presentation of the present book very well. Other general books on user interfaces include Baecker & Buxton, Beech, Card, Moran, & Newell, Carroll, Coats & Vlaeminke, Dumas, Monk, Nickerson, Norman & Draper, Sime & Coombs, Thomas & Schneider, and *Software Psychology* by Shneiderman.

Finally, the most up-to-date information on interface design issues and research is found at the annual meetings of the Human Factors Society and the Special Interest Group on Computer-Human Interaction of the Association for Computing Machinery (ACM-SIGCHI). Here both research papers and in-depth courses on user interaction topics are offered. Some similar courses can also be found at the annual meetings of the ACM Special Interest Group on Computer Graphics (ACM-SIGGRAPH), a sister society to ACM-SIGCHI, especially courses relating to windowing systems and interface implementation.

Chapter 2

PRINCIPLES OF USER INPUT

Soon after a user begins to use your program, he or she must enter some control or data information. The way your user input is handled sets the tone and feel of the whole program. Awkward input design is probably more noticeable than any other problem short of actual errors and incorrect functions; it is one of the problems most frequently mentioned in software reviews.

There are sometimes special input techniques or devices that are necessary to make your program usable by persons with disabilities. These are discussed in Chapter 14. Any reader who is writing software for a general audience should read Chapter 14 and be aware of the problems and suggestions discussed there.

A number of other special environments are discussed in Chapter 9. These are special hardware and software solutions for museums, for work with children and in education, and for artificial intelligence work as well as for users with disabilities. However, once a technique is developed for a particular purpose, it is often seen to be useful in a much broader context. The special environments we present contain some state-of-the-art interface techniques that you will find useful and informative.

2.1   Types of User Input

A program requires two kinds of input. *Control input* is information from the user that controls the action of the program. The user selects which program function is to be executed at any time and gives the program whatever parameters are to be used for this function. Within a particular function, *data input* is the means to provide the program with the data, either numbers or text, on which it works. Mechanically, command parameters and data may look alike and their input may even be handled with the same tools, as illustrated in the next few chapters, but these functions look quite different to the user.

Of the two input modes, data input is the simpler to design. Computer users quickly get used to standard techniques for entering text or numbers because the concept becomes familiar: merely enter values using normal typing techniques (although other data input is possible and occasionally natural). Control input, however, is much more closely linked to the way a user thinks of the problem and his or her model of the way to solve the problem for which the program is designed. It may take a great deal of design and experimentation to find out how a user thinks about the problem process. This is one of the main aspects of interface design. Many of the readings at the end of this chapter discuss these design and experimental approaches.

2.2 Input Devices

The traditional input device for interactive programs is the keyboard. This comes in a variety of forms, from the simple to the complex. Figure 2.1 illustrates several different keyboard layouts. Even the fundamental question of key layout can vary; the Dvorak keyboard is sometimes used as an alternative to the normal QWERTY layout, as shown in Figure 2.2, because it lays the keys out more naturally for the typist and tends to increase typing speed once the user is accustomed to it. If your program expects keyboard input, you must consider the range of keyboards your users may have when command input is requested (data input is much more standard). Function keys and cursor keys are very attractive but may not be present or usable in the same way on all keyboards.

Other kinds of devices are familiar in a graphics or mixed graphics/text environment. Following the approach usually taken in computer graphics, we classify these devices by function.

The function of a *pick* device is to choose an object on the display screen. This object is frequently part of a graphic menu or an object to be manipulated. A pick operation selects an object on a graphic screen when the pick device's screen echo is in the object's region. This is usually accompanied with highlighting of the object. The selection is confirmed by an event operation such as a button or key press.

A *locator* device is used to identify a point on the screen. As the device is manipulated, the selected point is updated and shown on the screen, often with a small cross or other symbol called the locator's cursor. When a point is needed by a program, a locator is called, and the coordinates

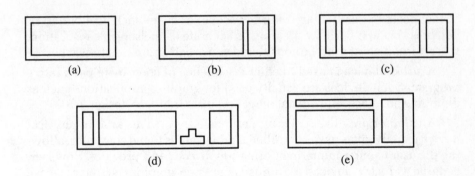

Figure 2.1   *A range of keyboard layouts:*
(a)   neither function keys nor numeric keypad (Macintosh Plus)
(b)   no function keys (Macintosh SE standard keyboard)
(c)   function keys and numeric keypad (IBM PC)
(d)   function keys at left, cursor keypad
(e)   function keys at top

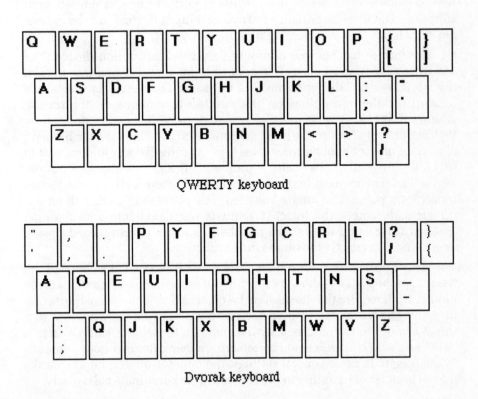

Figure 2.2   *QWERTY and Dvorak keyboard layouts*

of the locator's position are returned when an event such as a button or key press occurs. Locators are only as accurate as the screen's resolution, so a returned point must be considered as a rough approximation at best.

A *stroke* device is used to enter a sequence of coordinate pairs into a program. Such devices are usually used for graphics applications such as digitizing an image, and are not often part of an interface design.

A *valuator* provides scalar numeric data input. This kind of physical device usually gives user-controlled analog values to the computer, allowing the user to enter numeric information directly to a program. However, genuine valuator devices are unusual outside graphics systems, so we must often look for ways to provide a valuator function with a different device.

In fact, a common situation is to have a single nonkeyboard device that must be used for all these input functions. Fortunately, it is relatively easy to make any device simulate other device classes if you have graphics capabilities on the screen. This is discussed below. In considering a particular device, it is important to note that how it fills these roles depends on how it is programmed and how it interacts with the user and with the screen. The device itself is less important than the interaction it supports. The most important nonkeyboard input devices are the *mouse*, *graphics tablet*, *touch screen*, *light pen*, and *joystick*.

The mouse has become a very widely used interaction device. The Macintosh computer is largely responsible for popularizing this device, though it was certainly not the first to use it. The mouse is basically a locator, translating motions on the desktop to motions on the screen, where a mouse key can give a pick action or provide locator information. Pick actions by a mouse are quite common; the use of the mouse in menu choice, in moving about a spreadsheet, in opening disks or folders, and in invoking programs is basically a pick with the use of a mouse button. Mouse locators are used in drawing programs, where a click of the mouse identifies a point. The mouse can also be a valuator if used with an on-screen scale where the location point is translated into a data value. Another interaction device, the trackball, is just a mouse turned upside down, and fills exactly the same kind of functions.

Many applications use the graphics tablet in ways that go beyond the name "graphics." The tablet is a locator and sometimes a valuator, as is the mouse. Both require that the user move one hand to manipulate the device directly. The tablet can also be used as a pick device in two ways: in a direct analogy to the mouse or with a menu on the tablet's surface. In this case, the menu choice is made by selecting a menu item without reference to the screen. In more general settings, the tablet is often used as a stroke device because of its ability to provide multiple coordinate pairs easily.

Figure 2.3

(a)   Macintosh mouse, courtesy of Apple Computer, Inc.

(b)   three-button mouse, courtesy of Logitech

(c)   trackball, courtesy of Abaton

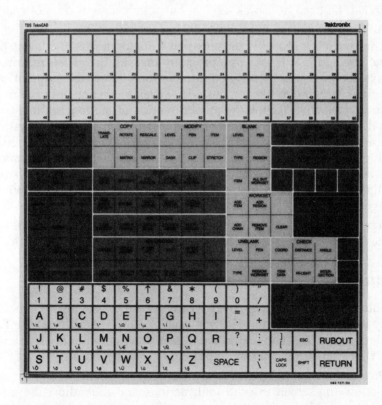

Figure 2.4   *A tablet with a menu, courtesy of Tektronix*

Figure 2.5   *Two joysticks, courtesy of Kraft and CH Products*

Light pens and touch screens operate by direct user interaction with the screen surface. Each allows the user to point at or touch a position on the screen. The light pen can act as either a pick or locator device. A touch screen can be used as a pick device, but touch screens are not accurate enough to allow careful point selection.

The joystick is probably the only real valuator device in this list, but it is rarely treated in this way by a program. Instead, the values returned by the joystick are usually translated into motion of an onscreen point, so its function is very much like a mouse. However, a joystick only returns the direction it is moved, giving relative direction of motion, while a mouse gives distance in two directions. The direction returned by a joystick is often associated with a fixed velocity, giving the user more a feeling of steering the cursor than of moving it directly; this difference may be important in the way a user works with a program. While the joystick is usually associated with (inexpensive) games, it is a very viable device for more general kinds of programs.

In addition to these rather standard devices, there are special input devices for the handicapped, discussed at some length in Chapter 14.

Simulated Devices

We noted above that a single device can be used to provide various kinds of input functions by simulating a range of other device types. These simulations are routinely described in computer graphics books. Here we sketch the simulations that are important to user interfaces.

Pick and locator devices are the primary tools for direct manipulation. Both allow the screen to echo their actions and thus allow the user to interact with information displayed on the screen. A pick operation is easily simulated by a locator and an event, such as a key or button press,

FUNCTION: Get Object

INPUT: None

PROCESSING:
```
    turn on locator and display locator cursor
    while no event do
        get locator position
        display locator cursor at current position
    /* event has now happened and position is known */
    for each selectable object on the screen
        if position is in the object, return the object identifier
```

RETURN: an identifier of an object chosen by the user

Figure 2.6 *Design for a simulated pick operation*

as shown in Figure 2.6. Since locators return points, they are valuable for other user functions such as drawing. Thus locators are probably the most common user interface devices, as evidenced by the number of mice, tablets, and trackballs around.

Some systems, however, do not have locator devices; these are mostly keyboard-only terminals or personal computers, and we must find ways to provide a locator function for them. This can be modeled on the joystick, which provides direction instead of distance. Various keys can be used to indicate motion direction for the cursor. Other keyboard functions, such as the shift key, can even change the cursor's velocity. Some standard models for these keys exist, shown in Figure 2.7: cursor control keys in a

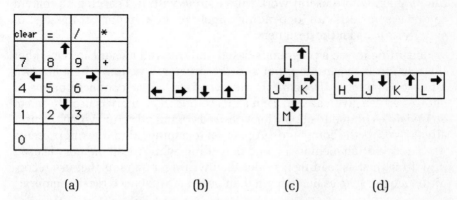

(a) (b) (c) (d)

Figure 2.7 *Various cursor control key groups*
(a) cursor control in numeric pad
(b) cursor control key group
(c) cursor control by a key diamond
(d) cursor control by a key row

```
turn on locator cursor at current position
get keypress
while keypress is not a terminate key /* not an event */
    if keypress is a cursor control key
        adjust position value by appropriate amount
        redraw location cursor at new position
return position for use
```

Figure 2.8 *Keyboard replacement for a locator*

numeric keypad, a separate cursor control key group, the Apple II I-J-K-M diamond, and the Unix vi H-J-K-L control row (left, down, up, right respectively). These keys can be used for both text and graphics cursors.

Implementing this kind of keyboard control is very straightforward, differing from the sketch in Figure 2.6 only in how we compute the cursor position and in the nature of an event. Each cursor control key will indicate a relative motion by a fixed amount, so we must add or subtract this amount from the x- or y-coordinate of the cursor point. An event will be a different keypress, such as RETURN or ESC. The code fragment in Figure 2.8 shows how to use keys to replace a locator and can be used in place of the first five lines of the processing in Figure 2.6.

2.3   Options in Control Input

Programs are like any other tools people use: people must learn how to use the program before useful work can be done with it. Learning a program can be easy or difficult, depending largely on how important the goal of easy learning is for the designers.

Learning to use a program is based on how well a user can remember the relation between his input and the program's action. There are two kinds of memory. *Recognition memory* is used to connect command choices with a given action, as in a menu. *Recall memory* is used to select an invisible command choice for a desired command action when the user already knows the commands. A parallel to another kind of work presents itself: recognition memory is used in reading, while recall memory is used in writing. Just as reading is easier than writing, programs that use recognition memory are easier to learn than programs that need recall memory.

Learning to use a program is also affected by the relation between control actions and program actions. It is clearly easier for someone to learn to use a program if any action he takes has the same meaning at every point in a program. When this is not the case, when different parts of a program interpret an action in different ways, problems arise.

These different environments are called *modes*. Modes are familiar to most people who have dealt with computers for some time. Most standard line editors offer many modes: certainly command mode and edit mode, and within edit mode are often found insert mode, append mode, modify mode, and delete mode. Because programmers are used to modes, they often assume that other people, the people who will use their programs, can work with them as well. But users can lose track of the mode they are in and quickly become confused when an action is not what they expect. There are some actions that can make modes less confusing, such as keeping mode information on the screen or changing the cursor shape depending on the mode, but they don't eliminate all the problems.

The principle of consistency is maintained when software is *modeless*, that is, when each action has a unique effect anywhere in the program. It is difficult to design software that needs a wide variety of controls without using modes. For example, the EMACS editor is fully modeless but requires complex control-key sequences that many people find difficult to remember or even type.

If complete modelessness is hard to get, what is a viable alternative? A program is usually intended for one primary application and has one predominant operation, such as entering text on a word processor or typing in cell contents in a spreadsheet. Make that operation the program's standard mode. If you need other modes, they can then be done in a transitive way (Apple's *User Interface Guidelines* calls these "spring-loaded" modes). Thus, pop-up menus, message windows, or clearly distinguished single-action operations can be valid modalities.

We should note a different use of the terms *modal* and *modeless* in some interface systems. On the Macintosh, dialog boxes are considered modeless if the user can dismiss the dialog without making a response, and they are modal if a response (even "cancel") is required. Because these terms are quite new, they often have many meanings; be careful.

Beyond the consideration of learning, control input is one of the most visible parts of the user interface. In order to provide comfortable program control, the designer must

- understand the audience for the program,
- know, in depth, how the program's intended users think about the program's problem and how they would go about solving it, and
- provide a command system that allows the users to solve the problem with as little reference to the computer or the program as possible.

Understanding the user's thinking processes is the most difficult part of user interface design and is not within the scope of most programmers' skills alone. Control design must be done with a lot of input from the program's audience and with feedback from many trial designs. Such trial designs, known as *prototypes*, are a critical part of building usable interfaces. A good user interface toolkit is a tremendous asset in building both prototype interfaces and reliable final interfaces. We provide a number of pieces and ideas for such a toolkit in the remainder of this book.

Two main approaches to control input are most commonly used: menus and command lines. Each has its advantages. On the whole, menus take advantage of the user's recognition memory, while commands require the user's recall memory. These are discussed in more depth in Chapters 3 and 4, respectively.

It is important to note that menus and commands are not mutually exclusive; it is possible for a program to be run from either command lines or menus. For example, the dBASE IV microcomputer database program is basically an interactive database design, editing, and operation system that uses menus extensively, but it also includes a full-capability command-driven system inherited from dBASE II and dBASE III, as well as a Structured Query Language (SQL) database query capability based on commands. Another system using a duality between command lines and menus is the Zenographics Mirage graphics software, where a user can alternate between the two controls with the press of a function key. On the other hand, many Macintosh programs such as MacWrite are mainly oriented towards menus but allow keystrokes to act as short-cut commands and execute menu choices without removing hands from the keyboard. Experienced users tend to acquire the recall knowledge needed by commands and expect to get added speed by using them.

Direct manipulation is a less common approach to control input. It is a technique in which pick operations choose an object upon which operations are performed. This is relatively common in the Macintosh, in Computer-Aided Design programs, and in advanced scientific software but is rare in other everyday applications. A real advantage of direct manipulation is its strong use of recognition memory and the direct control it gives the user; this is based on the observations made at Xerox that it is easier to see something and point to it than to remember something and type it. We discuss it at more length in Chapter 9 and refer the reader to that chapter for further information.

Programming a direct manipulation system "from scratch" is a difficult job. Such systems often require years of programmers' experience and large amounts of manipulation code in order to perform even the simplest functions. Extensive libraries must be built and maintained to support these operations. Fortunately, recent developments in programming technology, such as object-oriented languages, have begun to have an impact on this process. A system such as MacApp for the Macintosh can relieve much of the user interface load and allow the programmer to focus once again primarily on the application. A number of other systems for user interfaces are object-oriented and support direct manipulation. More information on these is given in Chapter 10.

There is a fundamental difference between direct manipulation systems and either command or menu systems. Both commands and menus select the operation first and the object to be used later; a direct manipulation system chooses the object first and the operation later. Hence commands and menus are operation oriented, while direct manipulation is object oriented. Users seem to find the object orientation more human and less mechanical. This is apparently part of the reason for the success of the Macintosh.

We devote a chapter to each of the menu and command line input methods, concentrating on how they are implemented and how these implementations can become part of your user interface toolkit. Here we look at the tradeoffs between the methods, but we first remind you of the principle from Chapter 1: *be consistent* in your control interface. Do not use menus some places and command lines in others; it will make your program much harder to learn and use and will create an inconsistent model of your program in your user's mind. On the other hand, another Chapter 1 principle is: *be flexible.* It is feasible to allow both menu and command line interfaces to be available so the user can choose which to use.

A designer must choose among menus, command lines, and direct manipulation techniques for program control. Experimentation and experience have shown that well-designed menu systems are easy to learn and require little training, since the program is largely in control of the execution sequence, and the user needs to use only recognition memory. Menus also show the current and default actions of the program easily, require little typing skill, and do not have many problems with user errors. Many educators believe that menus should be the only control technique for educational software since students do not work with any one program enough to become a skilled user. Menus are slow, however, and have very limited flexibility. Speed problems can be alleviated by allowing type-ahead and command options for menu choices, and flexibility can be increased by using scrolling or hierarchical menus and by supporting a range of input devices and techniques for menu choice, as described in Chapter 3.

Command systems are generally more complex than menus. They are harder to learn and require more user training, since large numbers of commands must be memorized. However, they repay the user for this effort by being quite fast and quite flexible (Shneiderman [1987]). Commands require some typing skill and are very prone to mistaken entries. Programs that use them require more careful and extensive error-handling and retry facilities. Help systems are important for command-line systems but are harder to provide effectively, since the user's help options are not all visible. Paper-based learning and user aids are often used here.

Direct manipulation retains the speed and flexibility of commands and relies on intuition and recognition memory to make learning easy and training less necessary. This technique limits the user to displayed objects only, however, and may not be the best method in some situations. For example, it may be easier to type a name than to select the object with this name on a screen. Direct manipulation requires considerable care and experimentation to determine what user action is natural for a given manipulation action. At this point, programs using direct manipulation do so for only part of their operation, with the rest usually managed by menus since both techniques are visual and choice-oriented. A brief introduction to direct manipulation programming is included in Chapter 9.

> PRINCIPLE: Use menu techniques for a program intended for casual or infrequent users.

> PRINCIPLE: Use command techniques for a program whose users will become skilled in its operation.

2.4   Options for Handling Data Input

As we said earlier, data input is not as complex a problem as is control input because the user's mental model of input is much simpler—just type the number or text into the computer. There are some variations in what the user considers to be a valid way to write a number, however, so the routines that actually read input need to understand these variations. We describe ways to do this in Chapter 5. Techniques for prompting the user for input also offer a number of variations.

There are two main types of data input and a third less common method. The traditional technique for beginning programmers is an unformatted sequence of prompts and responses, which is basically a primitive free-form input approach. A more structured approach, often found in business and database programs, is to use a formatted screen with fields for data values. Occasionally, some programs allow the user to manipulate controls on-screen to provide data values.

The most important factor in data input design is that it must be consistent with the control input design and the output design of the program. The user must see the program as a complete unit. This means that menu-driven programs should consider forms-based data input, and command-driven programs fit more closely with free-format input. Programs using direct manipulation for control might well continue to use direct screen techniques for data input.

The user properties for the data input options are very much the same as for control input. Forms input is initiated by the computer, requires little user training, and shows default (or previously entered) values easily. It also gives the user a view of a whole block of data, allows editing within the block, and can be used with intelligent terminals to collect a screenful of data and transmit it to the computer in burst mode. Compared to free-form input, however, it is less flexible, less powerful, and does not readily handle situations where various input values may cause different kinds of subsequent input to be needed.

> PRINCIPLE: Make data input fit consistently with the control input and information output phases of your program.

2.5   Providing Activity Feedback to the User

As the user works with your program, it is extremely important that he or she be kept informed of the program's activities. The normal function of interactive program use is that of a sequence of command and data inputs with computer processing occurring from time to time. The user needs to be kept informed of the program's status and whether the current control or data input is satisfactory.

If the program control is by menus, two kinds of feedback should be used. Each menu should be labeled. If menus are nested, the sequence of menus leading to the current one should be shown, and the default or current menu selection should be highlighted, as shown in Figure 2.9, which shows highlighting added to an AppleWorks screen.

If the program uses commands, a useful technique is to prompt for each command and then echo the command in a present, active form to show that it is being executed. For example, in a text-oriented system the command *do action to object* might cause the echo *doing action to object now*.

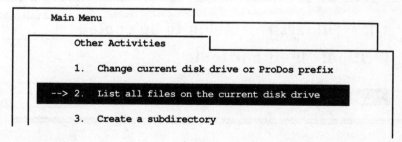

Figure 2.9   *Part of an AppleWorks nested menu screen with highlighting added*

Direct manipulation allows a somewhat simpler and more visual feedback. Like the menu illustration above, when an object is chosen for manipulation, the object is highlighted. When the manipulation is happening, words or images are highlighted on the screen to link the action to the preceding choice. This operation is discussed in Chapter 9 as part of the notion of revealed structure, and is a very important aid to the user's understanding of the program.

In any case, some processing will require that the computer "sit and think" for a period of time. If this period is going to exceed a couple of seconds, it is important to reassure the user that the computer has not frozen up and that it is making progress toward the next interaction point. The program must provide some kind of activity and completion information itself. There are a number of ways this can be done: "Please wait" messages, the hourglass and watch face icons, clock dials or wait bars that reach a certain place when the processing is finished, or counters that tick down while saying how much work is left. Some of these are shown in Figure 2.10. All these are helpful, but the more active the indicator is and the more accurately it says when the processing will finish, the more it helps the user. At the same time, maintaining the indicator does take a certain amount of CPU time, lengthening the time to do the action it is monitoring.

These are all aspects of the following fundamental principle of highly-interactive systems.

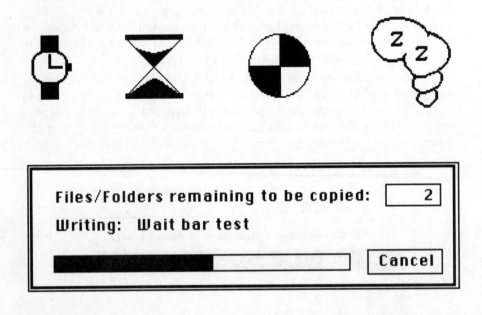

Figure 2.10 *Wait messages or icons from different systems*

```
compute amount of activity
loop
    do a unit of work
    increment proportion done
    call ShowActivity( proportion )
end_loop
```

Figure 2.11   *Loop for feedback display*

PRINCIPLE: Always provide the user with information
on what is happening with the program.

Programming this kind of activity feedback depends on the kind of
activity you have and the system you are working on. If the activity's
duration is not readily computable, the best bet is to put up some kind of
general nontimed message. This can be "Please wait" or the cursor can be
changed to a wait icon, as shown in Figure 2.10. If the activity's time can
be computed, a feedback display can tell the user how much of the work
has been completed at any time, as shown in the file copy display in
Figure 2.10.

The basic operation design for feedback is shown in Figure 2.11. The
ShowActivity operation can present any kind of display that shows
proportions: a wait bar, a "thermometer," a circle with a proportionally
filled arc, or an icon moving along a line. Various options should be tried,
with a single version chosen to be used throughout the program.

2.6 Example: A Program Having All Three Kinds of User Input

The MacWrite word-processing program for the Apple Macintosh has a
classical example of a well-designed user interface. This program combines all three kinds of control input described in Section 2.3. It offers
menu control using standard Macintosh pull-down menus, as shown in
Figure 2.12. However, these same menus show a shortcut command form
for many of the menu choices, with commands having a double-key
command-letter form. This allows experienced users to move through the
command functions on the program quite quickly, especially since these
commands are much more special-purpose than those of a full operating

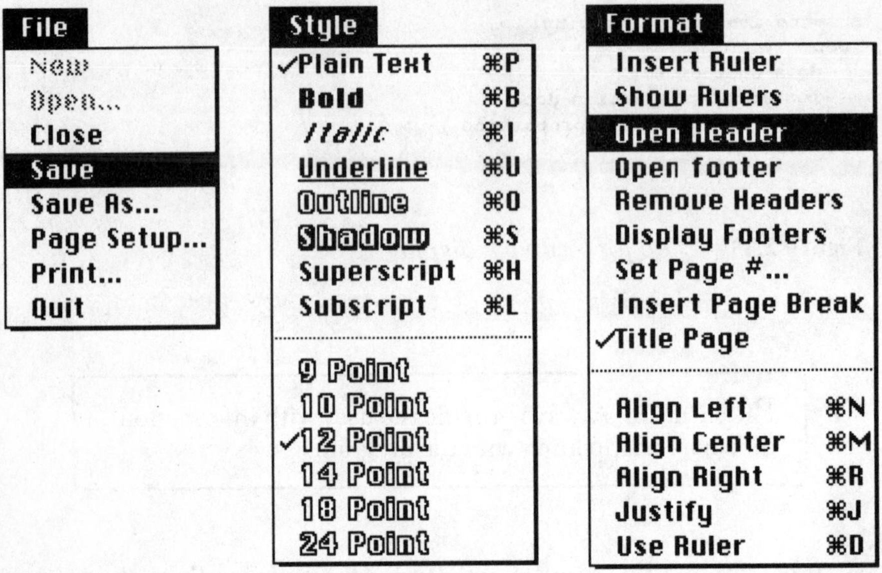

File	Style		Format	
New	✓Plain Text	⌘P	Insert Ruler	
Open...	**Bold**	⌘B	Show Rulers	
Close	*Italic*	⌘I	Open Header	
Save	Underline	⌘U	Open footer	
Save As...	Outline	⌘O	Remove Headers	
Page Setup...	Shadow	⌘S	Display Footers	
Print...	Superscript	⌘H	Set Page #...	
Quit	Subscript	⌘L	Insert Page Break	
			✓Title Page	
	9 Point			
	10 Point		Align Left	⌘N
	✓12 Point		Align Center	⌘M
	14 Point		Align Right	⌘R
	18 Point		Justify	⌘J
	24 Point		Use Ruler	⌘D

Figure 2.12 *Several pulldown menus for MacWrite*
Copyright Claris Corporation, used by permission

system. Finally, word processing naturally defines blocks of text for formatting operations. MacWrite uses direct manipulation to highlight text for formatting operations as well as to set margins and tabs from the rulers, and to set the text insertion point. An example of a MacWrite screen showing the ruler and some selected text is shown in Figure 2.13.

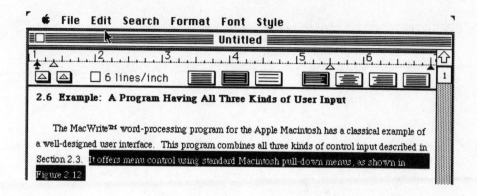

Figure 2.13 *MacWrite screen with highlighted block and ruler*
Copyright Claris Corporation, used by permission

2.7 Readings

Our discussion of input is often called dialog design. It is a general design issue discussed in a number of sources, including C. Marlin Brown, Ehrich and Williges, Rubenstein and Hersh, and Shneiderman [1987]. Modality has been part of programs for a long time, but there is not much about it in the literature. However, a good, though brief, description of modalities in generally modeless systems is found in Apple's *User Interface Guidelines*.

## Chapter 3

Programming Menus

It is not uncommon for people to equate the phrase "user friendly" with the idea of "menu driven" software. This is a mistake. Some menu-driven programs cannot be viewed as user-friendly (whatever that means), while command-driven programs can easily be an excellent fit for many users. Still, it is true that menus fit novice users well because they rely on recognition memory and structure the program for the user. In this chapter we look at a variety of kinds of menus and how to implement them.

3.1 Examples of Menu-Driven Systems

We begin this discussion by giving examples of systems that use menus extensively. This gives us some background to build on as we look at different kinds of menus and menu options in more detail.

AppleWorks

AppleWorks is an integrated application for the Apple II family, containing a word processor, spreadsheet, and filing system. Each of these subsystems uses the operation style common to its application, but they are tied together with a menu-driven approach. A routine AppleWorks menu screen is shown in Figure 3.1. Selection may be made by typing the number of a selection or by using the up- and down-arrow cursor control keys. When RETURN is pressed, the currently-selected action is done. File control menus, such as that of Figure 3.2, allow the user to select more than one file with the right-arrow cursor key.

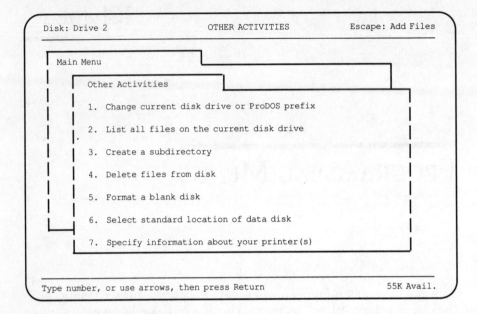

Figure 3.1 *AppleWorks Other Activities menu*

Copyright Claris Corporation, used by permission

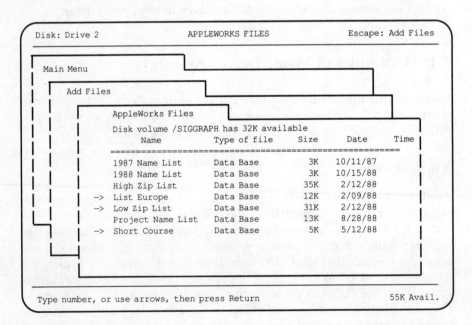

Figure 3.2 *AppleWorks Save File menu*

Copyright Claris Corporation, used by permission

Note that the Other Activities menu, along with all the nonfile menus, allows wrap-around with the arrow keys; a down-arrow keypress from the bottom menu item moves the menu to the top item, and an up-arrow keypress from the top menu item moves to the bottom.

AppleWorks is a remarkably successful system and makes even an older kind of computer into a very good working tool. It is a good example of a piece of software that transcends the image of the computer it works on.

MacWrite

MacWrite is the original word processor for the Macintosh. It originally came with the Macintosh computer but now is sold separately by Claris. It was the first introduction to the general public of the Macintosh interface style and philosophy. It is discussed in more detail in Chapter 2.

Many of MacWrite's actual operations are handled by direct manipulation. The mouse sets the point for text insertion and marks text blocks for other operations, such as cutting or attribute setting. A number of operations are available from menus, however, as we illustrated with Figure 2.12. The mouse is also used with these menus, but the operation is a genuine menu action and not direct manipulation. The menus in this earlier figure are, in fact, second-level menus. The top menu level is the horizontal menu line at the top of the screen; this menu line is common to all "genuine" Macintosh software, and is illustrated in Figure 3.3. When the mouse is moved onto the top line and the button is clicked, the submenus pull down from the top line. Thus these are called "pulldown menus" and are also common on the Commodore Amiga and the Microsoft Windows system for the IBM PC.

When a pulldown menu is opened, it remains open as long as the mouse button is depressed. If the mouse cursor is in the window when the button is lifted, the highlighted menu choice is activated, as is shown in Figure 2.12. How you implement pulldown menus depends very heavily upon the system you are using. The MacApp example in Chapter 10 includes pulldown menus.

 File Edit Search Format Font Style

Figure 3.3 *The MacWrite top menu line*

Three particular features of MacWrite's menus are worth noting. First, menu choices that are sometimes available but not currently active are shown in gray instead of black, so the user always sees the same menu but cannot choose inappropriate items. Second, many of the choices are also available via command key combinations, allowing users who are familiar with the program to move more quickly than menus permit. Finally, the items in the style menu are somewhat self-explanatory. Bold, italic, underline, outline, and shadow fonts shown in their output styles, giving a bit of extra guidance in style selection. Some add-on options for the Macintosh even show each entry in the font menu in the font it names.

dBASE IV

The dBASE IV database management system includes an extensive interactive database environment called the *Control Center*. This lets the user define the data, queries, forms, reports, labels, and applications that go with a database. The Control Center provides menus and work screens for all the database functions of dBASE IV, although a parallel command system is also provided.

The work screens are of little interest to us here, but dBASE IV has an interesting menu structure. The Control Center and each of the functional areas mentioned above have a multilevel menu structure with pulldown menus and hierarchical submenus. This is an example of the menu tree structure described later in this chapter. A sample of a hierarchical menu screen is shown in Figure 3.4.

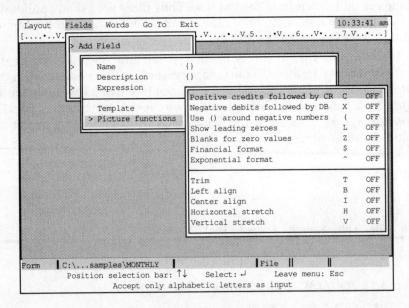

Figure 3.4   *A hierarchical dBASE IV menu screen*

Lotus 1-2-3

Lotus 1-2-3 is a standard spreadsheet and is described in Chapter 1. Here we simply remind you of 1-2-3's menus; some typical examples are shown in Figure 1.2. These menus are multilayered; most menu choices open up a new menu with more detailed options for that choice. A selection can be made by moving to the option with the right- and left-arrow keys (again, the choice is circular, and the currently selected item is highlighted), and the chosen item is selected by pressing RETURN. Alternately, typing the first letter of a choice's word causes that choice to be made immediately, so an experienced user can make a complete set of selections very quickly.

AutoCAD

AutoCAD is a fairly standard computer-aided design system that runs on a number of MS-DOS machines with a variety of graphics boards and hardcopy devices. It is graphics oriented and can be used with a mouse, tablet, or the cursor-control keys as its graphics input device. Like most computer-aided design programs, AutoCAD maintains on-screen menus of various types. These menus are operated by the graphics device, usually a graphics tablet but in some cases a mouse, but are not pull-down. An example of an AutoCAD screen with a menu is shown in Figure 3.5. This is the classical menu system for CAD software, but AutoCAD also includes the option of using pulldown menus and dialog boxes as well.

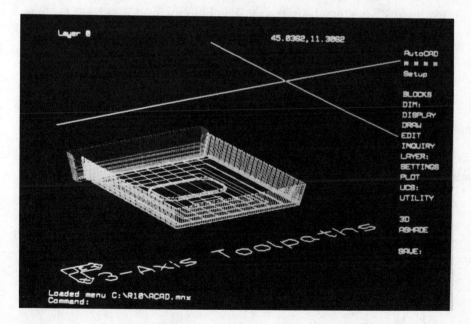

Figure 3.5 *AutoCAD screen*

Courtesy of AutoDesk, Inc.

AutoCAD's menu items are not all words; some are small graphics, almost like icons. This is an example of a graphic menu system. The distinction between graphic menus and direct manipulation systems is sometimes rather fine. We suggest the following working distinction between graphic menus, text menus, and direct manipulation systems:

> *A text menu is a text-only list from which choices are made by entering text or by using cursor keys manipulating a text cursor. A graphic menu is a displayed list of items from which one is selected by a graphics device such as a mouse or tablet; cursor keys can be used if they manipulate a graphics cursor. Either of these menus chooses an item for a previously determined operation; a direct manipulation system determines the operation after the object is chosen.*

Thus the Macintosh desktop is not a graphic menu, because the items on the desktop (disks, files, or applications) are first chosen by location and then opened or launched by a double mouse-click. However, the tools area in a MacPaint screen can be seen as a graphic menu since moving the mouse cursor into this area indicates a choice to change the painting operation, and then the cursor location and mouse click select the new operation.

3.2   Programming Text Menus

Text menus have long been the most commonly used interfaces for inexperienced users. When most computers and terminals had little or no graphics capabilities, neither graphic menus nor direct manipulation were viable outside a narrow range of inherently graphic applications such as computer aided design. Even now, a text-based program can work quite comfortably with text menus.

Text menu control can be very flexible. It can use any method of cursor control available, as well as the particular menu-oriented functions of item number and key character or abbreviation. These are illustrated below.

Principles of Text Menus

One principle of menu use stands out from all others. It is very important that the list of choices be kept short enough to allow easy reading and to fit comfortably on a screen. Undoubtedly, this is the first principle of menu use, for either text or graphic menus.

> PRINCIPLE: Keep menus short and clear.

For text menus, where the user will have to read a few words to make a choice, our guideline is that they should contain, at most, nine selections. One of the drawbacks many programmers found in the UCSD p-System (a Pascal-based operating system and programming environment once widely used with personal computers) was that the menus were rather large and there was no way around them.

If more choices are needed, either have the menu scroll (with a clear indication that it does so), include <MORE> as an option and provide a second page of menu choices, or have a choice from the first menu open up a more detailed menu. More complex choices, or a number of choices that have a secondary menu, may suggest that you should go to a command-driven system with help facilities. Some writers suggest that a menu system should support no more than 10 to 20 choices. While this is quite restrictive, and we have used menu-driven systems with more choices than this, it is a marker in the direction we are suggesting.

PRINCIPLE: Keep nested menus as simple as possible, and do not nest them deeply.

There are, of course, exceptions to this principle. At least two very good systems use several levels of nested menus quite successfully. The Zenographics Mirage graphics software has very extensive menus, but it keeps track of the path the user has taken through a list of previous choices in the upper left corner of the screen. This is shown in Figure 3.6. This package also allows the user to switch to a command language if desired. The AppleWorks system uses the file folder metaphor for nested menus, showing the previous menu choices as tab labels on file folders under the current folder, as shown in Figures 3.1 and 3.2.

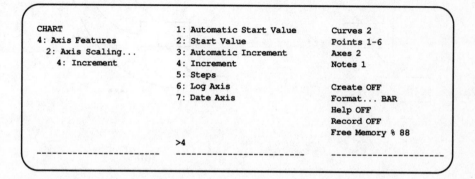

```
CHART                    1: Automatic Start Value    Curves 2
4: Axis Features         2: Start Value              Points 1-6
   2: Axis Scaling...    3: Automatic Increment       Axes 2
      4: Increment       4: Increment                Notes 1
                         5: Steps
                         6: Log Axis                 Create OFF
                         7: Date Axis                Format... BAR
                                                     Help OFF
                                                     Record OFF
                                                     Free Memory % 88

                         >4
-----------------------  -----------------------     -----------------------
```

Figure 3.6 *A Zenographics Mirage screen with command history*

You must be very careful with the design of a menu system based on menus that need to be nested more than two levels deep. With this depth of menus, the user must have carefully designed navigation information, as discussed in Chapter 2, on how the nested menu was reached in order to keep the operations in mind. These nested menus are good candidates for the "pop-up" menus shown in Figure 3.4, menus that simply appear in windows on the screen in a convenient place.

If a menu-based system relies on nested menus, the structure will be organized in something like the trees in Figure 3.7. Note the difference between trees (a) and (b); in the former, the user must trace his or her way back out of the detailed operations by going back up the tree, while in the latter, the user may return to the startup level very quickly from any place in the tree. Certainly the experienced user would find the latter faster to use. This is a specific instance of an important general case: the richer the control options, the more ways an experienced user can work flexibly. The trick is to do this without making the software too complex for a novice.

An alternative design with a large number of choices is a scrolling menu. This might be used when there is no natural hierarchy of menu choices, for example. Since much of this menu is off-screen, you must have some kind of technique for allowing the user to get to a menu selection quickly, such as a scroll bar at the side or an arrow at the bottom of a menu to indicate more choices. The user must know roughly where an off-screen item can be found, so it is good to organize such a menu alphabetically.

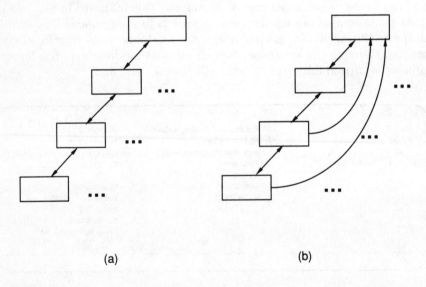

(a)   (b)

Figure 3.7   *Two trees with arrows*

Recall from Chapter 1 that we emphasized the dual properties of consistency and flexibility in interface operations. If your system is based on menus, the menus need consistency so that they all function the same way, and they need flexibility so the user can work with them in a style that is comfortable to him or her. These two issues are addressed in the menu examples we present later in this chapter.

We present the implementation of a typical text menu in Figures 3.9 and 3.10. Such a menu allows you to make your selection in three ways: by typing its number, by typing the first letter of the option description, or by using arrow keys to move up and down the menu. The arrow key option can stop at the top or bottom of the menu, or it can wrap around; the next choice below the bottom item wraps to the top item, and the next choice above the top item wraps to the bottom item. In any case, the default selection is highlighted at the start and each selection is highlighted when made. This allows the user to see what has been chosen and reselect if it is not correct; the action will take place when the RETURN key is pressed.

Such a menu operates flexibly with the user's personal style. Persons who are number- or letter-oriented, or who know the program well ("power users"), can jump to their choice directly. People who do not want to memorize the program's options can get very satisfactory results with only arrow keys. In fact, a system that is fully menu-driven with such menus would be easy to learn, since users only need the up-arrow and down-arrow keys, and easy to use, since advanced users only need two keystrokes to make a choice.

Alternate Forms

So far we have only illustrated what we might call the "classic" menu: the list of text choices in the central part of the screen. There are several other possible techniques. One is to maintain part of the screen, say a header or footer line, with a one-line list of brief names; these names may be chosen by typing their number or first letter, or by choosing them with a mouse. The Macintosh screen header is such a "menu of menus," and Lotus 1-2-3 uses a similar technique. This is convenient for keeping the user informed of the options available during an operation. One such application might be a line describing editing options while using a text editor. However, each part of the program should display its own menu line, minimizing the user's need to memorize options.

Another approach is to allow multiple selections from a menu. This is somewhat unusual, because most menu operations select a single operation as opposed to multiple objects. However, sometimes it is appropriate, as shown in AppleWorks' file operations. Since several files can be active in memory (or "on the desktop") at once, the file selection menu allows the user to select more than one file at a time. This certainly streamlines file operations for the program's user and should be carefully considered when it is possible. The programming is not difficult; you simply return a list of choices from the menu display procedure.

Another interesting menu technique is introduced by Bly and Mall-gren called *cycling softkeys*. This technique puts a set of short display menus on the screen with each menu corresponding to a separate function key. Each press of a function key acts like a down arrow for its menu, moving the selection down and wrapping around at the bottom. When all selections are made, another action such as a RETURN keypress is needed to confirm them. These menus can be independent or the choice from one menu may determine the options for another. Figure 3.8 shows this latter approach, where each choice of `Action` changes the details of the other menus. The cycling softkeys technique is limited by availability of screen space or the need for more commands than the function keys can provide, but, if it can be used, it is a very appealing design.

Since we have seen menus built with both keystrokes and the mouse as the selection device, we should mention some of the tradeoffs between keystrokes and mice. Many users are uncomfortable with the need to move a hand from the keyboard to a mouse, make a positioning choice, and then return to the keys. This is especially a problem for persons who

Action	Brush	Color
Draw	●	Black
Type	●	Red
Graph	◉	Green

Action	Size	Face
Draw	9 pt	Normal
Type	10 pt	**Bold**
Graph	12 pt	*Italics*

Action	Type	Axes
Draw	Bar	Grid
Type	Line	Tics
Graph		None

Figure 3.8   *A simple set of cycling softkeys with commands and parameters*

are highly skilled with keyboards. Keystrokes are faster for choosing items in well-structured menus. However, a mouse is usually better than keys for positioning the cursor on a completely random point on the screen, since using a mouse is very close to pointing. We illustrate the overall design of a menu selection routine with both mouse and keyboard functions and do the final program example for keyboard only.

A mouse's graphic capabilities can be extended to include joysticks, game paddles, or light pens as described in Chapter 2. Programming these devices is fairly straightforward. The increasing availability of good graphic equipment and the growing user demand for easy interaction makes the following principle increasingly important:

PRINCIPLE: Design your programs to give the user access to the most natural and powerful devices available for program interaction.

Implementing Text Menus

The programming involved for a standard text menu is fairly simple but does require the ability to write characters at any location on the screen without rewriting the entire screen. Below we outline the organization of a subroutine for such a menu. Our pseudocode in Figure 3.9 is fairly close to Pascal and should be easy to follow.

The only problems here are keeping track of the previous and current choices, managing the text written to specific screen locations, and rewriting the menu choices with and without highlighting. Note that these are all independent of the menu details; this is really a common skeleton with varying text and actions. We follow up on this idea in the next section. Figure 3.10 shows the code that implements this as a C function on a Unix machine, using the general functions GotoXY defined below and Highlight and ClearScreen, defined in this code. Some specific vt100 code is included, but it is clearly marked.

This code solves all three problems noted above. Direct screen access in this example is much like that found in most Pascal systems on personal computers, calling a "GotoXY" system procedure to position output anywhere on the screen. Screen locations are kept in data arrays. Note that highlighting on this menu depends on the capabilities of the terminal or personal computer that is used.

The screen control available for personal computers is much harder to do on time-shared systems since different terminals have very different

PROCEDURE: Menu

INPUT: none

PROCESSING:
```
    Variables:
        array of screen locations for menu choices
        user input key value
        user event value
    Display menu screen:
        Top of screen header describing menu and giving location
        Move to first menu line
        For each menu line
            Print number & menu item with first letter capitalized
            Skip to next menu line
        Write menu screen footer at bottom of page
        Highlight the default choice
    Get user input:
        while choice is not finished do
            get a user event (keystroke or mouse button)
            if event is keystroke then
                if key = RETURN then finished
                else if key = good digit then
                    remove previous highlight, highlight new choice
                else if key = good character then
                    remove previous highlight, highlight new choice
                else if key = up or down arrow then
                    remove previous highlight, highlight new choice
                else
                    do something to say key is invalid: beep bell?
            if event is mouse button then
                if mouse is double-clicked then finished
                else if mouse location is within menu range then
                    remove previous highlight, highlight new choice
                else
                    do something to say location is invalid
        end-while
    Perform action indicated by choice, if any
    Return
```

OUTPUT: none; the chosen operation is performed.

Figure 3.9 *Pseudocode for a menu*

ways of handling cursor movement. There are standards for terminal control, primarily the ANSI X3.64 standard informally known as the "vt100" standard. Under this standard certain character sequences control cursor movement, as given by Figure 3.11. For more details of vt100 operations, refer to the termcap entry of Figure 13.6.

```
#define LINESIZE        20
#define COUNT            5
#define DEFAULT          1
#define CR              '\013'      /* Carriage return */
#define ESC             '\027'      /* Escape key */
#define TopLine          2
#define BottomLine      24
#define LeftMargin      10
#define IndentMargin    15
#define LeadinKey       ESC         /* vt100 specific */

int DoAMenu();
{
    int i, last, current, row[COUNT]={6,9,12,15,18};
    char ch, firsts[COUNT]={'a','b','c','d','e'};
    char *MenuList[COUNT]={"A - first line","B - second line",
            "C - third line","D - fourth line","E - fifth line"};

/* Display original menu screen with default choice indicated */
    ClearScreen();                              /* see function definition below */
    GotoXY(TopLine, LeftMargin); ReverseVideo; /* see fn defn below */
    printf("%s","Sample Menu - Brown and Cunningham"); ReverseVideo;
    for ( i = 0; i < COUNT; i++ ) {
        GotoXY(row[i],IndentMargin);
        printf("%d    %s",i+1,*MenuList[i]);
    }
    GotoXY(BottomLine,LeftMargin); ReverseVideo;
    printf("%s","Use arrow keys, number keys, or letter keys");
    last = current = default;
    GotoXY(row[current],IndentMargin); ReverseVideo;
    printf("%d    %s",current+1,*MenuList[current]); ReverseVideo;

/* Now get user input and respond until user presses RETURN */
    system ("stty raw; stty-echo"); /* turn off character echoing until done
*/
    while ( (ch=getchar()) != CR ) {
        if ( ch == LeadinKey ) {            /* recognize an arrow key */
            if ( UpArrow() )                /* check up arrow */
                if (current++ > COUNT) current = 1;
            if ( DnArrow() )                /* check down arrow */
                if (current-- < 1) current = COUNT; }
        if ( (ch >= '1') && (ch <= COUNT+'0')    /* recognize valid nbr */
            current = ch = '0';
        for ( i=0; i < COUNT; i++ )         /* scan for valid first letter */
            if ((ch = firsts[i])||(ch = 'a'-'A'+firsts[i]))
                current = i+1;
        if (current != last) {
            GotoXY(row[last],IndentMargin); ReverseVideo;
            printf("%d    %s",last+1,*MenuList[last]);
            GotoXY(row[current],IndentMargin); ReverseVideo;
            printf("%d    %s",current+1,*MenuList[current]);
            last = current; }
    }
    system ("stty raw; stty-echo"); /* user has pressed RETURN now; resume
echo */
    return( current )
```

continued

```
}
int UpArrow()                  /* sample for vt100 */
{   if (( (ch = getchar() ) == '[' ) && ( (ch = getchar() ) == 'A' ))
        return( 1 );           /* overall sequence is ESC [ A */
    else
        return( 0 ); }

int DnArrow()                  /* sample for vt100 */
{   if (( (ch = getchar() ) == '[' ) && ( (ch = getchar() ) == 'B' ))
        return( 1 );           /* overall sequence is ESC [ B */
    else
        return( 0 ); }

ReverseVideo                   /* sample for vt100 */
{   printf("2%c[7m",ESC); }    /* toggle between normal/reverse video */

ClearScreen()                  /* sample for vt100 */
'{   printf("%c",'\012'); }    /* control-L */
```

Figure 3.10   *Actual menu code*

```
Cursor Control for the vt100 terminal (ANSI x3.64)
        ^ = ESC key (ASCII 27)
        N = digit string for the number N
```

Movement	character sequence
Cursor up N lines	^[NA
Cursor down N lines	^[NB
Cursor right N characters	^[NC
Cursor left N characters	^[ND
Cursor position row N column M	^[N;MH
Cursor index down	^D
Cursor index up	^M
Cursor start next line	^E

Figure 3.11   *vt100 cursor movement*

The use of vt100 control sequences will let us write a routine for these terminals which acts just like the GotoXY procedure of microcomputer Pascal. In turn, this will let you use the same menu subroutines for time-shared computers that you use for micros, reducing the number of wheels that must be invented for your programming.

We will assume that your program keeps track of the current cursor position in variables OldX and OldY; as we see in Chapter 5, this is almost certainly already needed for data input. The routine is shown in pseudo-code in Figure 3.12.

PROCEDURE: **GotoXY**

INPUT: **two screen coordinates, NewX and NewY.**

PROCESSING:
   use the current text coordinates, which must be available
   compute the relative X and Y screen distances that the
   **   cursor must travel**
   use index up or index down to move to the correct line
   use cursor right or cursor left to move to the correct
   ** . space**

Figure 3.12 *Pseudocode for* `GotoXY`

```
GotoXY( R, C )                          /* vt100 version */
    int  R, C;     /* R = row; C = column */
    {
            printf("%s%d%c%d%c","^[",R,';',C,'H');
    }
```

```
#include <dos.h>
union REGS inregs, outregs;
GotoXY( R, C )                          /* IBM PC version */
    int  R, C;
    {
        inregs.h.ah = 2;                /* function */
        inregs.h.dh = R;                /* row number */
        inregs.h.dl = C;                /* column number */
        int86(0x10, &inregs, &outregs); /* generate interrupt */
    }
```

Figure 3.13 *Two implementations of GotoXY*

The codes for this operation for the vt100 terminal and for the IBM PC are shown in Figure 3.13. Note how the vt100 version uses the particular "Cursor Position" operation in the vt100 standard, and the IBM PC uses registers and interrupts. These allow you to avoid complex logic for efficient cursor motion.

Both the GotoXY functions implement the cursor movement with a direct access instruction, but this may not always be available. If it is not, it may be necessary to move the cursor a row or a column at a time, and movement to the start of the row, end of the row, top of the page, etc. may also be available. It might not be most efficient to simply make the device step by rows and/or columns to the new position; special cases might be used to speed this up. For example, is the new position closer to the start of the line than to the current position? If so, then move the cursor to the start of the row and use cursor up or down instead of cursor index, so the cursor will be at the beginning of the new line and you can space to the right from there. The resulting optimized routine will be full of special cases, but I/O is much slower than tests, so sending fewer characters will pay off in the end.

A more general approach is found in the Unix environment, where the system contains a terminal capability file (usually named /etc/termcap or /etc/terminfo) which is read at the program's runtime. This allows all applications to be written for a generic terminal and to have the appropriate controls given from the termcap file. In addition, most Unix systems include a tool named curses which allows the programmer to develop applications with direct cursor control and with text windows for general terminals. In Chapter 10 we show a screen developed with curses. Using this tool you can create a sequence of overlapping windows; each window can easily be a menu screen so the user can see the sequence of active menus at any time. The code for such a screen is relatively straightforward, being mostly a sequence of calls to the curses library routines. Unfortunately, curses is one of the more difficult pieces of Unix on which to find decent information. We give more information and some concrete examples of curses code in Chapter 10.

We have used the general term "highlighted" to refer to the way the current menu choice is indicated on the screen. This can take many forms. A few methods that have been used are printing the selected text in inverse video, printing it in an alternate standout color, surrounding it with a line-drawn box, and printing an arrow or a check mark in front of the choice. Some examples are given in Chapter 2. Again, consistency with other programs and internal consistency should guide your choice.

A More General Menu Approach

The menu in the previous section suffers from a probably fatal flaw: it is hardcoded into a single procedure. If this is used in a prototyping environment, the programmer must write a new procedure for each menu. He or she must also rewrite the procedure and recompile the program whenever a menu is changed. It is difficult to ensure that each menu works exactly the same way, since they are all written individually (and possibly by different people). Moreover, changing the menu interaction style for the whole program requires rewriting all the separate menu procedures, a daunting task. When the program reaches production, all these menu procedures require their own code space, so the program is quite large. However, if you look at the procedure's code a bit you will see that all the operations are the same for all menus; only the number of choices, text of the choices, and chosen operations differ. In this section we look at ways to make this process more general. By doing this, the menus operate consistently, all menu operations are updated by changing only one procedure, and the code space for menu presentation is a single procedure.

We cannot claim that a general approach to menus is new. In fact, the MPW and MacApp development systems for the Macintosh and the Microsoft Windows system for the IBM PC use this approach under the name of *resources*. A resource is an object from a class of previously defined tools the system can use. Examples include cursors, fonts, icon lists, and windows. The programmer must specify the contents of this object and then apply a resource compiler to create an image of the object in a form the program can use. An example of a Microsoft Windows resource definition and the pulldown menu it defines are shown in Figure 3.14 from Jamsa, while resource definitions for the Macintosh are found in the MacApp example in Chapter 10. A resource compiler allows programs to read binary images of data and special data structures without requiring the programmer to handle all these intricacies manually. With the idea, then, that a menu is a resource, the programmer can give the contents of each menu and have a menu presented by a single procedure; all the procedure need receive is the number of the menu.

Two problems must be solved if you are going to implement the concept of a menu resource for a program yourself. First, how are you going to store the text information so the single menu procedure can retrieve it? Second, how are you going to connect the text information with the actual procedures that the menu choices are to call? We outline some possible answers to these questions, while realizing that more efficient answers are available to programmers working on a specific system.

```
name MENU
begin
  POPUP "File"
    begin
      MENUITEM "Run...", 1
      MENUITEM "Load...", 2
      MENUITEM "Copy...", 3
      MENUITEM "Get Info", 4
      MENUITEM "Delete...", 5
      MENUITEM "Print...", 6
      MENUITEM "Rename...", 7
    end
end
```

Figure 3.14 *Microsoft Windows resource and its pulldown menu*

The actual menu storage is most logically in the form of a list. Each individual menu then becomes a single item in this list. Within a single menu itself is found the menu title, the number of choices in the menu, and another list of the menu's choices. Each choice is made up of the text for the choice's menu listing and the name of the procedure to be called if this choice is made. Thus, storage of menus is really a question of how to store lists. Since we are concerned here with a working solution, and are more concerned with making it understandable than with making it optimal, we suggest that each menu be stored as a file record. Then, displaying menu i becomes reading the menu record file for record i and using it. Each record, then, will contain the menu name as a text string, the count of menu items as an integer, and an array of subrecords that each contain the text of a menu choice as a text string and the name of the procedure to be called, also as a text string. More formally, these menu record and file structures can be given by the Pascal type and data definitions in Figure 3.15. The function of the resource compiler in this case would be to translate the programmer's entries in a human-readable form into these records and enter them into a file.

The next problem is connecting the text in MenuItems[i].Action with the actual procedure call needed to implement the function of the menu choice. In principle this could be handled by replacing the Action item by the load address of the function at run time. We will again take a simpler path, however, and suggest that each menu choice be passed to a single procedure that "decodes" the desired action. This procedure takes the name and matches it with the action in a very simple way, illustrated by the code sketch of Figure 3.16.

```
TYPE    MenuRec = record
        MenuTitle = packed array[1..NMax] of char;
        Count  = 1..ItemMax;
        MenuItems = array[1..ItemMax] of record
            Choice = packed array[1..ChoiceMax] of char;
            Action = packed array[1..NMax] of char
            end
        end

VAR
        MenuFile = file of MenuRec;
```

Figure 3.15 *Record definition for a resource file*

PROCEDURE: **DoIt**

INPUT: **One string, the name of the procedure to be called**

PROCESSING:
```
for each letter
    for each procedure that uniquely starts with letters so far
        if the input string matches the letters so far
            call that procedure
        if the input string does not match the letters so far
            go on to one further letter
```

OUTPUT: **None; the desired procedure has been executed.**

Figure 3.16 *Design of a procedure invoker*

3.3 Programming Graphic Menus

Another type of menu is the graphic menu, based on symbols, icons, colors, or patterns instead of text or descriptions. Here a graphic input device is normally used to select a point, and the point chosen is given meaning by its location. As noted above, graphic menus are not the same thing as direct manipulation because manipulation implies that an action goes along with the selection, where the menu choice simply uses graphics techniques instead of typing to choose an option.

In the post-Macintosh era, it is tempting to phrase all our discussions in terms of devices that control a cursor or other on-screen position indicator, as is usually the case with a mouse or graphics tablet. However, other possibilities exist. Many applications are built around a tablet with a plastic template on the tablet's surface. The meaning of a chosen point on the tablet is then carried by the template and is not reflected on the screen. This is very useful when the screen has no graphic capabilities and is often used with nongraphics terminals. Our examples and principles are primarily oriented to on-screen graphic menus, but are also applicable for programs designed with a template on a tablet. Such templates are shown in Chapter 2.

The way a program communicates with graphics devices varies widely among computers and among devices. On one hand, there are computer-specific devices such as the Apple II game paddles, which transmit their activities to particular memory locations; here you simply read the value at these locations. On the other hand, devices such as graphics tablets use standard communications and operate by sending messages back and forth between the computer and the device. For these, you must usually send an attention message to the device and then wait for the response. The exact nature of the message and response depends on the device.

Principles of Graphic Menus

When you work with graphic menus, the number of items that should be on the menu is determined by how quickly menu items can be recognized and selected. A whole-screen menu can provide up to 256 color choices, and a part-screen shape menu up to a dozen or so, depending on the accuracy of the graphics pointing system. Human response to a positioning task is covered by Fitts' Law, which states that the time it takes to locate an item is given by

$$C + K \log_2(D/S + 0.5)$$

where D is the distance to the item's location, S is the size of the object, and C and K are constants. Thus location time increases for larger movements or smaller targets; small items can slow down the selection process considerably. In addition, some devices make it fairly difficult to place the cursor on a small spot. Inexpensive joysticks can make only coarse motions, while onscreen crosshairs may move too quickly to allow careful positioning. If you emulate a graphics selector with arrow keys, they must give large jumps when pressed so you can move quickly all the way across the screen. This possible lack of fine control leads to a general principle:

PRINCIPLE: Be sure your graphic menu items are easily selectable by the system's graphic devices.

Graphic menus are more difficult to make legible than are text menus. There are many ways to convey information graphically, including color, shape, and text. Because of the complexity of graphic information, we have several principles of graphic communication.

PRINCIPLE: Be sure your graphic representations are immediately distinguishable from each other.

If a graphic menu contains a number of items, it is time-consuming to read the entire menu to find a particular menu choice. When there are different kinds of choices, they can be grouped by function to save the user search time. Grouping can be done by physically separating some graphic items from others, by using different overall shapes for different groups (much like traffic signs), or by using different colors. For more information on color as a communication tool, see Chapter 8.

> PRINCIPLE: Use grouping to give a first level of discrimination in graphic menus.

The concept of a graphic icon has grown out of the need for graphically distinguishable symbols. Icons are commonly associated with the Apple Macintosh but are getting wide use in other new systems. The most difficult problem with icons is developing a graphic that really represents the concept or item you mean. This seems to be an activity better left to people with real graphic arts experience; our observation is that programmers seem to create icons that are hard for computer novices to interpret. Besides graphic design, you may want to look at the field of *semiotics*, the general theory and practice of signs. Some aspects of this field deal with aspects of signs in computer interfaces.

Icons can be a real asset to a system and have been held to be copyrightable. Some examples of icons from different applications, including some from noncomputer sources, are shown in Figure 3.17.

> PRINCIPLE: Be sure your graphic items carry the meaning you intend.

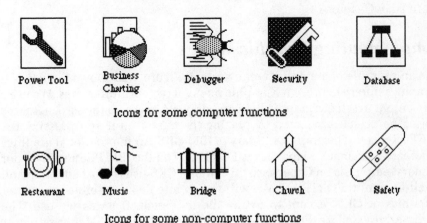

Power Tool   Business Charting   Debugger   Security   Database

Icons for some computer functions

Restaurant   Music   Bridge   Church   Safety

Icons for some non-computer functions

Figure 3.17   *A number of different icons*

When we discussed text menus we always highlighted the current choice before that choice was selected. This is also an important feature in graphic menus. This highlighting can be done in many ways: reverse video, blinking, surrounding the choice by a box, brightening, redrawing in a special "chosen" color or with intensified lines, or moving the choice to a separate "current selection" field. The principle of menu highlighting is given below; we have shown examples of highlighting in Chapter 2.

PRINCIPLE: In any graphic or text menu, highlight the currently selected item.

We have said that you should always use the most powerful user communication tool available. However, when you are writing a program for a wide variety of users who will have systems with different configurations, you will not always have these powerful tools available. Recall that while describing text menus we gave the principle that each program should allow the user to choose among as many ways to use the program as possible. This is equally true with graphic menus and graphic devices. For example, you might design a paintbox system to use a mouse or trackball but include facilities so it can be used with only the arrow keys if that is all that is available. This is greatly aided if you use design and implementation tools that include capabilities for a number of devices; then runtime hardware checks or user configuration programs can define the environment for the program and allow the use of available devices without heavy reprogramming. Some of these runtime checks are described in Chapter 13.

Implementing Graphic Menus

As an example of a graphic menu system, Figure 3.18 shows the use of a graphics library to present a graphic menu of two furniture types. We use a pick input to select a graphic item and draw its image on the screen. In this case, the object is selected by placing the cursor on it and pressing the RETURN key. The graphics library is IBM GKS, an international graphics standard system. Our language is FORTRAN on the IBM PC in spite of our general emphasis on C, because this kind of GKS use is most common and well-known in FORTRAN. We will not go into detail on either computer graphics or GKS, except to define the fundamental terms we use. The subroutine calls use the GKS standard names for FORTRAN subroutines.

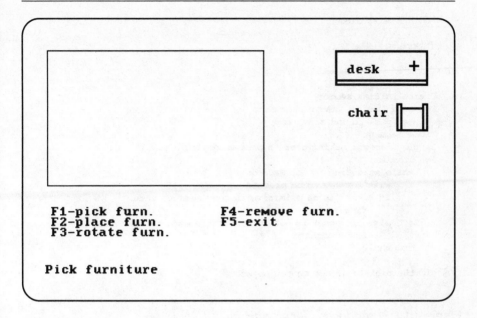

Figure 3.18 *The graphic menu*

The following GKS functions have occurred in this program before the code sketch we present:

- GKS has been initialized and opened.
- The workstation, in our case an IBM PC with graphics display and keyboard input, has been opened and activated.
- Model and device coordinates have been set up by means of workstation and normalization transformations.
- The pictures of the room and the two pieces of furniture have been displayed on the screen. Note: each of the pieces of furniture is a graphic primitive. They are grouped into the segment that makes up the graphics menu.
- A menu of function keys has been displayed and *F1 - pick furn.* has been selected.

Since FORTRAN on the IBM PC does not allow the use of communication ports (to which graphics devices such as tablets would be attached), the example uses cursor control keys on the keyboard for menu selection. The pseudocode design is given in Figure 3.19 and the FORTRAN code is in Figure 3.20.

PROCEDURE: **GraphicMenu**

INPUT: **None**

PROCESSING:
```
    Initialize screen
    Create initial segment
    For each item in the graphic menu
        Set pick id and draw item
    Close segment
    Display message asking user to pick an object
    Get user input:
        while selection is not made do
            wait for key to be pressed
            if cursor is on primitive in menu segment then
                finished
            else if cursor is not in selectable menu segment then
                issue message
        end-while
```

OUTPUT: **the pick id of the chosen object**

Figure 3.19 *Pseudocode for graphic menu*

```
C     This is the Fortran code for generating a graphic menu and
C     picking from the menu, as illustrated in Figure 3.16.  The
C     example is part of a demonstration program for the IBM
C     Personal Computer Graphical Kernal System and uses IBM
C     Personal Computer Professional FORTRAN.
C
C*****************************************************************
C*    Data for the menu segment
C*****************************************************************
      real xdry(6),ydry(6),xchry1(9),ychry1(9)
      real xchry2(2),ychry2(2),xchry3(3),ychry3(3)
      data xdry/75.0,100.0,100.0,75.0,75.0,100.0/
      data ydry/87.0,87.0,100.0,100.0,88.0,88.0/
      data xchry1/93.0,93.0,94.0,94.0,99.0,99.0,100.0,100.0,93.0/
      data ychry1/73.0,80.0,80.0,73.0,73.0,80.0,80.0,73.0,73.0/
      data xchry2/94.0,99.0/, ychry2/79.0,79.0/
      data xchry3/93.0,93.0,100.0,100.0,93.0/
      data ychry3/73.0,80.0,80.0,73.0,73.0/
C*****************************************************************
C*    Create and display the menu segment
C*****************************************************************
C     Create segment 100:  2 pieces of furniture
C
      call gcrsg(100)
```

continued

```
C
C     Set up the first piece of furniture in the graphic menu:
C     Set pickid to 101 for the first piece of furniture
C     Set fill color to background color
C     Set fill interior style to solid
C     Output an invisible fill area
C     Set line color to index 1
C     Draw a polyline to make a desk
C     Set text color to 3 and output text identifier.
C
      call gspkid(101)
      call gsfaci(0)
      call gsfais(1)
      call gfa(6,xdry,ydry)
      call gsplci(1)
      call gpl(6,xdry,ydry)
      call gstxci(3)
      call gtxs(78.5,92.0,4,'desk')
C
C     Set up the second piece of furniture in the graphic menu:
C     Set pickid to 102 for the second piece of furniture
C     Output an invisible fill area
C     Draw two polylines to make a chair
C     Output text identifier
C
      call gspkid(102)
      call gfa(5,xchry3,ychry3)
      call gpl(9,xchry1,ychry1)
      call gpl(2,xchry2,ychry2)
      call gtxs(78.0,77.0,5,'chair')
C
C     close the segment
C
      call gclsg
C*****************************************************************
C*    Pick a piece of furniture from the menu
C*****************************************************************
C
C     Display message asking user to pick a piece of furniture
C     Request input from the pick input device
C        Status will be zero until the cursor is at a primitive at
C        return
C
      call gtxs(0.0,1.0,33,'Pick Furniture             ')
2000  call grqpk(wkid1,1,status,segnam,pickid)
      if (status .eq. 0) goto 2000
C
C     The graphic menu segment is 100; there's an error if this is
C     not the picked item
C
      if (segnam .ne. 100) then
        call gtxs(0.0,1.0,33,'Can not pick this furniture     ')
        goto 2000
      endif
```

Figure 3.20 *FORTRAN code for graphic menu program*

This graphic menu uses a graphics library to do its graphic operation. Other approaches make use of built-in software tools to manage graphic menus. While these are available on MS-DOS systems with GEM or Microsoft Windows, the best example is given by the toolbox ROM on the Apple Macintosh, especially combined with the MacApp application template. These toolkits allow you to build pulldown menus, button boxes, and icons; provide for mouse-based highlighting and selection techniques; and do all this in a style completely consistent with other applications on these systems. Thus, you get the advantages of consistency and straightforward application writing without having to create all your menu-creation tools from scratch. Such toolkits are described in Chapter 10.

PRINCIPLE: Use toolkits whenever possible to make your job easier and to make your software consistent with the user's expectations.

This consistency is so valuable to the user that the Macintosh user depends on software manuals for assistance much less often than users of other systems; the entire function of the software is usually laid out via the available menus. However, programming on the Macintosh requires a detailed knowledge of this toolbox and extensive knowledge of the subtle points of the language used.

3.4   Readings

There are few references that deal directly with the mechanics of menu programming. The menu support offered by a particular system will be covered in the manuals for that system; see for example the Apple MacApp manual for MacApp pulldown menus and the Microsoft Windows references by Jamsa and Petzold.

Implementing generalized menus with the concept of a menu resource is a fairly straightforward application of list processing. Any good data structures text, such as Horowitz and Sahni, should be of help in this.

Icon design is basically a problem in graphic design, not in programming. Marcus has written about this problem in several places, such as the Marcus 1985 article. The theory of semiotics is less familiar to computer people, but Caluda and Mareno's article on semiotics will be interesting here.

Graphic menus are a special case of graphics interaction and, in particular, selection of graphic objects. The general problem is covered in the better computer graphics texts, such as Foley and van Dam. Details on selection in various graphics systems are given in their respective manuals, but see particularly Enderle, Kansy, and Pfaff for information on GKS.

## Chapter 4

PROGRAMMING
COMMAND-BASED SYSTEMS

W_e saw that commands offer the user control over complex programs with a wide range of options. Giving the user such powerful and flexible control has its price, however. Careful design and planning can keep this under control, so this chapter focuses on general toolkit approaches to accepting and acting on commands.

4.1 Examples of Command-Driven Systems

To set the stage for the discussions that follow, let us consider three particular command-driven systems. For each, we give some background on the system, some examples of commands in the system and their function, and a description of creating command scripts for the system.

Unix

Unix is one of the most widely used and far-reaching operating systems in use today. It runs on micros, minis, superminis, mainframes, multiprocessors, and supercomputers. It runs in two basic forms—the Berkeley releases (bsd 4.3 for 32-bit machines, bsd 2.10 for PDP-11's) and the official AT&T System V (V.3), but both offer the user the same basic functions. Unix was originally developed at Bell Laboratories in the early 1970's and made its way out via the universities to become the tool of choice for a generation of hardcore programmers. Its primary audience historically has been computer experts. As more people need to get information from remote computers, and as more and more general-purpose computers use Unix, end users with less experience are now needing to use such systems.

One of the strengths of Unix lies in the concept of *shells*. These are programs that accept user input and in turn call for the execution of the user's choices. When a user logs onto a Unix machine, the user's choice of shell program is executed and runs as long as the user is signed on. Beyond the standard shells, called the Bourne and C shells after the designer of the first shell, Steve Bourne, and the programming syntax of the second shell, respectively, custom shells have been written to support special uses of the system. Some early Unix computers even featured menu-driven shells in an attempt to make the system more available to nonexperts; these menu-based shells are still available and can be a good way to introduce novices to Unix. Current efforts to provide different Unix shells include Apple's work to make their version of Unix, A/UX, operate in a standard Macintosh fashion, and Sun's work to provide the Open Look interface to Unix. So, Unix does not offer a single face to the world; it can have whatever look its programmers want.

Unix presents its user with a prompt when it is ready to accept a command. This prompt is somewhat user-definable and ranges from very simple to rather complex. Examples are shown in Figure 4.1.

A user responds to this prompt by naming an executable file with parameters as needed or desired. The number of commands available is unlimited, because each program is executed simply by typing its name (no LOAD or RUN commands here!) Moreover, any text file can be made executable simply by changing its mode setting. This is frequently done with lists of commands in a single file, making new user-defined commands. Since these text files can have variables and control statements, especially in the C shell, they are usually called *shell programs* or *shell scripts*. Two examples are shown in Figure 4.2. Of course, a user cannot execute any program or shell program on the entire computer; access is limited to those programs in the user's path unless the user knows, and types, their full path name, and the user must have appropriate file permissions.

default Bourne shell	**$**
Bourne shell showing host	**(hostname) $**
default C shell, showing level of current process	**[1] ~#**
C shell after directory change showing host, process level and current directory	**(host) [3] ~/xxx/yy#**

Figure 4.1   *Some Unix shell prompts*

```
# Shell script to compile a group of C programs, passed to the
# command line, and retain the compiled programs with the .c
# extension changed to .x (for executable).
for i in $*          # for each argument to the command
do
    echo $i:          # print out the file name being compiled
    cc -o 'basename $i .c'.x $i       # cc -o ExecFile SrcFile
done
```

```
# Shell script to loop forever, holding a terminal active on a
# system that wants to go away after a time of less than 10 minutes
while true
# that is, loop forever until user terminates
do
    date
    if mail -e
    then
        echo You have mail
    fi
    sleep 600          # 600 seconds, that is, 10 minutes
done
```

Figure 4.2   *Two small Unix shell scripts*

It is common for Unix commands to have a large number of optional parameters, which is made easy by the way C handles arguments to a command line. By convention, these arguments are listed with a dash (-) indicating that they are arguments to the command. Some examples of standard Unix commands and their arguments are shown in Figure 4.3.

These commands are extremely terse and abbreviated, and commands can be "piped" together to create powerful actions from simple parts. Again, Unix is historically an expert's system (some would even say a hacker's system) whose users are expected to cope with sometimes obscure names and nonintuitive syntax.

It is fairly simple for a C program under Unix to handle arguments to the program. Some programmers will even use this technique instead of, or in addition to, interacting with the user for program values. Of course, this is consistent with technical Unix users, so it is appropriate for this audience. An example of this technique is shown in Figure 4.4.

```
ls          list names of all files in current directory
ls -l a*    list names and properties (long format) of all files in the current
            directory whose names begin with 'a'
ls -lR      list names and properties (long format) of all files in the current
            directory and in all its subdirectories
```

Figure 4.3   *Variations in the Unix* ls *command*

```
/* Command decoding:  This program takes a number of parameters through
 * the command line in standard Unix fashion.  These parameters, and
 * their flags are:
 *    -c  insert the real and imaginary parts of the constant c
 *    -i  determine the maximum number of iterations allowed
 *    -m  determine the value which, when exceeded, stops iterations
 *    -x  enter the low and high x-coordinates of the domain
 *    -y  enter the low and high y-coordinates of the domain
 */
/*
 * Set up default values for the data
 */
double real_c=-.11, imag_c=.6557, x0=-1.5, x1=1.5, y0=-1.5, y1=1.5;
float max = 100.;
int   iter = 100;
/*
 * Main interprets the command line arguments and sets up the parameters,
 * then calls do_fractal to perform the actual computations.
 */

main( argc, argv )
   int argc;
   char **argv;
{
   char *cp;
   double atof();

   while (- argc) {
      if ( *(cp = *(++argv)) == '-' )
         switch ( *( ++ cp ) ) {
            case 'c' : real_c = atof( *( ++argv) );
               imag_c = atof( *( ++argv) ); argc -= 2;
               continue;
            case 'x' : x0 = atof( *( ++argv ) );
               x1 = atof( *( ++argv ) ); argc -= 2;
               continue;
            case 'y' : y0 = atof( *( ++argv ) );
               y1 = atof( *( ++argv ) ); argc -= 2;
               continue;
            case 'i' : iter = atoi( *( ++argv ) );
               argc--; continue;
            case 'm' : max = atof( *( ++argv ) );
               argc--; continue;
         }
printf("Usage: fractal [-c <re> <im>][-i <iter>][-m <max>]",
      "[-x <x0> <x1>][-y <y0> <y1>]\n");
   exit(1);
   }
   do_fractal();
}
```

Figure 4.4 *Unix command decoding*

Unix usually comes with its entire manual on-line, so the manual is available at a moment's notice to users who forget details. For such an audience and with such help, these cryptic commands are acceptable; for a more general audience, they would not be.

dBASE IV

dBASE IV is a direct and very closely related descendant of dBASE III and dBASE II, among the first microcomputer database systems (there was no dBASE I.) dBASE IV runs on MS-DOS computers, and the dBASE series is probably the most widely used PC database. Its uses are in business or personal applications, and its users are persons who are not computer experts.

dBASE IV offers its users two modes of operation. The newest, called the *Control Center*, gives the user an interactive interface to control database creation, editing, and operations; it was discussed briefly in Chapter 3. The original dBASE II and the most powerful mode for dBASE III were based on commands. This capability is also present in dBASE IV. The prompt for the commands is simply a period, '.', and some examples of its commands are shown in Figure 4.5.

These commands are straightforward and use English command words that express the desired actions quite effectively. Novices learning dBASE IV have much more trouble with the concepts of manipulating files than they do with the commands themselves, but a good deal of training is necessary on the system before a user becomes proficient.

It is possible to do all your work with dBASE IV interactively, but it is also possible to write command files, which have variables and control statements and are called "dBASE programs," to do work for you. These programs are about as powerful as programs in early versions of BASIC, but their syntax is somewhat more primitive since dBASE tries to use English instead of the cleaner notations of programming languages. These dBASE programs are invoked by the command .DO *programname*. An example of a simple dBASE IV program is shown in Figure 4.6.

```
.USE filename
.SORT ON fieldname TO filename
.INDEX ON fieldname TO indexfilename
.DISPLAY FIELDS fieldlist FOR condition TO PRINT
```

Figure 4.5 *Some dBASE IV commands*

```
* Print a simple mailing list of active customers from a larger
* mailing list.  Labels start every six lines, and the address is
* three lines.  The list is to be sorted by zipcodes, so use the
* indexed version of the list.
USE maillist INDEX byzips
SET TALK OFF
CLEAR
@ 2, 20 SAY 'Be sure printer is ready and contains 1-up labels'
@ 4, 20 SAY 'Press <RETURN> when ready'
WAIT
SET PRINT ON
DO WHILE .NOT. EOF()
   IF customer = 'Y'
      ?
      ? name
      ? address
      ? city + ' ' + state + '  ' + zipcode
      ?
      ?
   ENDIF
   SKIP
ENDDO
SET PRINT OFF
SET TALK ON
```

Figure 4.6   *A simple dBASE program*

Tell-a-Graf

Tell-a-Graf is an interactive system for generating a variety of standard graphs and plots. Such graphs are defined by giving the data and setting a number of attributes for the graph, such as graph type (line graph, bar chart, pie chart...), labels, data markers, legends, etc. The data can come from a file or interactively from the user, and the attributes can be set in any order. These attributes are set by commands which can be given in any order. The commands allow considerable abbreviation; for example, GENERATE A BAR CHART can be written GEN A BAR. Commands also allow extra words in them to make them more English-like.

At any point while setting up a graph, the user can ask for the current version of the graph to be displayed at a graphics terminal, and the user can then return to the process of refining the graph. A brief example of a Tell-a-Graf session is shown in Figure 4.7 and the graph it defines is shown in Figure 4.8; the program prompts are in plain text, and the user entries are in boldface.

TELAGRAF
SPECIFY FILES:
    [..RETURN here means data from keyboard]
GENERATE LEVEL..ENTER:
GEN A BAR.
GENERATING A BAR CHART
ENTER:
TITLE TEXT IS 'ACTIVITY INDEX BY MONTH'.
TITLE TEXT IS 'ACTIVITY INDEX BY MONTH'.
ENTER:
X AXIS TYPE IS MONTHLY.
X AXIS TYPE IS TIME.
ENTER:
SEQUENCE DATA.
72, 110, 124, 130, 104, 95, 100, 64, 95,
104, 110, 100
EOD.
DATA VALUES IS 72, 110, PLUS 10 MORE NUMBERS.
ENTER:
Y AXIS LABEL IS '% OF AVERAGE ACTIVITY'.
Y AXIS LABEL TEXT IS '% OF AVERAGE ACTIVITY'.
ENTER:
MAKE A FRAME.
AXIS FRAME IS ENABLED.
ENTER:
TURN THE Y GRID ON.
Y GRID IS ENABLED.
ENTER:
SEND.

Figure 4.7   *Tell-a-Graf Commands*

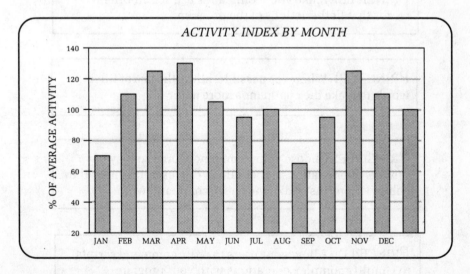

Figure 4.8   *Tell-a-Graf graph*

4.2 Options for Commands

The examples of command-based systems above show a number of options that are available for commands. Commands can be very terse and almost artificial, as in Unix; can use English words but still be tightly structured, as in dBASE IV; or can allow flexibility in format with alternatives and extra fill words, as in Tell-a-Graf. In all these cases, ordinary text is entered, and the text is then broken up into words and tokens that represent the commands and their parameters, and then the commands are executed with the parameters that are passed to them.

The nature of a command system must, of course, be matched to its intended audience. A minimal system, such as Unix's, provides little support to its user, since its users are expected to be computer experts. A system such as dBASE IV offers less cryptic commands and more English filler words (SORT ON ... TO ...); its users are less expert but still need considerable training. A system designed for more casual users, such as Tell-a-Graf, needs a still more flexible and English-like language.

We have really been talking about several general principles here:

PRINCIPLE: Design your commands to fit the level of expertise of your audience.

PRINCIPLE: Make your commands use action-oriented words that fit the actions of the program.

PRINCIPLE: Wherever possible, allow the use of filler words to make the commands more natural.

PRINCIPLE: Choose your command words so they have unique abbreviations, and allow the user to enter the abbreviations instead of the entire command word.

PRINCIPLE: Allow your users to write command scripts to simplify complex operations with your program.

Some commands, such as file commands, can operate on more than one object. When this is the case, "wildcards" can allow the user to specify that one character or a group of characters in the entry need not match a specific character pattern in an object's name. For example, it is common for the character '?' to stand for any single character and '*' to stand for any group of zero or more characters. A few examples of wildcard matches are shown in Figure 4.9.

Allowing wildcard matches where useful can be a way to give your users more power with your program. When a name with wildcards is used, it can be compared with each name available to the command, and those that match can be returned. For example, the name might be replaced with a list of all the names that match the input. Thus, wildcards are ordinarily used where either the next instance of a match or a list of all names matching the source in some other name list is allowed. The action the program will take upon getting a wildcard name will be to search a list of names for matches, and then take each of the matching names through the LookUp procedure of Section 4.6 to build a token for further processing.

| a?cd | *matches* | abcd | axcd | a2cd | a+cd |
| a*cd | *matches* | acd | abcd | alotofcd | a!$cd |

Figure 4.9   *Some wildcard matches*

FUNCTION: **Match**

INPUT: **two words, w1 and w2, with word i possibly having wildcards**
        two indices, i1 and i2

PROCESSING:
```
    test = false
    If w1[p1] = BigWild then
        If p2 < length( w2 ) then
            test = test or Match(w1,w2,p1,p2+1 ) /*skip w2[p2]*/
            p1 = p1 + 1
    If ( p1 < length( w1 ) and ( p2 < length( w2 ) ) then
        If ( w1[p1]=w2[p2] ) or ( w1[p1]=SmallWild ) then
            test = test or Match(w1,w2,p1,p2+1 ) /*skip w2[p2]*/
        else if ((p1=length(w1)) and (p2=length(w2))) test = true
```

RETURN: **test**

Figure 4.10   *Design for Match*

```
#define BW    '*'   /* "BigWild" */
#define LW    '?'   /* "LittleWild" */

char Match(i,j)
char *i,*j;
{ char match;

    match=0;                    /* initially there's no match */
    if(*i == BW) {              /* have a wild card in string i */
        while(i[1] == BW) i++;  /* skip past duplicates */
        /* if *j isn't null, move over one place on string j */
        /* and ask about the recursive match */
        if(*j) match |= Match(i,j+1);
        i++;     /* move one place on string i without moving on j */
            /* this skips past the wild card */
    }
    if (*i && *j)    /* neither *i nor *j are at end of word so /*
                     /* move over one place on both if they still/*
                     /* match */
        if(*i==*j || *i==LW) match |= Match(i+1,j+1);
    else if(*i==*j) match=1;        /* both end at same place and */
                                    /* match to that point, so we win */

    return match;
}
```

Figure 4.11   *C code for* Match

Implementing wildcard matches can be complex if it is done with standard iterative techniques. However, a nice use of recursion yields a very clean, short Match function contributed by Jason Fox, that covers all the wildcard cases. The design for Match is shown in Figure 4.10. With a slight simplification, taken care of in the code, this function is shown in Figure 4.11. We use two constants, BigWild and SmallWild, in the place of the more specific '*' and '?'. When this is translated to C, its character indices are recast as pointers to type char, and we get the code of the figure.

4.3 Overall Structure of a Command-Driven System

A command-driven system is operated by reading a command and its parameters, carrying out whatever actions are called for by the command, and then waiting for the next command. For convenience to the user, more than one command may be allowed on a line, and a command may be allowed to span more than one line. This means we need a working definition of a command to proceed:

```
cc source.c -o prog.out; rm *.o; prog.out

cc -c source.c lib1.o lib2.o lib3.o lib4.o &
lib5.o -lm -lcurses
```

Figure 4.12   *Variations on commands and lines*

A *command* is a sequence of characters terminated by an end-of-command character or an end-of-line that is not preceded by a command-continues character.

A frequent choice for an end-of-command character is the semicolon, while a common command-continues character is the ampersand ('&'). If your target system(s) allow input that is longer than a screen line, for example 255 characters, then the command-continues character may not be needed. Figure 4.12 shows examples of two command lines, showing multiple commands per line and multiple lines per command. These are taken from standard Unix commands.

A Tool for Designing Command Action

When we discuss details of command handling, we see that command information comes to the program as a sequence of command words and parameters. The command processor starts in a "waiting" state, and each command word moves it to a new, partly-processed state. When the command processor gets to an action state, the parameters are assembled and the action of the command is carried out.

This kind of action is somewhat confusing to talk about in English, but is well described by a tool from compiler construction and theoretical computer science, called a *state transition diagram*. These diagrams are graphs with a waiting (or neutral) state, other partial-command states linked by edges corresponding to command words, and parameter-gathering states linked to command states by edges corresponding to parameter values. An example of a state transition diagram for a tiny and trivial command system is shown in Figure 4.13. This concept has previously been used by Foley and van Dam in their discussion of interface design.

In this system, there are only two commands, SET and PRINT. Each takes a variable name, X or Y, as the next part of the command. The PRINT command means to print the variable's value. If end-of-command is then encountered, the system goes back to the waiting state and issues a prompt, if that is desired. If a variable name is next encountered, the variable's value is printed. If any other input is received, an error is present and is reported before the system returns to the waiting state. Thus, the command PRINT X Y is legal and will print both variables' values.

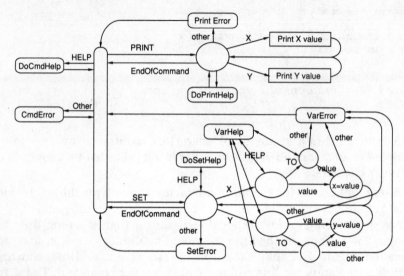

Figure 4.13 *A state-transition diagram for a small system.*

The SET command operates similarly, except that after the variable name is entered, the user is to enter a value (and may enter TO before the value.) More variable setting is possible before returning to the waiting state, as described above. Thus both the SET Y TO 5 and SET X 9 Y 4 commands are legal in this system.

This use of state transition diagrams provides a useful way to ensure that commands are handled consistently. Since the diagram describes *what* the interface does for the user, not the details on how it performs the operations, it is invaluable in managing and designing the behavior of the interface.

You should note very quickly that this tiny example has a few *help* functions. Adding help facilities to a system is not difficult, and working from a state transition diagram as we have is a good way to ensure that the help is truly responsive to the program's current operation and the user's needs.

Command Undo

The "undo" feature is one of the most user-friendly options one can add to a system. This is actually easier to implement than it would first seem. A straightforward technique is to maintain two copies of the data you show to the user: the "permanent" version and the displayed version. Each editing action takes the current displayed version, makes it permanent, and the user's actions make changes in the displayed version. Whenever changes cannot be held in an overlaid displayed version, such as is the case when a file is saved, they cannot be undone. When a user asks for an undo, simply switch the roles of the displayed and the permanent versions. When the work is saved, save the displayed version to a file.

Users would also like a multilevel undo capability, which would be relatively straightforward to implement by extending this idea to a stack of recent versions. In this case, an undo would pop the stack and display the new top version. However, this undo cannot be undone, tends to get a user lost in a sea of old versions, and the space this feature would take is rather large, so it is not often implemented.

4.4   Allowing User-Defined Commands

If you decide to allow users to add their own commands to your program, you must first decide if the program itself needs to handle the new commands or if you will let the user manage the commands through the standard file system by building new files containing the command's actions.

The file approach is probably easier to program and is suitable for users who are comfortable with file operations. With this approach, the user is permitted to type any desired command sequences into a text file. Since the file name will then be the new command, you will probably want to use some particular file name extension to identify the program's command files uniquely so as to avoid confusion with other files. When the file name is invoked, the file will be opened and its contents used instead of the keyboard until the end of the file is reached.

You need arguments for file-based commands even more than you do for regular commands, since these new file-based commands will probably be used to replace common command sequences. The easiest way to do this is to take the rest of the command line following the file name and break it into an array of parameter tokens as described below. You can then refer to these parameters by position in the argument list in the command file; a name such as $1 refers to the first parameter, $2 for the second, and so on. When the string $2 is read in the command file, the second token in the list is inserted in the command being read from the file, and processing continues. Figure 4.14 shows an example of a file built for our tiny example.

```
File name:           SETXY
Usage:               SETXY Value1 Value2
Contents:            SET X $1
                     SET Y $2
```

Figure 4.14   *A small command file*

```
#PRINTALL
PRINT X
PRINT Y
#SETXY
SET X $1
SET Y $2
```

Figure 4.15   *A user-defined command script file*

Having the program itself handle new commands may be somewhat easier for the novice user since it does not involve any direct work with the file system. Your program might simply have a "recording" feature that records the user commands as they are entered and saves them in a buffer. This would require a "Start Recording" command, an "End Recording" command, a buffer into which commands are saved as they are entered, and a way to either name or discard the buffered commands that were entered when the recording is finished. As above, since parameters may need to be saved as symbols instead of as values, the user can enter new values when the command is re-issued.

A mechanism for such user-definable commands might be a file to which user "scripts" are appended, along with the key name used to save the script. A file containing the scripts for two commands might look like Figure 4.15.

When the user wanted to name a set of recorded commands, the '#' character and the name are appended to the file, and the commands in the buffer are read into the file. It should also be possible for an experienced user to edit the file directly to create new commands or to modify or delete existing ones.

In fact, any scheme for allowing users to add commands to a program should have five command capabilities. The user must be able to

- add new commands,
- edit a command,
- get a list of all added commands,
- list the contents of any added command, and
- delete any added command.

Techniques for adding commands in text files handle all these with normal file operations: creation, editing, directory listing (with the file extension for command files), file listing, and file deletion. However, capturing commands from the program's operation and handling them from within the program is less amenable to these operations. While you might have command-handling functions in the program, it is simpler to allow users to list and edit command files to manipulate these commands.

An interesting option is available to system designers when dealing with user-defined commands. Will a user be able to redefine the meaning of a standard system command, or are these to be fixed and unchangeable? Many systems, such as the HP3000, allow user-defined commands to take precedence over standard commands, while Unix allows the user to set up an individual search path to have commands in various directories executed in very flexible order. This is easily done by searching the user's files for the command before checking the standard commands, which can be done without much loss of command interpreting speed.

There are limitations to what we can reasonably do with user-defined commands in this book. Adding control options (loops, if/then, etc.) to these commands turns them into small programming languages and your command interpreter becomes a language interpreter. To implement such a command system you need to refer to a book on programming language interpretation. Without good command flow control, users can kill the program quickly if they allow two commands to call each other, creating a quick infinite recursion. It might be best to require that a command can only call previously-defined commands.

4.5   Programming Command Input

Programming command input falls rather naturally into three parts. The first part takes the entire command input from the keyboard (or command file) and breaks it into words. The second part takes each input word and either matches it to a command action or parameter or determines that there is no suitable match and an error exists. The third part acts on the input and carries out the command. The first two parts are the components of this section, and the third is covered later in this chapter.

The commands described above are very general and are the type that would be given to a program instead of an operating system. Unix operates much more simply; it takes the first word of the command string, searches in its path for a file of that name, and tries to execute that file with the rest of the command input as its only argument. We concentrate on general command structures in the discussions below.

Breaking Commands into Word Lists

This section presents techniques that are fairly routine programming and can be easily sketched. They are included primarily for completeness. We sketch the process of filling a text buffer with the idea of detecting the end-of-command character, as an alternative to standard programming language input. Our input approach is pretty straightforward if input is catenated for lines ending with the command-continues character. The design is shown in Figure 4.16.

PROCEDURE: `FillBuffer`

INPUT: `characters from keyboard or file`

PROCESSING:
```
LNR {Last Nonblank character Read} = NULL {ASCII 0}
i = first - 1
While LNR <> COMMAND-CONTINUES do
    get a character  ch
    while  ch <> NEWLINE do
        i = i+1
        InputBuffer[i] = ch
        if  ch <> BLANK then LNR = ch
        get a character  ch
    enter blank in InputBuffer in place of NEWLINE
```

OUTPUT: `filled character buffer`

Figure 4.16 *Design for* FillBuffer

Note that this procedure will stop when it encounters a NEWLINE that was not immediately preceded by the COMMAND-CONTINUES character. Notice also that this procedure does not handle backspacing, word killing, or other input editing. This editing is expanded in Chapter 5, so we do not include code for this version here.

Now with all the text in the buffer, we must retrieve each word from the buffer to feed into the command recognition and action process. The definition of word is the critical driving factor in this code. Here we define a word as a sequence of characters terminated by a blank, newline, or end-of-command, to keep the code design simple. Apple computer, however, defines a word as follows:

A *word* is any continuous string that contains only the following characters:

- a letter
- a digit
- a nonbreaking space (a special character printed as a space)
- a currency symbol ($, ¢, £, or ¥)
- a percent sign (%)
- a comma between digits
- a period before a digit
- an apostrophe between letters or digits
- a hyphen, but not a minus sign or a dash (these are distinguishable from a hyphen on the Macintosh).

```
PROCEDURE:  GetWord

INPUT:    InputBuffer
          position i of first unread character in buffer

PROCESSING:
    If exhausted(buffer) then
        FillBuffer(InputBuffer)
    Word = blanks
    While InputBuffer[i] = BLANK do i = i+1
    index = 0
    while InputBuffer[i]<>BLANK, NEWLINE, or EndOfCommand do
        index = index+1
        Word[index] = InputBuffer[i]
        i = i+1

OUTPUT: updated value of position i
           character array Word
           number of characters in Word, index
```

Figure 4.17 *Design of* GetWord

It should be clear why we want to use the simpler definition of word for our example. As we look at the overall design, what we need is a simple procedure that reads the buffer into a word for further processing. This procedure's design is shown in Figure 4.17 and code in Figure 4.18.

```c
int GetWord( InputBuffer, i, Word )
    char InputBuffer[], Word[];
    int *i;
{
    int j, index;

    j = *i;
    if ( InputBuffer[j] == '\0' ) { FillBuffer(InputBuffer); j = 0; }
    while ( InputBuffer[j] == ' ' ) j++;
    index = 0;
    while (!Terminate(InputBuffer[j])) Word[index++] = InputBuffer[j++];
    Word[index] = '\0';
    *i = j;
}

int Terminate(ch)
    char ch;
{
    if ((ch==CR)||(ch=='\n')||(ch==EndOfCommand)||(ch=='\0')) return(1);
    else return(0);
}
```

Figure 4.18 *Code for* GetWord

This may return an empty word at the end of a command, so its result needs to be checked before the word is used. We implement this as a function that returns the character count, fitting the normal operation of C. The code for this is listed in Figure 4.18.

Matching Words to Command Parts

We now have the tools for breaking a command down into its basic words. Next we must determine the role of each word in the command. There are brute-force techniques for this in which command words are hard-coded into the interpreter, but this makes prototyping a nightmare. We use a more general technique, which has the advantage of allowing word changes and synonyms without changes in the detailed code.

Our procedure is to take the input word, identify its meaning in the command as far as possible, and create a token for the word. The token is handled by the command interpreter to find the correct action to take, as described in the next section. Before proceeding, however, we need to clarify the concept of a token:

A *token* is a pair of variables (value, class). The *value* is the word read from the command or the numeric parameter translated from the word, and the *class* is a code that is used to determine the actions that can be taken on the value. We will use the notation of a Pascal record and refer to the components as *token.value* and *token.class*.

Figure 4.19 shows the table of values and classes for our example in Section 4.3.

Value	Class
SET	SetClass
PRINT	PrintClass
X	XVarClass
Y	YVarClass
TO	FillerClass
HELP	HelpClass
number	NumParmClass
text parameter	TextParmClass
other	UnknownClass
EOLN or	EndOfCommand

Figure 4.19 *Token values and classes*

```
PROCEDURE:  LookUp

INPUT:  one word

PROCESSING:
    value = word
    class = LookInStandard( word )
    if ( class = UNDETERMINED ) then
        class = LookInUser( word )
        if ( class = UNDETERMINED )
            if word is numeric then
                class = NumParmClass
                value = translate( word )
            else
                class = TextParmClass

OUTPUT:  token of ( value, class )
```

Figure 4.20   *Design of* LookUp

The class is, of course, a purely internal concept. Storage and operation efficiency are increased if these are numeric values, although code reading suffers if they are purely hardcoded numbers. We use literals for classes in our examples with the understanding that these are associated with numbers in CONST or #define statements or their equivalents. Normally, there are distinct classes for each command action, allowing synonyms to give the user a richer vocabulary to fit his own style.

Each word will be tested by the LookUp procedure as it is input to determine its class. The design of LookUp is shown in Figure 4.20.

Lookup techniques for standard and user-defined commands are given below. This LookUp procedure is the heart of a simple procedure GetToken, sketched in Figure 4.21. This and the previous procedures are not expanded into code since they are quite simple.

```
PROCEDURE:  GetToken

INPUT:  none

PROCESSING:
    GetWord( word )
    LookUp( word, token )

OUTPUT:  token
```

Figure 4.21   *Design of* GetToken

■   To map the first three characters of a word into the integers 0..10 to handle 11 commands:

```
value = 0
for i = 1 to 3
  value = (value*PRIME+ord(shift(cmd[i])-ord('A'))) mod 11
hash = value
```

where PRIME is a prime number larger than 26; say PRIME = 31 as an example.

■   To compute the hash function based on all consonants in a command, you could use a similar function:

```
value = 0
len = length( cmd )
for i = 1 to len
  if not vowel( cmd[i] ) then
    value = (value*PRIME+ord(shift(cmd[i])-ord('A'))) mod 11
  hash = value
```

Figure 4.22   *Two hash functions*

To match words to classes, we use table techniques for standard command words and use different lookup techniques for user-defined command words. Fixed-table algorithms for standard command words are possible since these commands are fixed by the design. The actual entries in the fixed table are essentially tokens. The word value is to be matched, and the class value is to be returned.

Looking up words in fixed tables allows us to choose from many techniques that have been developed in computer science. This problem of looking up an entry in a table is a standard topic in data structures books and courses. The table could be a simple list, possibly with the entries ordered by the frequency of their use, and the lookup could be ordinary sequential search. The table could be ordered alphabetically by the word, with lookup being the more efficient binary search. We suggest a still more efficient approach: entries in an array with a hash function acting on the word to produce the index of the proper entry.

Hash functions on words are functions that manipulate the characters of the word in order to get a number. Most use the numeric value of each character (for example ASCII or EBCDIC) in the process and perform a variety of operations in an attempt to make different words have different function output. Hashing is a standard topic in data structures (see Horowitz and Sahni), but two examples are shown in Figure 4.22.

Hash functions are particularly well suited for fixed command tables for two reasons. First, you can restrict the hash function to use only part of a command and get abbreviations or short forms for commands. For example, you can take the first three letters of the command, or you can

FUNCTION: **LookInStandard**

INPUT: **one word**

PROCESSING:
```
h = Hash( word )
if ( FixedTable[h].word = word ) then
    class = FixedTable[h].class
else
    class = UNDETERMINED
```

RETURN: **class**

Figure 4.23 *Design of* LookInStandard

take the consonants in a command. Second, since you have a limited number of commands, the function can be chosen so that no two commands in the list hash to the same value, and then the values 1 to N are the output of your N commands. Such functions are called *perfect hashing functions.* If your command set is small, you may be able to come up with a perfect hashing function directly. If it is large you probably need to take a general approach to hashing and pick the exact function by computer-generated trial and error: choose values for the parameters of the function, try it on all the commands to see if there is a collision (two commands hashing to one value), and if there is, choose new parameters, either systematically or randomly.

We now assume you have a perfect hash function and a lookup table so that if your input word is one of the built-in words, it can be so determined very quickly. This is the essence of the LookInStandard function mentioned above and shown in Figure 4.23. Note that we store the abbreviated form of the command words in the table FixedTable.

The structure of the user-defined command list determines the way these commands are scanned for a match. If you use the technique of having each new command in a separate file, you need to search the appropriate file system for a file name with the right extension that matches the word. If you keep all your commands in a single file, you need to search that file for a header line matching your word. Both searches are relatively slow by computer standards but should be acceptable to the user unless really large numbers of user-defined commands are saved.

If a command word is not numeric, is not a standard command part, and is not a user-defined command, it is reasonable to tag it as a text parameter as we did in LookUp in Figure 4.20. If a command needs a command word and gets a text parameter, it is simple enough to see that an error has occurred and to handle it appropriately. More follows on this in the following section.

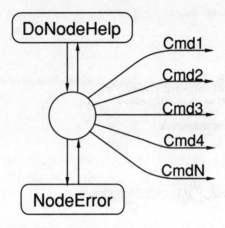

Figure 4.24   *Node of state/transition diagram*

4.6 Programming Program Actions with Commands

We now have an input sequence of tokens that the program is to recognize and act upon. One primary tool for developing the code leading to the actual program action is the state transition diagram introduced in Section 4.3. Each token acts to move the system from one state to another. However, we are not particularly concerned with the token's value but with its class; this allows synonyms and parameters to be handled without code contortions.

Let us take a typical node for a partly developed command in a state transition diagram, shown in Figure 4.24, and see what it takes to translate the node into computer code as shown in Figure 4.25. We can expand this into code for a small procedure as follows:

```
Procedure DoThisNode
    GetToken(tok)
    case (tok.class) of
        Class1: DoNode...
        Class2: DoNode...
        Class3: DoNode...
        ...
        ClassN: DoNode...
        HelpClass:
            DoNodeHelp
            DoThisNode
        other: NodeError
```

Figure 4.25   *Design for* DoThisNode

Here, each case branch then leads to a procedure call to the next node or to the action of the command if the command is completed. Note that DoNodeN may, in fact, generate a whole screen if the command word is all that is entered. This allows novices to have a simple system, while more experienced users can move quickly to complete commands. The HELP node will need to return to the same state to continue the user action, so it calls DoThisNode recursively.

Parameters themselves cause moves between nodes, just as command words do. If a command has a single parameter, the parameter will complete the command and cause the command action. If a command has more than one parameter, each parameter will move along a parameter-gathering path of nodes until enough parameters have been received and the command action can be completed.

Note that our code sketch implies a return from each procedure when it has processed its token or called the command action. This need not be the case. In case a command is to work on several items, as was the case in the command SET X 2 Y 3, the node reached by SET must stay active after it has processed the first SET X 2. This modification is small, however, and is shown in Figure 4.26.

Finally, we present the entire command processor for the tiny example of Figure 4.13. We do not use a block-structured design as we would in Pascal, where the subsequent nodes of a given node can be handled by nesting their procedures. Instead we use a topdown C-like organization for the nodes. To refresh your memory, refer to Figure 4.13 for the state transition diagram for this command processor. Without user-defined commands or wildcards (which were handled earlier and whose contents have already been turned into tokens), and with the tools from earlier in this chapter, the design is shown in Figure 4.27. We use names for node handlers and assume the existence of error and help functions, which are fleshed out in Chapters 12 and 13.

```
GetToken(tok)
while ((not error) and (not EndOfCommand)) do
    case (tok.class) of
        Class1:
        Class2:
        Class3:
        ...
        ClassN:
        other: error
    GetToken(tok)
```

Figure 4.26 *Modified* DoThisNode

```
Procedure DoCmd                        { no parameters }
   GetToken(tok)
   case (tok.class) of
         PrintClass:        DoPrint
         SetClass:          DoSet
         HelpClass:         DoCmdHelp
                            DoCmd
         other:             CmdError


Procedure DoPrint                      { no parameters }
   GetToken(tok)
   while ((not error) and (not EndOfCommand)) do
         case (tok.class) of
               XVarClass:         print( X )
               YVarClass:         print( Y )
               HelpClass:         DoPrintHelp
               other:             set error flag
                                  VarError
         if (not error) GetToken(tok)


Procedure DoSet                        { no parameters }
   GetToken(tok)
   while ((not error) and (not EndOfCommand)) do
         case (tok.class) of
               XVarClass:         DoSetX
               YVarClass:         DoSetY
               HelpClass:         DoSetHelp
               other:             set error flag
                                  VarError
         if (not error) GetToken(tok)


Procedure DoSetX                       { no parameters }
   GetToken(tok)
   case (tok.class) of
         NumParmClass:     X = tok.value
                           write("Setting X to ",tok.value)
         ToClass:          SetVar( X )
         HelpClass:        VarHelp
                           DoSetX
         other:            VarError


Procedure DoSetY                       { no parameters }
   GetToken(tok)
   case (tok.class) of
         NumParmClass:     Y = tok.value
                           write("Setting Y to ",tok.value)
         ToClass:          SetVar( Y )
         HelpClass:        VarHelp
                           DoSetY
         other:            VarError
```

continued

```
Procedure SetVar ( V )              { parameter is variable name }
   GetToken (tok)
   case (tok.class) of
        NumParmClass:    case ( V ) of
                              X:        X = tok.value
                              Y:        Y = tok.value
        HelpClass:       VarHelp
                         SetVar ( V )
        other            VarError
```

Figure 4.27   *The expanded diagram's design*

4.7   Readings

Since command handling is fundamentally like keyword handling in language compilers and interpreters, this chapter's supporting reading comes from the technical areas of computer science. State transition diagrams are a standard feature of language design and are used in Foley and van Dam for user interface operation design. Hashing functions and efficient table lookup are standard data structures topics; see for example Horowitz and Sahni. Common references on compilers and interpreters, such as the classic text by Aho and Ullman, will provide assistance on the whole parsing and command action process.

## Chapter 5

PROGRAMMING DATA INPUT

The problem of managing data input is often seen as trivial. After all, most programming languages provide built-in data input operations: IN-PUT, READ, and so on. Certainly data input is not treated as a problem of any importance in programming courses. Yet, there are a surprising number of problems that lurk below the surface and trap the unwary user. This chapter is devoted to the lowly problem of handling data input. The underlying idea is to give as much control as possible to the program so there will be as little room for program crashing as possible.

5.1 Different Forms of Data Input

Data comes in two basic flavors: text (alpha) and numbers (numeric). This input may be made in response to a prompt or as an entry on a formatted screen. The program may take each item separately or allow the user to enter several data items at once, thereby speeding operation by avoiding multiple prompts.

It is important to note that this chapter and this book deal with user interfaces, and hence interactive operation. They do not deal with file input, real-time data capture, or file formats. Getting the name of a file from a user, yes, but not the contents of the file.

5.2   Controlling Data Input from the Program

Every programming language offers some facilities for interactive data input, either as a language primitive or through a library function. These facilities are not robust enough for real interfaces, however. For example, the simple statement read(x) in Pascal, with x any numeric data type, will fail under any of the following simple—and common—mistakes:

- entering a number using the letter l (a lower-case L) instead of the digit 1, or the letter O (an upper-case o) instead of 0 (zero), and

- entering a number with commas used to separate thousands groups, or using periods as separators and a comma for a decimal point, European style.

A Pascal program using the read statement will either crash or completely misinterpret the input when either of these is done, and similar problems will occur with other programming languages. Clearly, we must provide better input capabilities than this.

In Chapter 4 we show routines to capture input from the user, break it into words, and parse a command line. For these routines it sufficed to use a string-input technique, since our main concern was what to do with a command after we recognized it and its parameters. Here we are looking at more complex problems of text entry where we must control each input character and its screen placement.

The fundamental principles of data input are straightforward.

PRINCIPLE: All input must be managed a character at a time.

PRINCIPLE: Numeric input must be flexible to handle various numeric formats.

We want to recognize any input problem and abort only bad input, not the whole program, and provide the user with a suitable error diagnostic.

5.3   Techniques of Text Input

Text entered as data tends to be more voluminous than text entered as commands. Thus, in this chapter, we focus more on managing larger-scale text input than we did in Chapter 4.

In this section we manage the input from a high-level language to make our discussion more understandable. A commercial product would use assembly language or other sophisticated techniques to control the display more efficiently.

In Chapter 4 we developed the principle of taking all input as an array of characters and breaking it up into a sequence of words for further interpretation. This input is handled by a loop of normal character-by-character read's with the standard language operations handling such things as input editing (backspace, etc.) The more detailed operations we describe here require more detailed principles.

PRINCIPLE: Implement input-editing operations in your own software.

PRINCIPLE: Treat text as whole words for input, allowing operations such as word-wrap and cancellation of the most recent word.

Note that we do not talk about full-screen editing of current input, which is more complex than we need. All the editing we describe takes place at the end position of the input string (as in a stack) while the input string itself is managed as a queue.

Now assume we have a screen upon which we have presented a prompt. The user responds to the prompt and begins to type. In order to maintain full control, each character entered must be accepted, its meaning ascertained (here is where we handle characters like backspace which are used in editing input), and its appropriate screen location determined. It must then be echoed to the screen.

How can we represent this information for the program? The easiest way, and for our purposes probably the best, is to treat all input as a simple array of characters. This array is treated as our text buffer, and all input is handled through it. In this simplest form, no attention is paid to the screen itself; we are essentially dealing with a "glass teletype." We do not include all possible editing functions, leaving them for projects. Our basic processing is shown in Figure 5.1, adapted from the work of Chuck Quittmeyer. This takes text from the keyboard, holds it in an input string, and echoes it to the screen. The screen display uses word wrap and supports both last-character and last-word deletion. When the user presses RETURN, the procedure terminates and returns the input string for further processing.

PROCEDURE: **GetText**

INPUT: none

PROCESSING:

```
clear input string to NULLs
clear input area to BLANKs
set initial row and column to 1
place cursor at current row and column
get a character ch
while ch <> RETURN
   if ch is printable then
      append ch to the input string
      if row < right margin then
         put ch on screen at current row and column
         increment column
      else                          /* end of a row */
         if ch <> SPACE then        /* allow spaces to stay on the row */
            EraseWord( buffer )     /* copy current word into small buffer */
                                    /* erase current word from screen */
         set column to 1, increment row
         PlaceWord( buffer )        /* replace word at start of next row */
                                    /* update column as you do so */
   else
      if ch = BACKSPACE then
         if column > 1 then
            decrement column
            write space to current row and column
            write null to end of input string
            if column = 0 and row > 0 then
               decrement row
               set column to end of that row
            else
               if column < SpacesLeft( row - 1 )
                  EraseWord( buffer )
                  decrement row
                  set column to the end of row
                  PlaceWord( buffer )
         else                       /* column = 1 */
            decrement row
            write blank to last position on new row
            set column to last position on row
            write null to end of input string
      else
         if character is KILLWORD then
            EraseWord( buffer )
            decrease column by length of word
            write NULL over word in input string
            if column = 1 and row > 1
               decrement row
               set column to end of that row
            update position
   place cursor at current position
   get next character
end-while
```

OUTPUT: string for further processing

Figure 5.1   GetText *design*

This outline is quite rough, but it shows us where the interesting parts of this process lie. Note that we need a language facility which will let us get a character from the keyboard without echoing it to the screen, as well as the usual capability of writing a character at any given point on the screen. Getting a character without echoing it may be part of the programming language; for example, you can use read(kbd,ch) in Turbo Pascal. It may require some use of system functions in other environments such as Unix, where you need to stty(raw) to accomplish this. It may even require some assembly language programming to implement, typically by waiting for a keyboard interrupt and then reading the character from the keyboard buffer address.

When this operation is finished, the text buffer array will be available for whatever further processing is needed. For example, the buffer can be broken into words and the words interpreted as numbers when numeric input is needed.

This outline requires two procedures to implement. The EraseWord procedure must copy nonblank characters from the end of the input string into a stack until a blank is encountered, erasing the characters from the screen as it copies them, and then pop the stack a character at a time into a word buffer so the word may be replaced if needed. The PlaceWord procedure copies characters from the buffer back into the input string and onto the screen at the current row and column, updating the column value as it does so; it can simply use the "if ch is printable" part of GetText. These procedures are quite straightforward.

5.4   Providing Default Values

Sometimes a data input will have a particular value most often associated with it, and it would be convenient if a user could simply accept this value without continuing to enter it. Such a value is called a *default value* for the input, and it can be provided fairly readily. The code sketch in Figure 5.2 illustrates how this can be done.

```
PROCEDURE:  DefaultInput

    INPUT:  None

    PROCESSING:
        put up prompt
        put up default value, highlighted
        get a character from the user
        if the character is RETURN, then return the default value
        else
            clear the input area        /* write blanks to it */
            call GetWord( NewText )      /* from Chapter 4 */
            return( NewText )   /* make a numeric conversion if needed */

    RETURN: value from the input
```

Figure 5.2   *DefaultInput design*

5.5   Techniques of Numeric Input

The previous sections give us tools for getting text from the user. We now assume that we have received a text word without blanks as input and need a numeric value for the program. The object is to take the text characters, convert each to a numeric value, and assemble these values positionally into a number. This, in itself, is not difficult, but we want to add a size-check feature to the routine, so it will issue a warning if the number entered is out of the given range. This will be a valuable aid in writing crash-resistant and error-resistant programs. The routines will also be mildly forgiving of nonstandard input, as may be appropriate.

Tools similar to those below are often available in a software environment such as that in Unix. As in other prewritten input functions, however, you may want to be cautious about using them without testing their ruggedness.

```
FUNCTION:  ctoi

INPUTS:  word W, bounds on admissible values VMAX, VMIN;
         assume VMIN < 0 < VMAX

PROCESSING:
     set word index to start
     if W[index] is '$' then increment index
     else if W[index] is '-' then
          set negative flag
          increment index
          if W[index] is '$' then increment index
     value = 0, errorcode = 0
     if negative then set VMAX to abs(VMIN)   /* handle lower bound */
     while not end_of_word and (errorcode = 0) do
          if W[index] is a digit then
                  convert W[index] to char_value and increment index
                  if (value > (VMAX-char_value)/10) then
                       errorcode = SIZE_ERROR
                  else value = 10 * value + char_value
          else
                  if W[index] = ',' then increment index
                  else
                       if W[index] = '.' then
                            increment index
                            if not end_of_word then
                                    errorcode = BAD_CHAR
                       else
                            errorcode = BAD_CHAR
     if errorcode <> NO_ERROR then value = 0
     if negative then value = -value
     return value and errorcode

RETURN:  value, errorcode
```

Figure 5.3   ctoi *design*

```
int ctoi( w, errcode, VMIN, VMAX )
    char w[];
    int *errcode, VMIN, VMAX;
{
    int index=0, value=0, err=NO_ERROR, negative=0, char_value;

    if (w[index] == '$') index++;
    if (w[index] == '=') {
        negflag++; index++; if (w[index] == '$') index++; }
    if (negative) VMAX = abs(VMIN);
    while ( (w[index]) && (err == NO_ERROR) ) {
        if ( (w[index] >= '0') && (w[index] <= '9') ) {
            char_value = w[index++] - '0';
            if (value>(VMAX - char_value) / 10 ) err=SIZE_ERROR;
            else value = 10 * value + char_value; }
        else {
            if (w[index] == ',') index++;
            else if (w[index] == '.') {
                    index++; if (!w[index]) err = BAD_CHAR; }
                else err = BAD_CHAR; }
    if (err != NO_ERROR) value = 0;
    if (negative) value *= -1;
    *errcode = err;
    return( value );
}
```

Figure 5.4   ctoi *code*

Getting an Integer Value

Our first example is a character-to-integer function, ctoi, that gets an integer from a word. The word and size bound are taken as parameters, and the value is returned along with an indication of whether errors were found in the number's formation or size. Our "forgiveness" is to ignore commas and a leading $ sign, and allow a decimal point at the end of the word. The design of this algorithm is shown in Figure 5.3.

The worked-out C code for this is in Figure 5.4. Note that we use the C convention that the end of any string, and hence end of word, is the null character with ASCII value 0, and we compress the code somewhat to save space.

When the routine terminates with an error, the program can ignore the error (living dangerously!) or can take suitable action to warn the user of the error and ask for reentry. This is discussed at length in Chapter 13.

Getting a Real Value

If we need to get a real number instead of an integer, the technique is fairly similar to what we saw earlier. Of course the user may enter many more digits than the computer can accurately represent, but this is an inherent problem with computer numbers and can be attacked using extended-precision real numbers instead of ordinary reals. This does not affect the process for evaluating the text word.

PROCEDURE: **PreScan**

INPUT: **a string which is to represent a real number**

PROCESSING:
```
    create a new, blank array which is to hold the scanned string
    if first character is '$' or '+', skip it
    if first character is '-', copy it and move to next character
    while character <> blank and <> 'E' and no error found, do
        if character is a digit, copy it to new array
        if character is '.'
            if no decimal has yet been found, copy it and note it
            else generate an error code
        if character is ',', skip it (maybe note location...)
        if character is 'l' {lower-case L} copy digit 1
        if character is 'O' { letter } copy digit 0
        if character is anything else, generate error code
        move to next character
    end-while
    if character is 'E', copy rest of string to exponent string
```

OUTPUT: **two strings, the floating-point string and the exponent string, and an error code describing any errors found, if any.**

Figure 5.5 PreScan *design*

As in the preceding example, we ignore a leading $ and embedded commas. However, this time we prescan the text word and remove all the extraneous characters while retaining the digits and decimal point. This prescan can be as intelligent as you want. We keep it simple and suggest some enhancements as projects. This prescan approach could have been used with integers and handles "E-type" scientific notation. We continue to handle the lower-case-L vs. 1 and letter-O vs. 0 translation.

The prescanning is presented first in Figure 5.5. It takes the input string and returns two strings, one of which is a standard floating-point number and one of which is an exponent if the E-notation (1.234E+05, for example) has been used. These strings will themselves be converted to numbers after the prescanning has completed.

Converting the output strings to numbers is quite straightforward. The integer conversion of the exponent string has already been discussed. The floating-point conversion is almost as easy; note that it does not need to do any error-checking since that was done during the prescan phase. This conversion is shown in Figure 5.6, the character-to-floating-point design. The overall process, then, is shown in Figure 5.7. Putting these designs together, the worked-out code is shown in Figure 5.8.

```
FUNCTION:  ctof

INPUT:  a string of digits, possibly containing one decimal point

PROCESSING:
    set value and decimal_count to 0, and after_decimal to false
    while character <> blank do
        if char = '.' then after_decimal is true
        else
            set value = 10 * value + value-of-digit
            if after_decimal then increment decimal_count
    end-while
    set value to value / 10^decimal_count

OUTPUT:  value
```

Figure 5.6 ctof *design*

```
FUNCTION:  GetReal

INPUT:  a character string

PROCESSING:
    errcode = PreScan(string, floating_part, exponent_part)
    if errcode <> NO_ERROR then report_error( errcode )
    else
        fp = ctof( floating_part )
        exp = ctoi( exponent_part, errcode )
        if (errcode = 0) then report_error( errcode )
        else
            value = fp*10^exp

OUTPUT:  value
```

Figure 5.7 GetReal *design*

This set of input routines can be incorporated in the programmer's user interface toolkit quite easily. The fundamental numeric input routines can replace the programming language's read routines directly, and each input routine can call for a string from the input buffer array. When this array is empty, the fundamental character-by-character input is called after an optional prompt is presented. These inputs are placed in the context of form-fillout or free-format input by general routines which can easily be adapted for various prompts or forms as needed.

```
int PreScan( InString, BaseString, ExpString )
    char InString[], BaseString[], ExpString[];
{
    int InIndex=0, BaseIndex=0, ExpIndex=0, decimal=0;
    char ch;

    while (((InString[InIndex]=='+')||(InString[InIndex]=='$')) &&
            (!InString[InIndex]))) InIndex++;
    if (InString[InIndex]=='-')

BaseString[BaseIndex++]=InString[InIndex++];
    while ((!InString[InIndex])&&(InString[InIndex]!='E')) {
        ch = InString[InIndex++];
        if ((ch >= '0')&&(ch <= '9')) BaseString[BaseIndex++] = ch;
        else if (ch == '.') {
            if (!decimal) { BaseString[BaseIndex++]=ch; decimal++; }
            else return( DECIMAL_ERROR ); }
            else if ( ch == '1' ) BaseString[BaseIndex++] = '1';
                else if ((ch=='O')||(ch=='o'))
                        BaseString[BaseIndex++]='0';
                    else if (ch != ',') return(CHAR_ERROR); }
    if (InString[InIndex++]=='E') {
        if (InString[InIndex]=='-')
            BaseString[BaseIndex++]=InString[InIndex++];
        while (!InString[InIndex]) {
            ch = InString[InIndex++];
            if ((ch >= '0') && (ch <= '9'))
                BaseString[BaseIndex++] = ch;
            else if ( ch == '1' ) BaseString[BaseIndex++] = '1';
                else if ((ch=='O')||(ch=='o'))
                        BaseString[BaseIndex++]='0';
                    else if (ch != ',') return(CHAR_ERROR); }
    return(NO_ERROR);
}


float ctof( str )
    char str[];
{
    int AfterDecimal=0, DecimalCount=0, index=0;
    float value=0.0;
    char ch;

    while (str[index] != ' ') { /* PreScan skips leading blanks */
        if (str[index] == '.' ) AfterDecimal++;
        else {        /* only digits and <= 1 decimal from PreScan */
            value = value * 10.0 + (float)(str[index] - '0');
            if (AfterDecimal) DecimalCount++;
    }   }
    for (index = 0; index < DecimalCount; index++ )
        value /= 10.0;
    return( value );
}

#define MINEXP -77     /* typical minimum and maximum exponents */
#define MAXEXP  77
```

continued

```
float GetReal( str )
    char str[];
{
    int errcode, experr, exp, count, power, size;
    float fp;}
    char BaseString[], ExpString;

    errcode = PreScan( str, BaseString, ExpString );
    if (errcode != NO_ERROR) ReportError( errcode)
    else {
        fp = ctof( BaseString );
        size = log10(fp);                    /* precompute allowable
exponent */
        exp = ctoi( ExpString, experr, MINEXP+size, MAXEXP-size );
        if (experr != NO_ERROR) ReportError( experr );
        else {
            for ( count = 1, power = 1; count <= exp; count++ )
                power *= 10;
            return( fp * power );
        }   }
}
```

Figure 5.8 *Code for entire floating point conversion process*

We have been careful to include range checking with the numeric input routines, but how would this be used in an application program? It is primarily a tool to avoid program crashes, so the programmer would probably use the largest possible value for the value bound. However, for input which is part of an ongoing expression, the partially computed value could be used to ensure that ongoing entries did not result in crashes. As a simple example, consider the following integer expression where X is to be input. If the integer size limit is taken to be 32,767 in the example 512 * X + 2417, it is straightforward to compute that the value of X must lie between -69 and 59, so these values can be used as the range bounds.

It is probably proper to remind the programmer here that good software not only does not crash but also tries to ensure correctness. Thus, values returned from the user should in many cases be checked for "reasonable ranges." That is, some entries simply should not be arbitrary. Interest rates, ages, and many other quantities can be checked for reasonable range (for example, interest rates between 0.05 and 0.25). Good software performs such checking gracefully.

Getting a Numeric Value from an Expression

In many environments, a user may want to enter a value by writing an expression instead of by simply typing in a number. This is central to the operation of spreadsheets, of course, and should be a part of any program for doing mathematics. It might also be very useful at times for accounting, simulation, or other kinds of programs. In effect, such a program offers the user a simple built-in calculator.

> PRINCIPLE: Allow your program to accept expressions anywhere a number would be entered.

A couple of examples of such expressions are 56 * 12 - 5 (numeric only) and 56 * A - B (numeric and variables). The first step in adding expressions to your input is to modify the input scanning of the last section to return a string which contains a whole expression, not just a numeric string. This is easily accomplished by having the scan continue until it encounters the end of input or any character not in an allowable expression, such as a letter following a space or any letter but 'E' immediately after a digit. Again, suitable letters can be converted to digits, multiple blanks can be reduced to one, and operators and numbers can be separated by blanks if these are not originally present. That is, the initial scan can return a string that is ready for further scanning by an evaluation procedure.

The expression evaluation itself can be done in several ways; we present two techniques that are quite different in philosophy but are both simple to implement. The code for one will be left as a project, while the other, slightly more sophisticated, will be expanded fully. Both techniques use algebraic notation, formally called "operator precedence," which is keyed by precedence rules for each operator, because we believe that most people naturally think of expressions in this way. If your audience wants to use reverse Polish expressions, as found in some scientific calculators, these computations are much easier to implement and will not be treated separately; see the projects for suggestions in this area.

The first approach we take to evaluation is nonrecursive. It involves the use of two stacks, one holding operators (parentheses, +, -, *, /, etc.) until precedence rules allow them to perform their operation, while the other stack holds operands (numbers) until they are acted on by their proper operator. This approach is suggested by a discussion in Horowitz and Sahni.

This evaluation process is keyed by the idea of two precedence values for each operator: one value for the operator when it enters the operator stack and another value for the operator when leaving the operator stack. These values are shown in Figure 5.9.

Operator	Entering Priority	Outgoing Priority
)	none	none
^	4	3
*, /	2	2
+, -	1	1
(	4	0

Figure 5.9   *Operator priorities*

Note that ')' has no priority since it will never actually be in the stack. The rule for handling operators is simple:

When a new operator is encountered having entering priority *ep*, operators are removed from the operator stack as long as their outgoing priority, *op*, is greater than or equal to *ep*.

Now let us see how this operation is to work on an expression that, while simple, illustrates the process. The expressions is 3 * (16 - 12) ^ 3 and its step-by-step evaluation works as shown in Figure 5.10.

The concept of "token" comes up in this design. A token is a single entity in the expression. In our case, a token is a number, an operator, or the EOS (end-of-string) mark. We assume that you will use the GetToken procedure of Chapter 4, which returns the token and the type (number, operator, or EOS) of the token. The design of the expression evaluator, then, is shown in Figure 5.11.

Expression so far	Operator stack	Operand stack
3		3
3 *	*	3
3 * (	* (	3
3 * (16	* (	3 16
3 * (16 -	* (-	3 16
3 * (16 - 12	* (-	3 16 12
3 * (16 - 12)	*	3 4
3 * (16 - 12) ^	* ^	3 4
3 * (16 - 12) ^ 3	* ^	3 4 3
	*	3 64
		192

Result: 192

Figure 5.10   *Evaluating an expression*

FUNCTION: **eval**

INPUT: **string exp terminated by EOS character**

PROCESSING:
```
    initialize operator and operand stacks to empty
    GetToken( tok )
    while ( tok.class <> EOS ) do
        if tok.class = Operand then
            push tok.value onto operand stack
        else
            if token = ')' then
                take operator from operator stack
                while ( operator <> '(' ) do
                    apply( operator, operand stack )
                    take operator from operator stack
            else
                ep = EnteringPriority( tok.value )
                while (operator stack is not empty) and
                    (ep <= OutgoingPriority(operator stack top) do
                    take operator from operator stack
                    apply( operator, operand stack )
                push tok.value onto operator stack
    (* now input is all processed; finish converting the value *)
    while operator stack is not empty
        take operator from operator stack
        apply( operator, operand stack )
    take value from operand stack
    if operand stack is now empty
        return value
    else
        handle error of too many operands
```

OUTPUT: **value**

Figure 5.11   ev*a*l *design*

The procedure *a*pply used above is quite easy. If the operator is an ordinary binary operator taking two operators, such as +, -, *, or /, remove the top item in the operand stack to be the right-hand operand, remove the next item (the new top item) from the operand stack to be the left-hand operand, apply the operator to these operands, and push the result back onto the operand stack. If the operator is a unary operator taking a single operand, such as SIN or ABS, remove the top operand in the stack, apply the operator, and push the result back on the stack. If the operator takes more operands, simply use the suitable number of operands from the stack, compute the value, and push it back. Figure 5.12 shows both the worked-out code for ev*a*l and the *a*pply operation.

```
typedef struct {
   char *string;
   int  class;
   } token;

int eval( str )
   char str[];
{
   token      tok;
   OpStack    ops;        /* operator stack */
   IntStack   ints;       /* operand stack */
   int        scratch, interr, ep;
   ch         op, ostop;

   OpInit( ops );
   IntInit( ints );
   GetToken( tok );
   while (tok.class != EndOfExpression) {
      if (tok.class == OperandClass) {
         scratch = ctoi( tok.string, interr, -MAXINT, MAXINT );
         IntPush( scratch, ints ); }
      else {
         if ( *token.string == ')' ) {
            op = OpPop( ops );
            while ( op != '(' ) {
               apply( op, ints );
               op = OpPop( ops ); } }
         else {
            ep = EnteringPriority( tok.value );
            while ((!OpEmpty(ops))&&(
                       OutgoingPriority(ostop = OpPop(ops))>ep)
               apply( ostop, ints );
            if (OutgoingPriority(ostop) > ep) OpPush(ostop, ops);
            OpPush( tok.value, ops); } }
   /* now input is all processed; finish value conversion */
   while ( !OpEmpty( ops ) ) {
      op = OpPop( ops );
      apply( op, ints ); }
   scratch = IntPop( ints );
   if IntEmpty( ints ) return (scratch);
   else error( TooManyOperands );
}

Apply( op, ints )       /* apply the operator to the stack */
   char op;
   IntStack ints;
{
   int First, Second, negative=0, index;

   if ( IntEmpty( ints ) ) error ( TooFewOperands );
   Second = IntPop( ints );
   if ( IntEmpty( ints ) ) error ( TooFewOperands );
```

continued

```
First  = IntPop( ints );
switch (op) {
    '+':  First += Second; break;
    '-':  First -= Second; break;
    '*':  First *= Second; break;
    '/':  First /= Second; break;
    '^':  if (Second < 0) { negative++; Second *= -1; }
          for (index = 0; index < Second; index++ )
              First *= First;
          if (negative) First = 1/First; }
    IntPush( First, ints ); }
}
```

Figure 5.12   eval *and* apply *code*

Two error conditions can arise in this evaluation process. First, the expression may have too few numbers for the number of operators at a given point. This will show up when you apply an operator since there will be too few operands on the stack for the apply subroutine to use. This error will be caught in apply. Second, there may be too many numbers for the operators in the expression. If this is the case, there will be more than one number in the operand stack when the evaluation finishes, and the error will be found here. In either case, the error should be handled by reporting the error in a window or an error area, erasing the input from the point of the expression, and allowing further input from that point.

Our second evaluation approach is recursive and reflects a Pascal-like approach to the concept of an expression. An *expression* is defined to be made up of terms, terms made up of factors, and factors made up of values or a parenthesized expression. For example, the expression (3X+5)(2-7X) is a single term, and has factors (3X+5) and (2-7X). These factors are again expressions, with the factor (3X+5) having the terms 3X and 5. Finally, the term 3X has the factors 3 and X, which are values, with X being a symbolic value. More formally, but still in a simplified presentation, the grammar of an expression is shown in Figure 5.13.

Expression:	**term + term**	or	**term - term**
term:	**factor * factor**	or	**factor / factor**
factor:	**value**	or	**(expression)**

Figure 5.13   *Parts of an expression*

This translates into the design of several procedures quite easily. Here, the *evaluate* procedure is the one called by the user, while the others are used in the evaluation's details. An important feature in this design is that the NextToken procedure used in the previous design is still used, but it is assumed to update the string position as it operates. User input begins with the function expr which comes at the end of this design. These procedures' designs are shown in Figure 5.14.

```
INPUT:    string containing an expression

PROCESSING:
    Function factor
        Input:    expression string
                  current index in the string
        Output:   value of next factor in string
                  updated index in the string
        Processing:
            NextToken( expression, index, token, TokenType )
            if (token = '(' ) then
                factor = expr( expression, index )
                NextToken( expression, index, token, TokenType )
                if ( token <> ')' ) then
                    error (missing right parentheses)
            else
                if ( TokenType = number ) then
                    factor = convert( token )
                else
                    error(improper expression)

    Function term
        Input:    expression string
                  current index in the string
        Output:   value of next term in string
                  updated index in the string
        Processing:
            value = factor( expression, index )
            NextToken( expression, index, token, TokenType )
            while token is * or / do
                if ( token = '*' ) then
                    value = value * factor( expression, index )
                else
                    value = value / factor( expression, index )
                NextToken( expression, index, token, TokenType )
            term = value

    Function expr
        Input:    expression string
                  current index in the string
        Output:   value of expression
                  updated index in the string
```

continued

Processing:
```
    value = term( expression, index )
    NextToken( expression, index, token, TokenType )
    while token is + or - do
        if ( token - '+' ) then
            value = value + term( expression, index )
        else
            value = value - term( expression, index )
        NextToken( expression, index, token, TokenType )
    expr = value
```

Figure 5.14   *Recursive descent design*

This is translated into code in a very straightforward way by the set of functions in Figure 5.15.

Error checking in this system occurs only at the lowest level. Since the expression is prescanned to omit anything that could not possibly be part of an expression (words, nonoperator special characters) there is no need to check for them. Thus, if part of the expression is not recognized as valid in the *factor* function, it must be an operator out of place, and this error will be properly found in *factor*.

```
/*
 * A set of functions which evaluate an expression by recursive
 * descent
 */
float expr( str, inptr )
    char str[];
    int  *inptr;
{
    int    TokenType;
    float  value;
    Token  tok;

    value = term( str, inptr );                  /* get first operand */
    NextToken( str, inptr, tok, TokenType );
    while ((*tok.string == '+')||(*tok.string == '-')) {
        if (*tok.string == '+')    value += term( str, inptr );
        else                       value -= term( str, inptr );
        NextToken( str, inptr, tok, TokenType ); }
    return( value );
}

float term( str, inptr )
    char str[];
    int  *inptr;
{
```

continued

```
    int    TokenType;
    float  value;
    Token  tok;

    value = factor( str, inptr );              /* get first operand */
    NextToken( str, inptr, tok, TokenType );
    while ((*tok.string == '*')||(*tok.string == '/')) {
        if (*tok.string == '*')    value *= factor( str, inptr );
        else                       value /= factor( str, inptr );
        NextToken( str, inptr, tok, TokenType ); }
    return( value );
}

float factor ( str, inptr )
    char str[];
    int *inptr;
{
    int    TokenType;
    float  value;
    Token  tok;

    NextToken( str, inptr, tok, TokenType );
    if (*tok.string == '(' ) {
        value = expr( str, inptr );
        NextToken( str, inptr, tok, TokenType );
        if (*tok.string != ')' ) error( RtParenMissing );
        else if ( tok.class == NumberClass )
                value = ctoi( tok.string );
            else error( ImproperExpression ); }
    return( value );
}
```

Figure 5.15 *Recursive descent evaluation code*

5.6   Managing "Fill in the Blank" Input

When a program expects a fixed set of input from the user, it is often convenient to display a formatted screen with spaces indicating various inputs. Figure 5.16 illustrates such a screen. These screens might be most appropriate when a sequence of data sets is required, with each data set having the same components. These screens let the user see the whole input form and remove the problem of losing track of input sequences. In fact, "fill in the blank" input performs the same function as paper-based forms, which many people find quite comfortable, and is a natural technique for software that will fill ordinary office functions. The formatted input screen corresponds to the formatted output screen as described in Chapters 6 and 7. The two should be designed together, and may even use identical formats.

A data entry screen usually consists of a series of fields where the user enters information. Data entry screens are more densely packed than most screens because the time saved by having a minimum number of screens to page through to complete a transaction is important. Time is lost when the data entry operator has to wait for the next screen to appear. If multiple screens are necessary, the items that are always, or most often, required to be entered should be on the earliest screens and/or close to the top of a screen.

The example in Figure 5.16 shows the display of a large number of fields on a single data entry screen without confusing the viewer by overcrowding the information. This is accomplished by grouping together like information, using both vertical and horizontal field label and field alignment, and using single and double lines to enclose the different data entry areas.

In Figure 5.16, the fields where actual data entry takes place are marked with solid underlines. The remaining dashed lines display data that is looked up from associated or related data tables. This lookup capability allows the user to enter codes, thereby reducing the number of keystrokes necessary to complete the data entry. Because of the cryptic nature of codes, the table lookup fields give instant verification to the operator that the correct code has been entered.

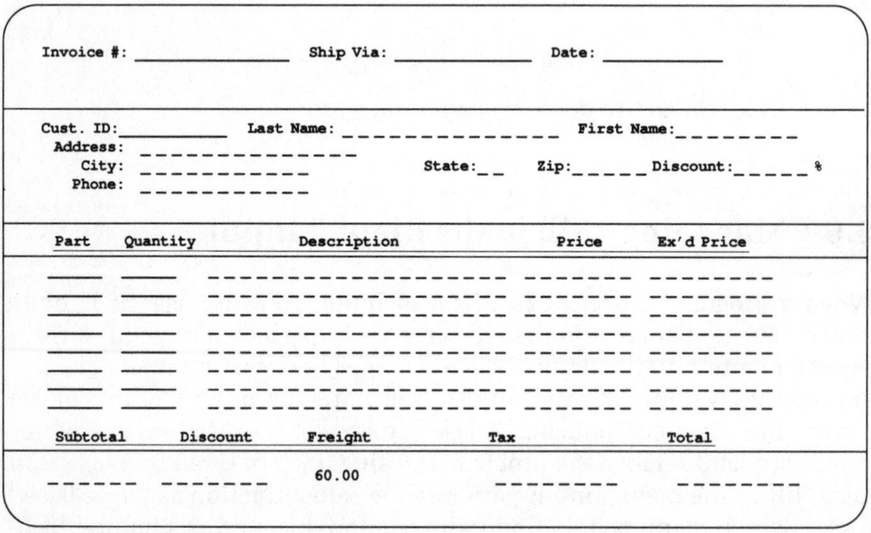

Figure 5.16 *TKentry.F1 data entry screen. This display was generated using Paradox*

This form includes the use of calculated fields (Extended Price, Subtotal, Discount, Freight, Tax, and Total). In some software, these fields may be for display purposes only, and the information is not saved in the table, or the calculations may become actual data in the table.

Other techniques for displaying data entry fields can have them highlighted by inverse video, underlining, or a different background color. Default values might already be displayed in some of the fields. For each field, the user could accept the default value or enter a new value before moving to the next field, as discussed earlier. If you need to have more data input than can comfortably fit in your space, you could have the input scroll horizontally (and disappear at the left) after the space is filled. We show this in Figure 5.20.

Filling in data entry screens can be a tiring task that you should make as easy as possible for the user. You should eliminate unnecessary key strokes by: (1) displaying default values for each field and allowing the user to skip immediately to the next field, (2) positioning the cursor at the beginning of each entry field that requires entry, (3) automatically skipping over areas not containing entry fields, and (4) not requiring the typing of extraneous characters such as leading zeroes or of separators such as back slashes and dashes. However, Galitz shows that saving keystrokes by automatically skipping to the next field when the current one is filled results in more errors and slower performance. A required manual tab to the next field is preferable.

Another thing that slows typing is the required use of the shift key caused by mixing upper and lower case characters or the the use of special characters, like '!' or '@'. The data entry operator should be able to type all data with minimal use of the shift key.

There are some considerations dependent upon whether or not the user is entering data on the screen from an associated source document. If this is the case, the screen should be designed exactly like the source document, with all the fields in the same locations. This will minimize the necessity to look back and forth between the source document and screen when entering the information. Since the screen can hold fewer characters legibly than the paper document, captions should use abbreviations and be as brief as they can be and still be clear. (They will be fully spelled out on the source document.) The current entry field should be highlighted.

If a source document is not being used to provide the data, then legibility and clarity of the screen become even more important. Captions should be spelled out and fully understandable by the person typing in the data. In this case, the entry fields must provide an indication of the kind as well as the length of the required information, as shown in Figure 5.17.

```
┌─────────────────────────────────────────────┐
│                                             │
│   DATE (MMDDYY):_ _ _ _ _ _                 │
│                                             │
└─────────────────────────────────────────────┘
```

Figure 5.17 *A date entry field showing length and kind of input needed*

In this example, the entry field indicates that six digits are required, two each for month, day, and year, and the cursor is positioned at the beginning of the field. As we noted earlier, all input should be checked for reasonable values and agreement with the type of data the field accepts. Wherever they exist, defaults should be shown and accepted with a single keystroke. To provide further legibility, long fields should be broken up with back slashes or dashes, as shown in Figure 5.18.

All input should be checked for "reasonableness." Details on programming data input are found earlier in this chapter. Since data entry screens impose a structure on the order in which data is entered, an application for which the sequence of data is highly random should be designed with some sort of data input command language.

An entire screen of information should be transmitted to the computer at a time. It is inefficient to transmit each entry as it is entered. Also, even if the cursor is somewhere in the middle of the screen, the information in all fields of the screen should be transmitted.

```
┌─────────────────────────────────────────────┐
│                                             │
│   Soc Sec #_ _ _\_ _\_ _ _ _                │
│                                             │
└─────────────────────────────────────────────┘
```

Figure 5.18 *Breaking up long fields with backslashes*

Moving from one field to the next can be done several ways; choosing a suitable technique is part of the overall interaction design and should be considered carefully. There are some standard techniques. Moving forward to the next field can be done by RETURN, TAB, or the --> arrow key. Moving back to the previous field (which is often needed for data editing) can be done by the <-- arrow key or, if one is available, by BACKTAB. When the user is at the last field on one screen, the "next field" action can bring up the next screen in a multi-screen form; when at the first field of a screen, the "previous field" action can bring back the previous screen.

As each entry is made, it is checked for validity and numeric entries are evaluated. If an error is made in the input, an error message should be displayed (in the error area as described in Chapter 6 or in a popup window as described in Chapter 7), the cursor should be moved to the beginning of the field, and the field should display an "error" mode. For example, if color is used and the original field is yellow, the field can be displayed in red. On a monochrome screen, if the original field is in inverse video, the field can be displayed in flashing mode. When the first character is entered in a field indicating an error, the field should return to normal appearance. If the field has a default and the user leaves the field without entering anything, the default value should be taken.

Note that managing this input is not really different from the general approach in Section 5.5; the formatted screen only differs in the way the prompts are managed and input echoes are given. The editing capabilities are quite straightforward, requiring only that the program keep track of the data item being entered.

Screens such as this are used for many operations, but one of the most common is with database applications. Each record's fields are displayed according to the user's own field definitions, and entries are filled in as described above. The screen of Figure 5.16 is such a microcomputer database screen.

We outline an example in which we create a screen with slots (one or more) displayed in inverse video and already filled in with default values. If the user enters the "accept" character (RETURN or TAB) the value is accepted, or the user can type in another value. On receipt of the first character, the old value vanishes and the new value begins to replace it. Each slot also has a designated type, so that an entry of the wrong type (for example, alpha in a numeric slot) causes an error message in a dialogue area. Our approach in Figure 5.19 is rather generic and can be seen as a "resource" approach similar to the general menu approach in Chapter 3. This example differs little from the default entry example above.

Using formatted screens, it is relatively straightforward to add a data editing capability to any program if the data is stored as a file or an array. The entries can be retrieved in order or by data set number. Any entry that needs editing can now be edited by using the current values as defaults and allowing the user to move to, and replace, the value(s) that need to be changed.

PROCEDURE: `InputScreen`

INPUT:
  `NF`, the number of fields in the screen
  `FP`, an array of field prompts
  `FL`, an array of field locations in the form r0,c0,r1,c1,r2,c2,...
  `FV`, an array of default values

PROCESSING:
```
clear screen
for i = 0 to NF-1
    GotoXY(FL[2*i],FL[2*i+1]-length(FP[i]))
    write FP[i]
    write FV[i] in highlighted text
i = 0
InChar = NULL
repeat
    GotoXY(FL[2*i],FL[2*i+1])
    read(InChar)
    if InChar is not TAB or CR
        clear buffer
        repeat
            echo InChar and place it in buffer
            read(InChar)
        until InChar is TAB, CR, or ENTER
    if buffer is a valid entry
        copy or translate buffer to FV[i]
    else
        replace FV[i] on screen and give error message
    if buffer is empty or valid
        i = i+1
until InChar = ENTER
```

OUTPUT: values in `FV`, some of which may be changed

Figure 5.19   InputScreen *design*

Adding horizontal scrolling to a one-row screen slot is also straightforward. Text is entered and edited as usual until the slot's space is filled. At that point, each new character scrolls the text left one space, with the leftmost character disappearing. When characters or words are erased, the text moves right, with previously hidden characters filling in from the left, until the text is smaller than the whole slot; then erasures are handled as usual. This is part of the behavior of an EditText object in MacApp, as illustrated by the MacApp example program in Chapter 10. The design of ScrollInput in Figure 5.20 implements a scrolled slot with some easily-seen functions. As in GetText, Figure 5.1, we allow single character and single word deletion here.

PROCEDURE: **ScrollInput**

INPUT: **none**

PROCESSING:
```
clear input string to NULLs
clear input area to BLANKs
set hidden = 0              /* number of characters scrolled off */
set position to 1
place cursor at beginning of area
get a character ch
while ch <> RETURN
   if ch is printable then
      append ch to input string
      if position is RIGHTEND
         move the contents of the input area left by one character
         increment hidden
      else
         increment position
      write character to screen at position
   else
      if ch = KILLCHAR then
         KillOneChar()
      if ch = KILLWORD then
         while last char. in input string is not blank and position > 0
            KillOneChar
   place cursor at position
   get a character ch
end-while

Procedure killword
   write NULL over last character in input string
   write SPACE to last character on screen
   if hidden > 0 then
      move screen characters right by one place
      write uncovered character to left of input area
      decrement hidden
   else
      decrement position
   place cursor at position
```

OUTPUT: **string for further processing**

Figure 5.20   Scroll Input *design*

5.7 Readings

This chapter is similar to Chapter 4 in its emphasis on fundamental computer techniques instead of specific interaction concepts. Besides the Horowitz and Sahni data structures text, a very good reference for this chapter is the near-classic *Software Tools* by Kernighan and Plauger, which will assist you considerably in building your tools. You should also check your system manuals to see what kinds of tools are already available in your environment.

## Chapter 6

GIVING INFORMATION BACK TO THE USER

As soon as a user begins to use your program, he or she will enter some information and expect a response. Whether or not the computer responds, how fast it responds, and in what manner it responds, all contribute to the success of your program. This chapter covers general principles of providing information to the user, as well as appropriate concerns for specific kinds of screens.

6.1 General Principles

The computer must provide information to the user and respond to requests, commands, and information provided by the user. All effective information and responses must be easy to read and understand. Responses must be informative, consistent, and as fast as possible. Sound difficult? It takes time, planning, and adherence to rules that have been outlined in the field of effective communication. The *implementation* of these rules is not so difficult.

Planning

Planning is the most important key to effective program communication. Far too often, programs are written and debugged without adequate thought to the elements of screen design such as layout, color, placement of text, or sentence structure. Even worse, no thought is given to the information needs of those who will use the programs. Such concerns must be an integral part of the program from the very beginning. Neither the program communication nor the printed documentation can be delayed until the computational part of the program is completed.

> PRINCIPLE: Plan screen design from the beginning.

Consistency

The program must present information consistently, in line with our general principles in Chapter 1. This means that the same type of information must be presented in a similar fashion (including style, layout, and color) and in the same location in order to elicit the same type of response from the user. Such consistency makes it easier for a novice to learn how to use the program and also allows the experienced user to work faster. Both kinds of users will and should expect the basic information such as menu choices and error messages to be similarly displayed throughout the program. The only way to achieve this consistency is to have users similar to the program's intended audience test the program continuously throughout its development.

> PRINCIPLE: Present information consistently.

Readability

First, let us discuss what makes screens easy to read. These guidelines have been derived from substantial studies and include the following:

- *Sentence structure and vocabulary*: Sentences should be brief and use the vocabulary of the intended user.
- *Use of upper- and lower-case text*: A combination of upper- and lower-case text is more legible than upper case alone.
- *Number of lines per display*: Most displays should hold no more than 12 to 16 lines of text and one graphic.
- *Length of lines of text*: Line lengths of 40 characters or less are more legible.

- *Placement of blocks of information*: Related information should be displayed together, always in the same location, and visually separated from other blocks of information.

- *Highlighting appropriate information*: The information you want the user to act upon should be highlighted with color, inverse video, or other similar indicator.

- *Effective use of color*: Use no more than five to seven colors per display, and choose color combinations carefully.

   More details on these guidelines are provided below.

PRINCIPLE: Present information so that it can be read quickly and correctly.

Consistency goes beyond simply having the same inherent structure throughout the program. It extends to the language used in the program. This language should be chosen very carefully to contain action-oriented words that show that the user is always in control of the program. The words used should accurately reflect the language the user associates with the program's function. An artist may use a different phrase to describe a graphic action than an engineer would, for example. Also, the language itself should be consistent from one screen to another, always phrasing the action in the same way, and always using the same words to describe the same actions.

PRINCIPLE: Make the program phrase all action in words that emphasize the user's control, describe positive actions, and reflect the user's normal usage.

Meeting Expectations and Needs

A user's expectations are affected by a number of things. The importance of consistency within a program is mentioned. Certainly, the first part of a program will create expectations that the other parts of the program will work similarly. This first introduction to the program also establishes the placement of information, the color or other highlighting used, and the vocabulary of the program.

You must also be concerned about the particular application and the type of user for this application. Certain words have very different meanings to people in different specialties. As an extreme example, one major graphics software company has a routine called EXPLODE which produces pie charts with segments pulled away from the center. The company was requested to change the name of that subroutine for a government agency which did not like the connotations of "EXPLODE."

As a more common example, consider the word "terminal." What does this mean to the computer professional? To the health professional? To the transportation official? If the program is geared towards a particular profession, you must choose your vocabulary carefully for those who are in that profession. If it is a more general application, you must be sure all words with multiple meanings are used in understandable context or carefully explained.

In many areas, work has traditionally been done in a standard way, and computers are now being brought into the process. You would be wise to take into account the terminology and methods traditionally used in such an application area. For example, if you are designing a computer aided drafting package, you must make it comprehensible to the traditional draftsman. If you are designing a word processor or office automation system, it must make sense to the office secretary.

> PRINCIPLE: Use vocabulary and techniques consistent with traditional working methods.

However, do not limit the capabilities of your program only to what people could do with their traditional tools. In many cases, the computer can allow more power and flexibility for a given task. Your interface should allow them to do traditional tasks in a familiar manner and at the same time expand their capabilities.

> PRINCIPLE: Use the computer capabilities to full advantage.

You must also consider what capabilities of the computer display, in addition to text, can be used to provide information more clearly for the user. The use of color or other highlighting might give a more effective indication of what the user needs to do. A graph might display the information more clearly than words or tables. The use of an icon rather than text might be more easily understood. Be aware, however, that the design of effective graphs and icons, like the design of an effective interface, is a difficult and specialized task. Just as it takes years to become a skilled, efficient computer programmer, it takes years to develop these graphic design skills and understandings. Programmers should seek advice from design artists in graphics and icon creation and should test the icons on users. The use of icons in graphic menus is discussed in more depth in Chapter 3.

What expectations do users already have when they look at programs? You would be wise to take into account other programs that might already be in use. It is possible that you can write a program that works better than a popular program such as Lotus 1-2-3. However, there are already thousands of users of this program. Most of these users will be more apt to buy a program that lets them continue working in a familiar fashion than they will be to buy an entirely different kind of program.

PRINCIPLE: Present information in a similar fashion as popular existing programs.

On the other hand, do not carry this concept to extremes. There are many programs that emulate the Tektronix 4010 graphics terminal, a storage tube device. One such terminal emulator for the IBM PC makes the PC look exactly like a Tektronix storage tube, even to the extent that it removes the ability of the IBM PC raster technology to scroll text. This emulator overwrites text instead, perfectly emulating the storage tube's inability to do any kind of selective erase. Even those who are very familiar with these terminals will not welcome unnecessary limitations being built into an emulator. Interestingly, it took extra effort by the programmer to add these limitations.

Presenting Information

There are some rules of good presentation that apply to both paper and computer display screens:

- Normal upper- and lower-case text is easier to read than all upper case.
- Text must be large enough to be read easily.

There are standards such as the DIN (Deutsche Industrie Normen) international standard for screen characters. This specifies a minimum height of 2.6 mm for capital letters for a computer display based on a viewing distance of 45 to 60 cm (18 to 24 in.). However, other factors such

Figure 6.1 *Enlarged pixel fonts and smooth font*

as the screen resolution and text quality alter the legibility. If the text font is poor quality, a larger size character may be less legible. Since characters on most computer screens are made up of tiny dots called pixels, a common method for enlarging text is to change each dot in the matrix that composes the character to four dots, nine dots, or more, resulting in a larger letter that may be more difficult to read, as illustrated in Figure 6.1.

The biggest difference between presenting information on a computer screen and presenting information on paper is the cost (or lack of cost) of blank space on the screen. The computer screen should contain only pertinent information, well spaced, in order to be easily read and understood. If more information is needed, a second or even third screen can be used rather than overcrowding the display.

A chapter by Reid in the Monk book further substantiates the need for upper- and lower-case text, as well as the need to avoid overfilling the screen. He recommends no more than 25% of the screen should be filled if the user is expected to locate and recognize information easily. Reinforcing this concept, a report from Danchek in the Galitz handbook suggests that a well-designed page of printed material only contains 40 percent printed matter, whereas a "good" computer screen contains only 15 percent printed matter.

PRINCIPLE: Make screens simple and legible.

A well-designed screen should present one major idea. Kearsley and Halley recommend no more than 12 to 16 lines of text and one graphic per screen. Text should be in short paragraphs of three to five sentences with double spacing between paragraphs. Different kinds of screens might call for denser information. Density of information varies somewhat with the purpose served by the display and is discussed in Section 6.2.

PRINCIPLE: Present only one major idea on a display.

If more information must be provided on a second screen, you must indicate that there is more to come and tell how to get to the second screen.

PRINCIPLE: Indicate when there is more information than is currently displayed.

Figure 6.2 gives an example of a screen illustrating one major idea and indicating how to continue with the program. This screen is from *Algebra Drill and Practice I* by CONDUIT.

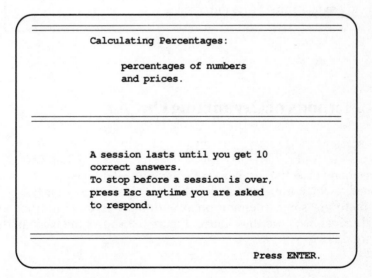

Figure 6.2 *A sample screen from CONDUIT's Algebra Drill and Practice I*
Used by permission

The "clutter-free" screen discussed above should contain only the information the user needs, and information is located where it is easily found. This information should be in clear, concise English, and it should indicate what is on the display and what the user must do with the information. One means of minimizing clutter throughout a program is to display information only when it is needed. This concept is discussed more in Chapter 12.

When more than one type of information must appear on the screen at the same time, the information must be grouped into cohesive blocks, separated from each other. There should be spaces surrounding the blocks, if not actual separation lines. Also, the user should become accustomed to seeing certain kinds of information, such as commands and error messages, in consistent locations on all screens.

Some tutorial programs require information from several previous screens in order to solve the current problem. This forces the students to keep a pencil and paper handy as they use such a tutorial because the information scrolls off the screen or is overwritten before it is needed, and thus limits the value of the tutorial. If information is not needed until problem-solving time, it should not be displayed until then. If it is needed in the earlier explanatory portion, it should be kept visible in a separate window or reshown when needed.

> PRINCIPLE: All information necessary to perform a given task must be on the screen.

6.2   Methods of Organizing Output

There are many different kinds of programs with many different functions. These need different types of screens serving different purposes, such as menu selection or data entry. Each type has special requirements and needs, which are given in detail below. However, regardless of purpose, there are some common organizational needs in addition to the general principles described above. Figure 6.3 shows the basic parts of a standard display.

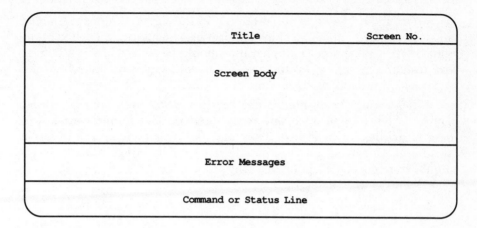

Figure 6.3 *Basic components of a display*

Major Components of the Screen

You must carefully consider what should be displayed on the screen, and how it should be displayed, at each point of your program. Users expect to find certain screen components in particular locations on most kinds of screens, and we will discuss these standard parts in the next few paragraphs. Special kinds of screens have additional needs, however, and we will describe several of these toward the end of this section.

Title Line

Each screen should have a title or heading that describes what kind of information is displayed. In the case of multiple screens, it should also indicate where the user is in the program. For example, a user searching through pages of information or following a tutorial needs to know what page he or she is on and how many more pages there are. Doing the same task with a reference book, he or she would know this by glancing at the pages. On a computer display, an indication can be given as shown in Figure 6.4.

```
INVENTORY          page 5 of 8
```

Figure 6.4 *Title line showing the user's position in the program's information*

Titles should be centered at the top of the screen. The page number should be in the same line, since this is a less frequently used area of the screen. The title and page number line should be separated visually from the rest of the screen by the use of inverse video or underline and separated physically by at least one blank line.

Titles should be printed differently from other text, but subtly so. They may be all upper-case, one exception to the usual upper- and lower-case principles for most text. They may be inverse video or a different sized font. However, the titles should not be distracting; they are only a point of reference, not a point of attention.

Command or Status Line

This is the line that explains either how the user gives commands to the program or what the current settings are for the program. It can define what each function key or control character does, or it can show the command that the user must type, either spelled out in full or suitably abbreviated. It should be at the bottom of the display so as not to be intrusive and to put the information where the user will be looking after reading the screen and while deciding what he needs to do next. The user's eyes are now, appropriately, at the bottom of the screen when he needs this information.

It is permissible to have all upper-case or all lower-case text here. If the user need only type part of the word, such as MOD for MODIFY or R for RUN, you can highlight these letters by an underline or increased intensity. Sometimes the mixed case is used to indicate what the user must type, such as MODify or Run, though this can be confusing, since the user may think it is necessary to type the word in mixed case, as shown. Parentheses are also frequently used, such as (MOD)IFY or (R)UN, or MOD(IFY) or R(UN).

Figure 6.5 is from the BASIC interpreter on the IBM Personal Computer. It is a reminder of what the ten function keys are programmed to do in a BASIC program. Pressing function key 1 will list the program, pressing function key 2 will run the program, etc. The status line can be in inverse video or have a line drawn above it to set it off from the main body of the screen. (Of course, inverse video eliminates the capability of having some letters in higher intensity, as mentioned above.)

The user should be able to turn this line on and off as desired. Users who are familiar with the program will not need to refer to this line very often and may find it distracting. Users also may wish to print or photograph a screen without this line.

```
The IBM Personal Computer Basic




1 LIST   2 RUN   3 LOAD"   4 SAVE"   5 CONT   6 "LPT1   7 TRON  8 TROFF  9 KEY  10 SCREEN
```

Figure 6.5   *The command line from BASIC on the IBM PC*

Error or WarningMessages

Error or warning messages should go at the bottom of the screen directly above the command or status line. Since this line will be blank most of the time, the space allocated for it provides a further separation between the screen body and the command line. Even more important than this specific location, however, is that it must *always* appear in a consistent location. It should be upper- and lower-case text and should provide all necessary information for the user. Error messages should not refer to written documentation. If explanation for the problem requires more than one line, the area can grow to two or three lines, you can provide a window which scrolls the rest of the message, or you can provide the rest of the information through a help facility.

Most importantly, this message must attract the user's attention. It should be higher intensity or a different color than other text on the screen, and an audible alert might accompany it. The user should be able to turn off the sound, however, if he or she chooses to do so. There are situations where others in the same room might be disturbed by the sound or a novice user might be embarrassed for others to hear all his or her mistakes.

The Screen Body

After leaving space for the title, command line and error messages on a 24-line display, there are 18 to 20 lines left. The remaining screen area, the screen body, contains areas of information the user needs and areas for the user to enter information. This area is organized in a logical top-to-bottom, left-to-right, fashion with the information the user needs first located at the top and information on how the user can go to the next screen or choose to do something else located at the bottom. Beyond this, the organization of the main body of the screen varies with the type of screen and is determined by the purpose the screen serves.

Considerations for Different Types of Screens

Applications have a range of different functions that require different kinds of screens. Some common types of screens are described below, with discussions of how they should be handled.

Menu

A menu screen consists of a list of options from which the user can make one or more selections. Principles and programming techniques for menus are discussed more fully in Chapter 3, but menus have a few distinguishing characteristics. Each item on the menu must be clear and concise, and all words should be fully spelled out. The menu list should be vertical and left justified. This left-justified list should be centered on the screen. If there is more than one column of menu items on a screen, each column should be left justified, with at least five spaces between columns, and the set of columns should be centered on the screen. The trade-off between the number of menu items on a screen and the number of screens is still being researched. However, in the Galitz handbook, a 1981 study involving a menu of 64 choices concluded that eight items on a menu, with two levels of menus, was easiest to learn and resulted in least errors and fastest performance.

In addition to screen titles, a menu may have category headings for each column of menu items. The category headings should be further set off, subtly, by underline, brackets or two dashes on each side, as shown in Figure 6.6. In this configuration example, the user will be asked to describe the input device, output device and display being used.

If the screen is a menu that comes from other menus, the user needs an indication of the path taken to get there, as illustrated in Figure 6.7 from the Zenographics Mirage software. In the original menu, Item 5. Controls, was selected; then item 5. Hardcopy, was selected, and so on. The current menu is in the center, and current status of choices is shown on the right.

```
                    Selection of Computer Equipment

     Input Device           Output Device            Display
     _____           _____            _____

     1.  Keyboard only      1.  Printer              1.  Monochrome
     2.  Tablet             2.  Plotter              2.  Color
     3.  Scanner            3.  Camera recorder
     4.  Mouse              4.  Video
     5.  Joystick

   You will be asked to enter information about your configuration
   First enter the number (1 - 5) of your input device:_
```

Figure 6.6 *Example of menu with category headings*

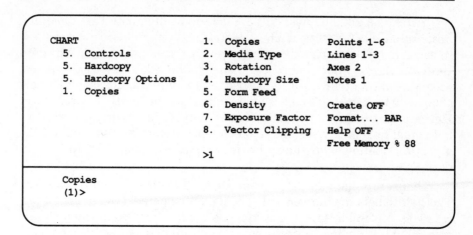

Figure 6.7 *Menu illustrating path to this screen, current status, and menu choices, from Zenographics Mirage*

Used by permission.

Data entry screens

Data entry and data display screens provide excellent examples of screen display organization. Data entry screens are also discussed in Chapter 5.

Early organizational techniques involved two columns, both left justified, with the column on the left giving the category and the column on the right giving the information. This method is still endorsed by some of those who have been working in the field of data entry for some time because it allows for easy proofreading. However, short categories on the left cause difficulty in keeping track of the corresponding data entry field on the right. Other kinds of information grouping have become more popular in current data management.

The formatted screen input example of Figure 5.16 includes a number of fields which are to be summed in the report. Field data that is to be summed is best displayed using a column scheme. However, if this would necessitate another screen in the data entry form, it is best to use the horizontal scheme as illustrated at the bottom of the screen in Figure 5.16. This avoids the necessity of a second screen. If all the fields to be summed are on a single line, the table can be viewed and understood.

Mixing horizontal and vertical label/field schemes can be confusing to the user. A *horizontal label/field* is of the form Field Label: field data. On the screen in Figure 5.16, for example, the field Cust. ID_ _ _ _ is a horizontal field and label combination. A *vertical label/field* is of the form

Field Label

field data

In Figure 5.16, the lower half of the form dealing with Part, Quantity, Description, etc. is a vertical label and field combination. Do not mix these schemes more than once in a given form. For example, do not start with vertical, switch to horizontal, and then switch back to vertical. The user becomes familiar with a particular pattern and will find it easier to follow along with the cursor if a consistent pattern is maintained. The example in Figure 5.16 uses both schemes, but it only switches from vertical to horizontal once, between the invoice/demographic information and the order information, and the order information is displayed in a well-recognized invoice design.

There are some other aspects of Figure 5.16 that are worth noticing. The field labels for the vertical scheme are centered over the columns, which is preferable to being left aligned. Also, the lookup field labels associated with name, address, etc. are left aligned as are the associated fields. This scheme is acceptable as long as the field labels have approximately the same number of characters. If the number of characters in a field label differs by more than five characters from another field label in a group of fields, it is better to right justify these field labels so they will be adjacent to the field data. This proximity makes it easier to find the field that a particular field label is addressing.

Question and Answer Screen

A question and answer screen presents short communications between the user and the computer. It might be a user survey where the computer issues a series of questions to be answered by the user, or it might be queries from the user for information provided by the computer. What distinguishes such a screen from a data entry screen or an inquiry screen is the amount of information provided in each communication. This type of screen can be used for data entry or database inquiry, but it is an inefficient method for these applications.

A question and answer screen is concerned with one issue at a time, displays only a small amount of information at a time, and requires only brief responses from the user. Since only a small amount of text appears with each question and answer, you can limit the length of lines and allow plenty of space to make the screen easily legible. Answers should follow questions on the same line or the next line and be easily differentiable from questions. If the computer is issuing the questions, a special symbol, such as a question mark or arrow, can be used to indicate that the user should now type his or her reply. Alternatively, the user's reply can be indented to distinguish it from the question. If the user is querying the computer, the indentation is more appropriate. Figure 6.8 is an excerpt from an on-line survey and is representative of a brief question and answer session.

```
In order to serve you better, we are making a survey of our users
Please answer the following questions about your use of our
facilities


1.  Enter your name (optional):
>>Judy Brown

2.  What institution do you represent?
>>The University of Iowa

3.  What is your area of scientific research?
>>
```

Figure 6.8   *Question and answer screen*

You must make sure that all information necessary for the user to answer a question is on the screen. If the information is provided earlier, it must remain on the screen instead of being allowed to scroll off, or it must reappear when needed.

Inquiry Screen

An inquiry screen is designed for people to retrieve information from a computer file or database. The important feature of such a screen is for the user to be able to scan a screen full of information quickly and easily to find the desired information. All information must be fully spelled out, and legibility is increased through the use of windows or adequate spacing between groups of information. Only that information that is requested or relevant should be displayed. The display is most easily read if related information is grouped into columns, and the columns are broken up with a blank line every three to five items for legibility. For speedier access, put the most frequently accessed information in the left-hand columns and, in the case of multiple screens, on the earliest screens. An example of an interactive inquiry is provided in Section 7.1.

Information Screen

An information screen provides information to the user. Examples of such a display are instructions for using a program, tutorials, help screens, or database display screens. Textual information should be in brief sentences and paragraphs, displayed legibly through the use of sufficient blank space as described earlier. If there is more information on a subsequent screen, there should be an indication that another screen is avail-

```
┌─────────────────────────────────────────────────────────────────────┐
│                                                                       │
│                    Inventory                    Page 5 of 8           │
│                                                                       │
│                                                                       │
│        -Computers-                          -Plotters-                │
│        1.  IBM PC                           1.  HP 7470               │
│        2.  Macintosh                        2.  HP 7475               │
│        3.  Leading Edge                     3.  Versatec              │
│            .                                4.  Zeta                  │
│        -Printers-                                                     │
│        1.  HP Laserjet                                                │
│        2.  Epson FX/80         Press ESC to return to Main Menu       │
│        3.  Imagewriter II           RETURN for next page              │
│        4.  Apple Laserwriter                                          │
│                                                                       │
└─────────────────────────────────────────────────────────────────────┘
```

Figure 6.9   *Information screen*

able. This indication, placed at the bottom of the screen, tells the user how to get the next screen of information and how to stop if he or she does not want any more information. If the user must now make a decision based on the information provided, all relevant information for that decision must be on the current screen. Figure 6.9 illustrates one of a series of inventory screens.

Control Screen

A control screen allows a user to monitor and control equipment or an environment. If something needs the user's attention, it should be displayed quickly and vividly. Highlighting through intensity, color, or even blinking is appropriate here because you must catch the user's eye. If the situation demands immediate attention, you should also add an auditory "alarm." In addition to getting the user's attention, you must provide information on what he or she must do now to control the situation. The use of graphics may help the user assess the situation more quickly and better understand what he or she needs to do. Be sure to test the graphical icons you intend to use to be sure they will be recognized by the user and will have the intended meaning.

Figures 6.10 and 6.11 illustrate a robot arm simulation. The user controls the robot arm by issuing commands to rotate parts of the arm. In real life, if the robot is commanded to rotate farther than it can physically rotate, it will break. By giving commands to the computer simulation first, the user can see if a command is proper, and this breakage problem is avoided. Figure 6.10 shows the robot in its current position and the command for the next rotation. This command includes a 200-degree rotation at the base, which the robot cannot do. Figure 6.11 shows the dialog box alerting the user that there is a problem. This example is courtesy of the Instructional Services Software Development Group at

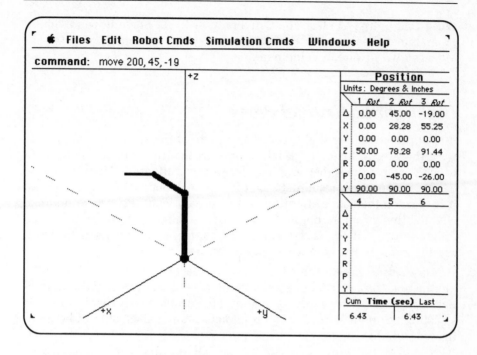

Figure 6.10   *Robot arm and next command*

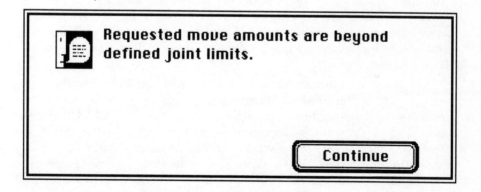

Figure 6.11   *Warning that such movement is not possible*

Weeg Computing Center, The University of Iowa, Steve Bowers, Senior Programmer Analyst, Les Finken, Systems Analyst, and Steve Wessels, Manager of Software Development.

Highlighting Critical Parts

It is important to highlight the part or parts of the screen on which you wish the user to focus. Highlighting means that this part looks different from the rest of the screen and therefore attracts attention. How much and by what means you accentuate the difference depends on how important it is to catch the user's attention and what you want the user to do next. Highlighting is an important means of revealing the structure of the program to the user, as described in Chapter 9, so you need to use it carefully and only to achieve a known purpose.

In a menu screen, the item or items selected by the user should be highlighted through higher intensity, inverse video, or color. Here highlighting is equated to choice, so it allows the user to verify that he or she is selecting the right item. A default choice, if any exists, should be highlighted initially.

In the case of a data entry screen, all the entry fields should be highlighted through higher intensity, inverse video, or color. Here highlighting means that the user can change the highlighted fields. Since inverse video or improper color combinations may cause decreased legibility, higher intensity or a carefully chosen color combination is more effective.

A question and answer screen should draw the user's attention to the fact that information is being requested by a prompt such as a question mark. Here the user's attention is already on the new question, so there is no need to reveal program structure with highlighting. Questions and answers are more easily differentiated by offsetting the answer. Since the questions and answers are brief, different colors or text types are more distracting than useful.

The object of an inquiry screen is for a user to be able to scan the data fields quickly to find desired information. In this case, the layout of the screen is more important than highlighting the entire data field. However, careful use of different background colors can highlight the different information groupings on the screen. The information should be in columns with appropriate labels. There should be three to five spaces between columns and a blank line every three to five rows to make the information more legible. Text should be left justified, and numeric fields should be right justified. Numeric data should be displayed in a constant width font so that the numbers line up. In the case of variable length decimals, like 1.54 and 2.637, numbers should be aligned by decimal point.

Information screens should reserve highlighting for especially important information on the screen and for the directions on what to do to get the next page of information or to return to some other task. Higher intensity or reverse video are appropriate here. Changing colors can easily become distracting if not used very carefully.

In the case of a control screen, it is sometimes very important to get the user's attention immediately. When equipment is operating normally, the use of neutral colors and higher intensity for the most important information will indicate that there is no problem and will verify at a glance that things are working properly. However, if something is wrong with the situation, you want to catch your user's attention any way you can. Change to an "emergency" color such as red and/or flash a warning message accompanied by an audible alarm. Blinking or flashing is highly attention-getting and should be used in such situations. In fact, blinking should be reserved for such situations because it becomes very distracting when it is not necessary. A window where such messages *always* appear works well.

In all cases, you will have occasions to produce error or warning messages. These are messages that indicate that what the user is trying to do is either incorrect or may have undesirable results. These should be strongly highlighted by higher intensity, or a different color from the rest of the screen, or even by blinking so you can get the user's attention. As mentioned in the case of the control screen, a window for error messages works well.

Presenting Tabular Summaries

We have only discussed text screens so far. With text we can inform, explain, interpret, and evaluate. Sometimes, however, we might be able to get the information across better by using tables. Tables allow us to summarize pages of information, to provide evidence supporting the conclusions the program draws, and to provide precise comparisons. A table can be displayed on any kind of terminal or monitor. Although it might be nicer to have line drawing and color capabilities, these are not essential. What is essential is visual clarity. The entire table must be on a single screen, and all text and numbers must be easily visible. Since a computer screen usually holds 24 lines, each of width 40 or 80 characters, and some room is already consumed by title and status lines, the table must be kept simple.

As with columnar data on inquiry screens, text should be left justified and numeric data should be right justified or justified by the decimal point. All text should be upper and lower case, with row and column labels larger or higher intensity than table items. If possible, rows and columns should be separated by lines. Figure 6.12 shows a table that provides information on equipment use in computer labs. It was provided by Fran Burns, Weeg Computing Center, The University of Iowa.

Usage Data for the Instructional Computing Labs

Department	Month	Total Users	# Users/ PC/day	# Users/ Mac/day	# Users/ Term/day
Dorm	March	4137	5.73	included in PC	5.67
	April	5850	5.86	included in PC	5.35
	May	2577	6.67	included	5.18
Business	March	10075	5.47	6.84	2.28
	April	12681	6.50	7.21	2.84
	May	5160	4.09	5.26	0.80
Education	March	663	5.60	7.41	0.11
	April	6014	5.00	8.09	0.25
	May	1323	5.03	8.85	0.44

Figure 6.12   *Information provided in a table*

Presenting Graphical Summaries

More and more displays now support graphics. However, "because it is there" is not a good reason to use graphics. Some types of data are readily depicted with a table. Frequently, however, a graph will reveal relationships or characteristics not evident in a textual or tabular display. Before you decide to use a graph, make sure it serves a useful purpose.

> PRINCIPLE: Use a graph to display information if it conveys information more effectively.

If a graph seems to be the best way to show your information, you then need to decide what kind of graph will be most informative. One way of making this choice is to verbalize what you wish to show and see what kind of chart shows that. For example, a line graph or bar chart can illustrate how something changes over time, while a pie chart or stacked bar chart illustrates percentages, as shown in Figure 6.13, provided by Jacob Hugart, The University of Iowa.

1988 Projected Income Pie Chart

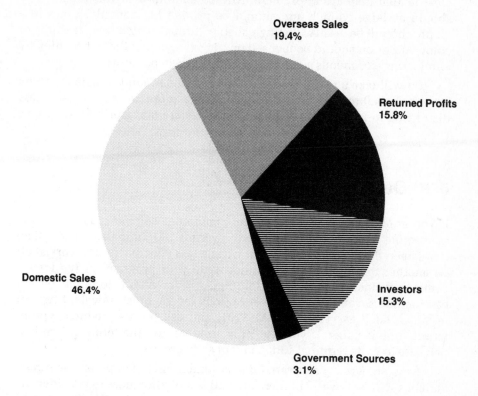

Figure 6.13   *A pie chart showing percentages*

Points to Note:

- Decreased Reliance on Government Sources
- Sharp Cutback on Overseas Sales
- Marked Increase of Investor Income

Once again, simplicity is the rule. Choose only the most relevant features of your data to produce clear, meaningful graphs. The concept of form, which includes properties of point, line, shape, color, and texture, is important in graphic design. Graphic designers and artists are skilled at structuring these elements into visually effective ideas and should be consulted in such design work.

Many of the same features or extensions to features recommended for clear textual displays apply here. All text should be legible; hence, text should be large enough and should be printed horizontally. Lines in a graph should be easily distinguishable through thickness, texture, or color. Attention should be focused on lines that depict the information by eliminating extraneous symbols, grids, and garish patterns.

If it will take a while to display the graph, announce the delay. Draw the graph before inserting the labels. It is more interesting and less distracting to look at the graph as the labels are being printed than vice versa.

6.3   Output Devices

If you are writing mainframe or minicomputer software, users may be connecting to the computer through a variety of terminals. A very effective screen design on one terminal will be less effective or not work at all on another terminal. You can either write your program for the lowest common denominator, a low-resolution, ASCII, "dumb" terminal; or you can include several device driver options for the most prevalent type of terminal, such as vt100 or IBM 3101, and ask the user which type of terminal he is using. If you use Unix, you can use the termcap terminal database to write terminal-independent software.

If you are writing software for a particular microcomputer, the screen varieties will be fewer, but there are still some differences to consider. As an example, consider the IBM Personal Computer series (PC/XT/AT) and compatibles. At the very least, a user may have either a monochrome monitor or a graphics monitor. On the monochrome monitor, you can at least draw boxes and other elementary graphics. You can highlight through increased intensity, inverse video, or blinking. If the user has the color graphics adapter (CGA) and color display, you can use a variety of color combinations for text, and you can also create graphics, but screens on which you can have graphics only allow four colors at a time. If the user has other graphics boards, such as the Enhanced Graphics Adapter or Hercules card, you are faced with different resolutions, different numbers of colors, and in some cases, different programming commands to locate, print, and draw. Furthermore, what if the user has a Color/Graphics Adapter and a monochrome graphics display? Color combinations that look great on a color monitor may be impossible to differentiate on the monochrome display. Chapter 8 discusses compatibility with monochromatic displays, and Chapter 13 has more discussion on adapting programs to various devices.

6.4 Readings

For general information on graphic presentation and visual display of information, we refer you to books by Schmid and Schmid and by Tufte. The book by Shneiderman and by Badre and Shneiderman give interesting insight into human/computer interaction, as well as on highlighting of information. The book by Rubenstein and Hersh gives some details on standards for the display of information. Three other books by Monk, Heines and Galitz give general information on displaying ideas and also deal with the issue of screen density.

Chapter 7

SCREEN TECHNIQUES

Examples of various types of formatted screens are given in the preceding chapter, Figures 6.3 to 6.12. There are basic parts of each display: title, screen body, screen number (if appropriate), error messages, and command or status line. There are some variations on what should be displayed, where it should be displayed, and how much should be displayed, depending on the purpose of the display. The most important thing about placement of information is consistency—within a program, between related programs, and with traditional working methods.

In each case, there are information areas appropriate to each of the basic screen designs described in Chapter 6. However, there are now many techniques for displaying information, including windows and other kinds of data display. At one time, the only method to display information was to have it continuously scroll off the top or to erase the entire screen for a page-by-page display. This method is still useful for some applications, but it has become possible and important for the display screen to be a dynamic medium. The use of windows in screen design has become very popular and is discussed in this chapter and, in more detail, in Chapter 10. Other interactive uses of the screen are vitally important.

7.1   Interactive Screens

Data Inquiry

One of the most common interactive uses of the computer is inquiry into a database. Examples of data inquiry screens and subsequent display screen from the database, Figures 7.1 to 7.5, are provided by Fran Hemingway, free-lance consultant in Orlando, Florida, using Paradox on the IBM PC.

Paradox is a database system from Borland International that allows immediate help about what each command will do when you select it. The following screens illustrate that help facility and the results of a Paradox query. In Figure 7.5, the query, the fields that contain X are those that will provide information. This particular database is about departmental computer equipment in a university. Information about the date the equipment was acquired (Date In) is not given because it was not requested.

Figures 7.1 and 7.2 illustrate the automatic help facility of Paradox. As you move the arrow keys across the menu, a one line description of the highlighted menu item appears. This is similar to the action of Lotus 1-2-3 menus, described in Chapter 1. Figure 7.3 is the query form that allows you to select a table, in this case "Stock," an inventory table. Figure 7.4 shows the fields on which you can select information, and Figure 7.5 shows the information requested and the results of the query. This database example is a good illustration of changing areas of a display while leaving other areas intact, although the interactivity, the most important aspect, is difficult to show in this series of static illustrations.

Notice in Figure 7.5 that you view the query and the results of the query simultaneously so that both verification and changes to the query request are easily made.

```
 View  Ask  Report  Create  Modify  Image  Forms  Tools  Scripts  Help  Exit

 View a table


 Use ↑ and ↓ keys to move around menu, then press ↵ to make selection
```

Figure 7.1   *Result of highlighting the view option*

```
View  Ask  Report  Create  Modify  Image  Forms  Tools  Scripts  Help  Exit

Get a query form to ask questions about a table



Use ↑ and ↓ keys to move around menu, then press ↵ to make selection
```

Figure 7.2   *Result of highlighting the ask option*

```
Table: STOCK                                                          Main
Enter name of table to ask about, or press     ↵ to see a list of tables



```

Figure 7.3   *Selection of a table for inquiry*

```
[F6] to include a field in the ANSWER; [F5] to give an example        Main

STOCK======Department=====Description==========Qty======Date In===
          :              :                     :              :
          :              :                     :              :

          :              :                     :              :

```

Figure 7.4   *Inquiry screen showing information available*

```
[F6] to include a field in the ANSWER; [F5] to give an example        Main

STOCK======Department=====Description==========Qty======Date In===
          : X BUS         : X                  : X           :
          :              :                     :              :

          :              :                     :              :
Viewing Answer table: Record 1 of 3                         Main

ANSWER==============Department======Description===========Qty====:
   1    :            BUS      : 30MB Fixed Disk      :  3      :
   2    :            BUS      : EGA Adapter Card     : 20      :
   3    :            BUS      : EGA Monitor          :  5      :
```

Figure 7.5   *Query and results*

The Screen as a Dynamic Medium

Figures 7.6 to 7.9 illustrate dynamic use of the screen. In this example, a philosophy drill and practice program on the principles of reasoning, the user is able to request further information by pressing the appropriate keys shown on the current screen. This information temporarily occupies the main information area of the screen, along with its environment. The original information is saved on a stack and restored when the RETURN key is pressed. The data structure for each area is shown in Figure 7.10.

Once the student starts the program, Figure 7.6, the philosophical area is selected with a single key stroke, in this case F for Fallacy Identification. This adds more information areas and paves the way for additional requested information to occupy the main information area of the display temporarily, as shown in Figures 7.7 to 7.9. Information that has been copied to the stack and overwritten is restored with the press of the RETURN key. In this particular example, pressing Alt-P gives a list of possible answers, Alt-H invokes the help facility, RETURN restores the list of possible answers, and a second RETURN restores the initial tutorial question.

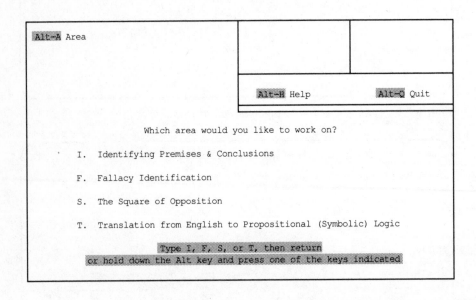

Figure 7.6   *Opening screen for philosophy program*

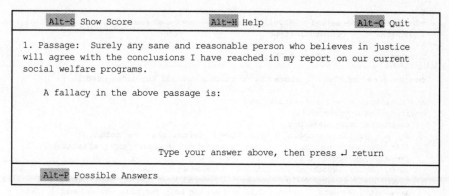

Figure 7.7   *First question, before Alt-P is pressed*

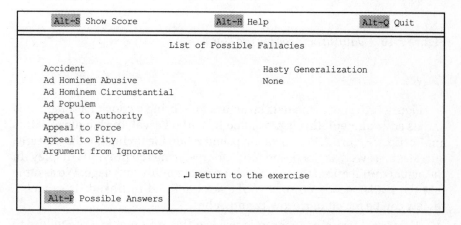

Figure 7.8   *Possible answers occupy main area, before Alt-H is pressed*

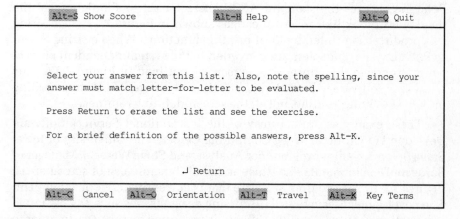

Figure 7.9   *Help facility occupies main area*

```
TYPE
    scrnbuffertype = array[1..3200] of char; { 20 rows x 80 chars/row }
    scrnbufferptr = ^scrnbuffertype;

    DOSname = string[MAXDOSNAMELENGTH];

    funcset = set of char;  { store the function & special key defns used }

    envirstackptr = ^envirsavestacktype;
    envirsavestacktype = RECORD
        savedarea: scrnbufferptr;
        ulr,ulc,lrr,lrc: integer; { upper/lower, left/right, row/column }
        directionused: integer; { topdown or bottomup? pulldown/popup effects }
        savedrow,savedcol: integer;
        savedfgcolor,savedbgcolor: integer; { color environment }
        savedlocals,savedglobals: funcset; { special keys in this environment }
        savedhelp: DOSname; {name of file containing help for this environment }
        nextsavedenvir,prevsavedenvir: envirstackptr; { double-linked stack }
    END;
```

Figure 7.10 *Data structures for the stack*

Figure 7.10 shows the data structure for storing a copy of a screen area and its environment; this is presented in Turbo Pascal, the language of this application. Figure 7.11 shows the pseudocode for saving the display area on a stack, as well as the pseudocode for restoring the previous display. In the actual application, these are written in assembly language. We assume that the reader needs no review of stacks defined in linked lists; such a review can be found in Horowitz and Sahni.

Another interesting technique used in this program is a procedure to isolate machine dependent screen drawing routines, such as drawing with the extended ASCII character set on the IBM PC. This procedure is called PetString. It uses the standard ASCII character set to simulate what the display will look like as best it can, as shown in Figure 7.12. Each string this produces is printed by local printing functions. When a string is sent to PetString, its characters are converted to the system-dependent character set to create the appropriate screen, as outlined in Figure 7.13. This allows the software to be ported to a number of different hosts by rewriting only the PetString routine, not all the screen-defining routines.

These examples are courtesy of the Instructional Services Software Development Group at Weeg Computing Center, The University of Iowa, Steve Bowers, Senior Programmer Analyst, and Steve Wessels, Manager of Software Development. The illustrations of dynamic use of screen areas, Figures 7.6 to 7.9, are from software that is currently under development. The development team is still discussing design issues such as how much information should be visible before it is requested by the user, in order to have a less cluttered screen. The authors of this book would prefer to see

PROCEDURE: SaveArea
Copy screen area into a buffer and place it and the environment into the environment stack. The stack pointer is a global variable.

INPUT: UpLeftRow, UpLeftCol, LowRightRow, LowRightCol:
                the corners of the area to be saved
    The environment global variables to be captured in the stack

PROCESSING:
    Create an instance MyArea of envirsavestacktype above
    Link MyArea into the top of the stack
    Copy the four corner data passed into the corner data of MyArea
    Create an instance MyBuffer of scrnbuffertype above
    Copy the contents of screen memory into MyBuffer
    Copy the global environment variables into their respective
        places in MyArea

RETURN: none; the stack contents and pointer value are changed

PROCEDURE: RestoreArea
Copy contents of the screen area at the top of the stack to the screen and restore the environment it presents

INPUT: none

PROCESSING:
    Restore the global environment variables from their values in
        the stack top
    Using the values of the screen corners in the stack top
        Copy the contents of the screen buffer to the proper
            locations in screen memory
    Unlink the stack top from the stack
    Dispose of the screen buffer and the environment stack frame

RETURN: none; the top stack area is removed and
                the screen is restored

Figure 7.11   SaveArea *and* RestoreArea *pseudocode*

```
PetString ('{═══════════════════════════════════════════════ }')
PetString ('!                                                 !')
PetString ('!          Do you want to start this area over again?   !')
PetString ('!                                                 !')
PetString ('!                                                 !')
PetString ('!  Starting over will take you to Difficulty Level 1, Exercise 1, in the   !')
PetString ('!  area you are working on.                        !')
PetString ('!                                                 !')
PetString ('!  If you want to return to the exercise you were on, use Cancel (Alt-C).  !')
PetString ('!                                                 !')
PetString ('!                                                 !')
PetString ('!             Type Y or N, then __>return            !')
PetString ('[═══════════════════════════════════════════════ ]'
```

Figure 7.12   *Defining a screen with generic characters and* PetString

PROCEDURE: `PetString`
convert certain ASCII characters to extended ASCII characters if they are not preceded by a protecting character

INPUT: **a source string with standard characters**

CONSTANTS: **a conversion table for the conversion process**
(Table shown for the IBM PC)

ASCII	Char	Extended ASCII
33	!	186
35	#	219
36	$	180
37	%	176
38	&	195
42	*	26
43	+	197
47	/	191
60	<	192
61	=	205
62	>	217
64	@	27
91	[	200
92	\	218
93	]	188
94	^	193
95	_	196
96	`	17
123	{	201
124			179
125	}	187
126	~	194

All other standard ASCII characters are in the table but have same char on each side

PROCESSING:

```
        Clear destination string
        Set pointer to beginning of source string
        While not at end of source string
                Get next character  ch  from source string
                If ch = ProtectChar then  /* protecting character */
                        Get next character  newch  from source string
                Else
                        newch = table[ch]
                copy  newch  to destination string
```

RETURN: **destination string**

Figure 7.13 *The* PetString *routine*

escape sequences rather than Alt key combinations used so that users with disabilities are not given the possible dilemma of having to press two keys simultaneously as described in Chapter 14.

7.2   Displaying Information Properly

It takes extra effort to display information properly. We note in Chapter 5 that standard language techniques for numeric data input are sometimes inadequate for production software. This is probably less true for numeric output, since there are fairly robust output formatting capabilities in most languages. However, we need to have the capability of displaying numeric values with more control than we would have with standard numeric output, and for this we need to have routines to convert internal representations of numbers into strings. We do this for integers in Figures 7.14 and 7.15 and leave the floating-point version for the reader's own work.

Mathematical formulas in software are a primary example of displayed information that frequently looks different than it looks in printed materials. Even more problematic is having a user type a formula and making it appear appropriate as it is being typed. A program from CONDUIT, *Discovery Learning in Trigonometry* by John C. Kelley, illustrates how this can be accomplished within the limitations of character graphics on the IBM PC. This capability is illustrated in Figures 7.16 to 7.23. Figure 7.16 shows the instruction screen. If the user types P or Q, the symbol Π or √, respectively, is entered into the formula. Pressing the up arrow key will cause subsequent characters to be entered as exponents and shifted up in the formula. Pressing the down arrow key causes exponent mode to be terminated. In Figure 7.17, the user is typing a

PROCEDURE: **FormatInteger**

INPUT: **a binary integer and a positive integer indicating the**
     number of spaces N desired

PROCESSING:
     Set up special cases of negative and zero values
     Call a recursive routine that:
          when the integer gets to zero, inserts the leading blanks
               in the array and the - sign, if needed
          when the integer is not zero,
               determines the digit to be placed in the array
               calls itself recursively to place the digits of
                    value/10
               places its own digit in the array.

OUTPUT: **the character array out whose leftmost N spaces**
     contain blanks and the character string for the integer,
     right-justified.

Figure 7.14   FormatInteger *design*

```
/*
 * Main routine to set up the negative and zero cases for
 * eventual output and make the initial recursive call to
 * the translator.
 */

char *FormatInteger( num, space );
    int   num, space;
{
    int isZero, isNegative;
    char string[];

    (num == 0) ? isZero = 1 : isZero = 0;
    if (num < 0 ) { isNegative = 1; space-; }
    else { isNegative = 0; space *= -1; }
    return (Ri2c( num, space, 0 ));
}

/*
 * Ri2c == Recursive integer to character routine.
 * It first checks the "end condition" of num = 0 and then
 * makes the recursive calls.  Note that it does not insert
 * a digit into the string until after all previous digits
 * are handled. */

char *Ri2c( num, space, where )
    int   num, space, *where;
{
    int   i;
    char  digit, string[];

    if (num == 0) {   /* terminating case */
        if (isZero) {
            for ( i = 0; i < space-1; i++ ) string[i] = ' ';
            string[space-1] = '0'; }
        else {
            for ( i = 0; i < space; i++ ) string[i] = ' ';
            if (isNegative) string[space] = '-';
            *where = space + 1; }   /* be sure the next call knows
                                       where to put the character */
    else {
            digit = '0' + num % 10;      /* digit to put into string */
            num /= 10;                   /* divide by 10 to get next try */
            Ri2c( num, space, where, string );
            string[*where] = digit;
            *where++; }
    }
    return( &(string[0]) );
}
```

Figure 7.15 FormatInteger *code*

formula and presses the up arrow key so that subsequent keys will be treated as an exponent. The word "exponent" gives additional reinforcement that an exponent is being entered. In Figure 7.18, the user has typed an exponent, 2, and the next character will also be part of the exponent. In Figure 7.19, the user has pressed the up arrow key a second time to get an exponent for x^2. Figure 7.20 shows that the exponent of x^2 is the square root of 2x. Figures 7.21 to 7.23 complete the formula. In Figure 7.21, the user has pressed the down arrow, so the exponent will now refer to x rather than x^2. In Figure 7.22, the user has added more to the exponent of x, and in Figure 7.23, the user has pressed the down arrow key again and completed the formula. The indication of "exponent" is no longer on the screen.

```
        F (x)    :   dependent variable
            x    :   independent variable
            ∏    :   3.141593

        Enter ∏ by pressing the <P> key.
        Enter √ by pressing the <Q> key.
        Enter an exponent by pressing
          the <≠> key. Press the <↓> key
          to unlock exponent mode.



        Below is an example of an entered
        function using standard algebraic
        notation.

        F(x) = 3sin(x)
        Now enter a function of your own.


        Press enter to continue.
```

Figure 7.16 *Information screen for Discovery Learning in Trigonometry*

```
        F(x)=sin(x↑
        exponent
        Type your function, then press Enter
```

Figure 7.17 *Entering an exponent*

```
F(x)=sin(x²↑
exponent
Type your function, then press Enter
```

Figure 7.18   *Continuing with the exponent*

```
F(x)=sin(x²↑
exponent
Type your function, then press Enter
```

Figure 7.19   *Formula changes to exponent for x^2*

```
F(x)=sin(x²^√(2x)↑
exponent
Type your function, then press Enter
```

Figure 7.20   *Use of parentheses to indicate what is included under the square root*

```
F(x)=sin(x ²^√(2x) ↑
exponent
Type your function, then press Enter
```

Figure 7.21   *Exponent now refers to x*

```
F(x)=sin(x ²^√(2x)+x ↑
exponent
Type your function, then press Enter
```

Figure 7.22   *The user has added more to the exponent of x*

$$F(x) = \sin(x^{2^{\sqrt{(2x)}+x}} + 3)$$

Type your function, then press Enter

Figure 7.23   *The formula is completely entered*

The examples in Figures 7.17 to 7.23 show how CONDUIT's software displays exponents on the screen. This is implemented by a routine called Expin; based on their design, the general design of this routine is shown in Figure 7.24. This procedure reads characters from the keyboard, displays them appropriately on the screen, and assembles them into an output string. The output string is then passed to further processing to parse it for evaluation; CONDUIT uses a translation from infix to postfix and evaluates that directly. While the design comes from CONDUIT, the pseudocode in Figure 7.24 is the work of the authors.

PROCEDURE: Expin

    Get an expression from the keyboard and echo it to the screen with exponents shown properly

INPUT: none; all input comes from the keyboard

PROCESSING:
```
    initialize routine:
        parenthesis level = 0
        character count = 0
    Move to the starting point for input
    Get the first character ch
    While not finished do
        if ch = ESC then finished
            break    { go back to start of loop }
        if ch = RETURN then
            add remaining parentheses if any
            finished
            break
        if ch = BACKSPACE then
            if last character was an arrow then
                update exponent level and restore printing height
            else
                if string is not empty
                    remove last character from string and from screen
            break
        if ch is upper case then
            downshift ch
```
                                                            continued

```
        if ch is an up arrow
            increment exponent level
            set next printing height a bit higher
            put exponent operator in output string
            break
        if ch is a down arrow
            if exponent level is > 0
              decrement exponent level
              set next printing height a bit lower
            else beep
            break
        if ch is a parenthesis
            update parenthesis level appropriately
        if ch is not valid or if string is too long
            beep  { char is ignored }
            break
        put ch in output string
        display ch at current height and position on screen
        if exponent level > 0 then
            display up arrow after last character
            set position so next character will overwrite up arrow
    end
```

OUTPUT: the expression in a text string in infix notation for further processing

Figure 7.24 *Pseudocode for* Expin *procedure*

7.3   Using Windows

When you think of windows in the context of user interfaces, you usually think of a Macintosh-like environment where each system activity is associated with a separate window. However, the general concept of windows is more widely applicable. In this chapter and Chapter 10, we consider both general window systems and special-purpose window applications and give some information on how to implement windows in both environments.

General Uses of Windows

There are two levels at which you can use windows in programming. The first is the general use of windows for all aspects of program operations. Here all input, output, and control are manipulated in windows, often in separate windows for distinct operations. This requires extensive programming, usually involving particular window-support systems such as Microsoft Windows, the Macintosh toolbox, the X or NeWS window system, or some user interface management system.

The second level of window use is to use windows to provide information and control for the user, while using the main screen for general program function. This sort of window is generally known as a *dialog box*. This can be done without general window support systems, with the programmer handling the details of managing the window on the screen and replacing the covered text afterwards. Such programmer-implemented windows are rarely as sophisticated as system-built windows but are completely adequate for a number of functions.

Windows for Active Program Operation

One style of window use is to have all program operations function through windows. That is, instead of ever using the screen directly, all of your program's output goes to your user only indirectly—it goes first to a window, and then the window puts it on the screen. Similarly, all the program input and control goes first to the window, and then the window sends it to the program. This is a complex operation and offers the programmer both positive and negative aspects.

The positive sides are very significant. If a program consists of several separate operations—data input, text input, file access, graphing, printing—each can be done in a separate window. These windows can be moved, sized, opened, and closed at either the user's or the program's discretion. An example of the use of multiple windows for one program is provided by MacPascal on the Macintosh. A typical MacPascal screen is shown in Figure 7.25 This language interpreter maintains separate windows for source code, text output, graphics output, and variable status, all or any subset of which can be open at once.

This multiple-window environment has an important use: it can allow the computer screen to echo the user's thinking processes. Each window can contain a separate focus of the user's attention with concurrent operation in the several windows, with almost instant switching between windows, and with cut and paste between windows to move information where it is needed. This lets the program be an active assistant in the problem at hand and amplify your user's working ability.

The negative side of this overall window use comes from the complexity of the task of handling all program operations through windows. Each window needs a number of routines for handling output and mapping it to the screen, for window opening and closing, for changing its size and screen location, and so on. You must decide if windows will overlap or not (nonoverlapping windows are called *tiled*, and some windowing systems will only allow tiled windows), and, if windows are to overlap, you must manage the task of saving and restoring information on the screen. When you pass all this work to a high-level window or user interface management system, however, this complexity becomes manageable.

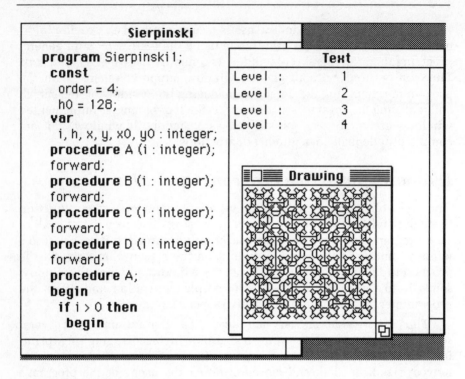

Figure 7.25   *A MacPascal screen*

Courtesy of Symantec

There are a few aspects of coping with window systems that give us pause. The first is that many of them seem to be tied firmly to one kind of hardware. This means that porting a program from an IBM PC or PS/2 with Microsoft Windows to a Macintosh with MacApp may require you to go quite a ways back on the design path and do much of the design over. If you plan a multi-platform program implemented on various window systems, build this into the design and keep your development system-independent as long as possible.

> PRINCIPLE: If you want to build a window-based program, use a window system and appropriate toolkit.

Windows for Transient Information or Control

Whether your program operates on a text screen, a vector graphics device, or a bitmapped display, it is possible to use a window concept to step out

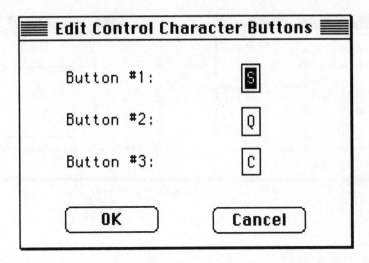

Figure 7.26   *A dialog box to set parameters*

of the normal program operation and communicate with the user. This communication is normally transitory, with no more than one window on the screen at a given time. As we noted above, this kind of window is commonly called a dialog box.

There are a number of different kinds of functions these dialog boxes can fill. They can be used for control, as in menus or parameter-setting boxes, or for information, as in status or activity reports, help information, or warning or error indicators. Figure 7.26 shows such a dialog box; examples of most of these others are given elsewhere in the book.

A dialog box that allows no input, such as a warning window, is sometimes given the separate name of an *alert box*. We will not continue this distinction in our discussions, however.

Window Layout

There are two options for placing windows on the screen: windows can be *tiled* or *overlapped*. Tiled windows are not allowed to overlap and often are sized to be as large as possible on the screen; overlapped windows are self-explanatory. Figure 7.27 is a sketched layout of each kind of window environment.

Some systems, such as Microsoft Windows 1.0, only allow tiled windows. This makes the screen easy to manage and eliminates covered-up information. Overlapped windows require much more computer effort to maintain, and part of some windows' contents may be hidden, but the flexibility of window presentation and the control the user can exert over screen layout make it generally preferred over tiled windows. Some

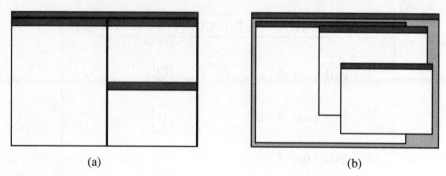

(a)   (b)

Figure 7.27   *Tiled windows (a) and overlapped windows (b)*

studies have shown tiling to be as efficient as overlapped windows or even more efficient for some tasks, according to Bly and Rosenberg. It is possible to set up an overlapped window system to function like a tiled system, but it is not possible to do the converse.

Window Control

Besides window functions mentioned above, there is the matter of window presentation. Basically we see three types of windows:

- *User-opened windows*: windows that are opened by a user's choice, are present for some interaction, and then close and vanish when the user is finished. Examples of this are pulldown windows (often containing menus), dialog boxes for parameter setting, and help windows. See Figures 7.6 to 7.9 for some examples; others are given in Chapter 10.

- *Program-opened windows*: windows the program opens when it needs to communicate to the user. This usually means activity or status information, warnings, or error notices, but it could be a program-initiated menu.

- *Resident windows*: windows that usually remain in a part of the screen for program operation or control. These may be movable or fixed; they may even be removable, being brought back by a user's window-open choice. In permanent, fixed form they can look like MacPaint's tools and palette menus. In removable, relocatable form they are often called *tearoff windows*.While sophisticated systems can be used to manage these kinds of window, it is possible to build them from *curses* or simple programming language tools—even from bare-bones screen manipulation.

7.4 Readings

We refer you to some of the same books mentioned in Chapter 6 for general information on displaying ideas; those by Monk, Heines and Galitz. References for further information on windows are given in Chapter 10, and a comparison of tiled and overlapping windows is given in Bly and Rosenberg.

Chapter 8

USING COLOR IN OUTPUT

We live in a world of color. Color can attract our attention, affect our moods, convey specific meaning to us, and be aesthetically pleasing or displeasing to us. The cost of color displays has decreased sufficiently in recent years to make them widely affordable, and users prefer multicolor displays. Consequently, much current software is using (or misusing) color. However, color is not useful for all users, as discussed in Chapter 14.

Color can be a very powerful communications aid. This chapter covers principles of effective color use, including effective communications and ergonomic considerations. As an example, we introduce ICARE, the Interactive Computer-Aided RGB (Red, Green, Blue) Color Editor, written by research scientist and artist Donna Cox at the National Center for Supercomputing Applications (NCSA) at the University of Illinois, Urbana-Champaign. ICARE uses color as a tool for scientific discovery. Color is used to convey information such as speed or temperature in a scientific image, and ICARE allows the scientist to use different color palettes to gain more information from the image.

8.1 Color to Increase Meaningfulness

Scientists at NCSA have found that proper use of color can make a scientific image more meaningful. The images that they, and others, have produced from their scientific research have been used worldwide to explain science to the public. In addition, color, used appropriately, can make other kinds of programs more effective.

157

The amount of information displayed on computers has increased astronomically during the last ten years and will continue to increase, especially as data transmission speeds increase. Color-coded displays are 200 percent more effective for grouping information than other codes such as brightness, shape, or alphanumerics according to Wanda Smith [1987a]. Color can guide the eye to the appropriate information and reduce the visual search, especially as the density of screen information increases.

In Chapter 6, we discuss the benefits of keeping a screen sparse and legible. There may be occasions when it is beneficial, or even necessary, to have more text or graphics information on the screen. Grouping related information through color coding retains the usefulness and legibility of the screen, even as the density increases. You can also tie together a set of related information on successive screens by using a common background color. The background colors should be unobtrusive, but they still group all the screens as containing related information. A change in background color signals a change in type of information. Be careful not to use the same color code for unrelated information.

One theme that recurs throughout this book is the need for consistency. Regardless of the application, users will expect that a color has the same meaning throughout a program, that similar colors denote similar meanings, and that events grouped with a common background color are somehow related.

PRINCIPLE: Be consistent in the use of colors.

Consistency in color coding carries over to all aspects of your project: training, testing, application, and publications. In this case, you may be dealing with different media: videos for training and printing for publications, as well as the computer application itself. Since colors can never look exactly the same on different media, you must select colors carefully so that they are as consistent as possible across the media. Be sure to consult with your publisher and video production people prior to publication.

Color Use by Application

According to Wanda Smith [1987a], the use of color in computer graphics "reduced training time, improved readability, cut search time, increased performance, and is preferred to monochromatic displays." However, the guidelines for the use of color vary with the application. Smith and Farrell discuss the use of color in several different applications. The following is a summary of their comments.

In *text editing*, color is useful primarily for highlighting. It can be used to highlight words or letters that are to be edited or misspelled words found by the spelling checker. With the increasingly popular use of windows and multiple applications on computer displays, color is a good way to code the type of application in each window. Color choices for text and text background are extremely important. Both text and background colors influence the legibility of the text. Since text is composed of fine lines, poor color combinations make it illegible.

In *charts and graphs*, different colored lines may overlap each other, as well as the grid which is probably an additional color. There may be text superimposed on the graph. It is important that each piece of information be easily distinguishable even though it may overlap other information.

In *modeling* applications, which may even be dynamic, you need many colors and levels of saturation (grayness) to give the appearance of depth and dimensions. You also need high resolution to achieve a realistic appearance.

With *monitoring* operations, text, graphs, and modeling are all utilized. Since colors have a specific meaning to which the viewer may have to react quickly, the connotation of the selected colors is also important.

Smith [1987b] has put together some tables of effective color combinations for text applications, computer aided design applications, process control application, and measurement applications. These tables are based on research at Hewlett-Packard as well as that conducted by Murch and Verriest et al. [1985] and are reprinted in Figure 8.1.

Putting Color Choice into the User's Hands

Some software allows user-controlled color installation, and there are some system-dependent ways to patch programs that do not allow color changes. Even though most of us have our favorite color combination, the flexibility of color choice in a program is not always desirable. We know of a calculus tutorial program that allowed the user to change the foreground color to any color on the system, including the background color.

Many software packages allow the user to select colors, and most prevent such a flaw as selecting the same color for background and foreground. The appropriate use of color can increase productivity, and "appropriate colors" vary with the task, as shown above. A user does not usually know how colors influence productivity. Research has shown that the misuse of color increases the time needed to interpret the display, thereby decreasing productivity, according to Smith and Farrell. For most applications, you should not allow arbitrary color selections.

Effective Color Combinations for Text Applications in Interactive Displays

Dark Backgrounds

Number of Colors	Good	Bad
2	white + green gold + cyan/green green + magenta/lavender cyan + red	red + blue/green/purple/yellow/magenta white + cyan/yellow white+ cyan/yellow blue + green/purple green + cyan cyan + lavender
3	white + gold + green/blue/magenta white + red + cyan red + cyan + gold cyan + yellow + lavender gold + magenta + blue/green gold + lavender + green	red + yellow + green red + blue + green white + cyan + yellow red + magenta + blue green + cyan + blue

Effective Colors for Computer Aided Design Applications

3D effects

Number of colors	furthest	to	closest
2	blue	-	red
3	blue - green / yellow	-	red
4	blue - green - yellow	-	red
5	blue - green - yellow - orange -		red
6	purple -blue-green-yellow-orange-		red

Process Control Applications

To Show:	Use:
concentration levels LOW concentration levels HIGH	desaturated colors saturated colors
life support status OK life support status CAUTION life support status EMERGENCY	blue/green/white yellow/gold red (flashing option)
direction IN direction OUT	red blue

Measurement Applications

Inspection/Quality Graphs

For:	Use:
grids	gray
data points	yellow
variance or error bars	blue (medium)
out of spec data	red
labels X	lavender
Y	limegreen
Z	cyan

Figure 8.1 *Table from Wanda Smith [1987b]*

8.2 Color as an "Exact Science"

Why should we make different color decisions based on the application? Why should colors not be chosen arbitrarily by the programmer or user? Before we can begin to discuss these issues, we must establish a common understanding of the terms used. We begin with precise, fundamental laws of physics to provide a definition of our terms. This allows an understanding of how we perceive each color independently, which we follow with a discussion of the interactivity of color. In our description of color, we discuss strengths and weaknesses of some of the more common color models.

The Physics of Color Perception

The color of an object depends on the object itself, the light source that illuminates the object, and the eye of the viewer.

In physics, light waves are measurable. With most human visual systems, light waves that fall between 400 and 700 nanometers (nm) are perceived as "having a color." This is due to the way in which these wave lengths of light interact with our nervous systems. This produces visible light ranging from red (700 nm) to violet (400 nm) through the spectral, or "rainbow," colors (red, orange, yellow, green, blue, indigo, violet). Different people have different sensitivities to the same wavelengths.

We can define *hue* very precisely as that color (such as red or blue) that results from a specific wavelength of light. Although this hue may be perceived differently by everyone who views it, this definition gives a single meaning for each hue. Since color is such an individual matter, varying with perception, eye training, and surrounding colors, much of the color vocabulary deals with perception, and the same words have different meanings in different contexts.

How each viewer perceives a given hue depends on the retina and lens of the eye. The retina is the light sensitive surface of the eye. It contains light sensitive receptors called rods and cones. Rods have much to do with night vision, and cones contain chemicals (called photopigments) that are sensitive to particular wavelengths of light and give the sensation of color. Each cone contains only one kind of photopigment, which means each cone is more sensitive to certain wavelengths than others. Furthermore, these cones are distributed unevenly across the retina. Since fewer cones are located at the periphery of the retina, our color discrimination becomes less in our peripheral vision, and only monochromatic images can be perceived in our extreme peripheral vision. Since the cones that contain the photopigment that produces blue are more scarce than the cones containing other photopigments, the human eye is least sensitive to blue.

Images are formed on the retinas, but we view these images by aiming both eyes at the object and by changing the shape of the lens in each eye to bring the image into focus. Since each color sensation is produced by a different wavelength, the lens must refocus to see each color sharply. Hence, certain color combinations can cause eye fatigue by requiring constant refocusing.

8.3 The Interactivity of Color— No Longer an "Exact Science"

You can now decide exactly which color of the spectrum you wish to use, and you can even measure the wavelength which produces that color with an instrument called a spectrometer. However, our eyes play all kinds of tricks on us. Once the screen is filled with colors, individual colors may no longer look like the colors we selected. Color constantly deceives us. You must at least be aware of certain color interactions so as not to misinform your user. If you are skilled enough in color perception and selection, you can deliberately create illusions with color.

Josef Albers, renowned artist and teacher, devoted a lifetime to the study and teaching of color. His famous color course was based on perception, as opposed to color systems or theories. The first three color plates are from the Albers color studies.

The same hue may look different against two different backgrounds, as illustrated in Color Plate 1. On the left, you see two small squares against different backgrounds. The bottom square appears to be the same color as the pale orange at the top. In the silk-screen version color study in the original edition of the Albers book, the yellow and blue horizontal bands are printed on a flap of paper which, when lifted, confirms that the two "different" browns are a continuously printed strip of the same color. On the right, you see two centered and framed olive grays, which are in fact the same color against different background colors.

The size of a given area, in addition to adjacent colors, can change an apparent hue. Small areas may look very different from large areas of the same hue, as illustrated in Color Plate 2. On the left, you see a composition made up of four presentations of the same six colors. On the right, you see four arrangements of the same four colors.

Conversely, two different hues may look the same, depending on the background colors used and the size of the area, as shown in Color Plate 3. On the left, the two horizontal bars in the centers are precise repetitions of the two vertical bars at the left, although they are reversed. On the right, Naples yellow and ochre are changed to look alike by different backgrounds.

Sometimes the eye fuses two or more colors which are next to each other to form a new color. This is known as the Bezold effect, named after its discoverer Wilhelm von Bezold (1837-1907). Bezold found that he could alter the color combinations of his oriental rugs entirely by changing or adding only one color. The Impressionist painters, especially the Pointillists, used this phenomenon to their advantage. They found, for example, that they could give the illusion of green by using tiny dots of blue and yellow closely together. The importance to us is that color computer displays take advantage of this effect. Each dot on the screen is made up of tiny triads of red, green, and blue phosphors that are perceived together as white. "Why *white*?" you ask. The color theory behind color displays is explained in more detail below.

8.4   Color Specification

There are a multitude of color models or descriptive systems for designating colors on both visual displays and hardcopy devices. Some are easier to understand, and some are easier to measure or to change certain color characteristics. No color specification system has all of the desirable characteristics for designating colors.

Mixing Colors

You probably have some familiarity with mixing paints. We all learned in grade school that our primary colors are red, yellow, and blue and that mixing pairs of these colors in equal amounts would produce the following: red and yellow yield orange, yellow and blue yield green, and red and blue yield purple. Mixing all three in equal amounts yields black, and the absence of all color is white. Sound familiar? Furthermore, we can get pastels or "tints" by adding white. For example, as we add more white to our original red, we produce paler and paler pinks. Similarly, we get "shades" of colors by adding black.

Mixing colors on a graphics display adds a number of new possibilities and difficulties. Color is produced on a computer screen when electron beams light up different colored phosphors on the display. So, we are now mixing lights instead of pigments, and we have a different set of primary colors: red, green, and blue. We combine pairs of these colors to get our secondary colors. Green and blue yield cyan (a greenish blue), and red and blue yield magenta (violet). No surprises so far. But, mixing red and green together and producing yellow usually comes as a big surprise to beginning computer graphics students. If there is no color (that is, no light), the display is black. Mixing red, green, and blue in equal amounts produces white. This is accomplished on the color display by producing tiny red, blue and green dots close together in triads. If you look closely, you can see the three colored lights. At a distance, the eye perceives the three primary colors as a white dot. This happens because of the Bezold Effect, where the eye "mixes" adjacent colors, discussed in Section 8.3.

Now, how do we produce the tints and shades we discussed when we talked about mixing pigments? Since all three colors together produce white, we "add white" to a color by mixing equal amounts of each of the other two primaries. For example, we get pink by adding some green and blue to red. We get a paler pink by adding more green and blue. *Saturation* is the purity of the color. A fully saturated hue has no white light mixed with it. For example, pink is the same hue as red; it is a desaturated version of red. Getting shades by "adding black" is more of a problem. If black is the absence of light, hence absence of color, how can we "add" it? What we have to do is take away light. This is done by decreasing the intensity of the electron beam on the display. At most, you can control whether the electron beam for each of the red, green, and blue phosphors is turned on or off and the intensity of each electron beam. This capability is not always under user, or even programmer, control. The number of colors on a display and the ability to produce shades are both limited by the system's hardware as well as its software. Since information must be stored in memory about whether each beam is on and the intensity of each beam, you are limited by memory size and other hardware features such as how quickly you can retrieve this information. For example, with the Computer Graphics Adapter (CGA) board on the IBM Personal Computer and compatibles, you have only two levels of intensity.

Color Models

Our concern in this book is with the user interface, so we are most interested in color description systems for the computer display. However, since you may have to design a program where color is an important feature and hard copy or video is also important, you must be aware of the hard copy and video color systems. For video, color information must be encoded in a standard format such as the National Television Systems Committee (NTSC) standard which is used in the United States and some other parts of the world. This standard was devised for compatibility with black and white receivers. The biggest problem in transferring an image from the display to a printer or plotter is that the color computer display uses lights, and the hard copy system uses pigments. Since you must now deal with two different sets of primaries, you must have a translation program to change your screen colors to hard copy colors. Even then, the resultant image will not look exactly the same. Different models are used in an attempt to produce desired colors.

Spectral Model

We discussed the spectral or "rainbow" model of red, orange, yellow, green, blue, indigo, and violet in Section 8.2. Each hue is the result of a measurable light wave. However, many different wavelengths look the same. Hence this is a good starting point, but it is inadequate for describing a complete color system.

Gray Scale

In order to understand more about a color system, let us eliminate all the hues and think about black, white, and the various grays in between. This is the image we have with a black and white photo or a black and white TV. A display that shows a large number of levels of gray also shows a more realistic image.

If you only have black and white to work with, gray levels are achieved by a combination of black and white dots (think of a newspaper photo). If a given area has a denser distribution of black dots, it looks darker than an area of sparser black dots. The same is true of a monochrome TV or computer display. If, however, you can control the intensity of the electron beam at each dot on the display, you can achieve a gray scale ranging from full intensity of the electron beam, through lower and lower intensities to achieve darker shades of gray, and finally to black, which is the absence of any light at that point. We define *intensity* of a dot on the display to mean the intensity of the electron beam at that dot.

Munsell Model

Artists are very familiar with the Munsell model. This was introduced in 1905, has been used for years in the printing industry, and is referred to in nearly all the literature by artists and designers. This system consists of an ordered array of color samples divided into equal steps and identified in terms of *hue* (the measurable color such as red or green), *value* (the lightness of the color) and *chroma* (the saturation, or amount of gray in the color). (See Color Plate 4.)

While the Munsell model is the one with which artists are most familiar, it is a perceptual system. Value is perceived rather than measured. All of the dimensions (hue, value, and chroma) are measured in terms of perceptually equal steps, which do not correspond to scientifically measurable equal steps.

RGB Specification

Describing color for the computer display is our main concern here. The RGB system uses the light primaries (red, green, and blue) and specifies a trio of values ranging from 0 to 100% for each of the primaries. For example, combining equal amounts of green and blue, with no red, produces cyan. A color can be specified by the percentages above, by the percentages expressed as proportions of each primary (so each value is a real number between 0 and 1), or by the value expressed as an integer in the range from 0 to N-1, where there are N distinct values for each primary supported by the hardware (so a system with 256 levels for each primary could express each as an integer from 0 to 255). The physical model used to describe this system is a color cube, and colors within the cube are the sums of the intensities of the three electron guns. (See Color Plate 5.) Due to its direct relation to graphics hardware, RGB color is easy to use in assigning and generating colors and is easy to program. Once people are accustomed to these primaries, it appears to be a comfortable system, according to Murch [1984c]. However, this system is confusing to those accustomed to the pigment primaries. Also, in order to produce most colors, you need a disproportionate amount of all three primaries. The drawbacks of this system are the difficulty of predicting the appearance of an RGB combination and the indistinguishability of combinations of higher intensities.

CMY Specification

Many hardcopy devices use the CMY (cyan, magenta, and yellow) color specification, and it works on the same principle as the RGB (red, green, blue) display specification. The basic difference is that the hard copy device deals with light reflected from colors on paper, and the display deals with projected lights. In each case, secondary and other colors are derived by mixing percentages of the three primaries. For example, on the CMY hard copy device, if you add equal amounts of cyan and yellow, and no magenta, to the same area you get green. This is somewhat different from the red, blue, yellow pigment system we are used to, but it is commonly used in printing computer images. Since you cannot really mix these colors together and get a clear black, most CMY systems also have black as a fourth color.

HSV Specification

The hue, saturation, value system (HVS) is widely used in video and TV broadcasting. The model is a cone, with the point down. *Hue* is measured in degrees around the top of the cone, starting with blue at zero degrees. *Saturation* is measured as intensity from the top (white, or full intensity) through shades of gray along the center axis to the bottom (black, or no light). *Value* is measured from the outer edge of very vivid hues through fainter and fainter pastels to white at the center. By using this model, fully intense hues can be measured with a spectrometer. Some colors that can be produced on a color display are not used for TV because they produce too strong a signal. Transferring an image to video or television not only involves a translation from the coordinates used in the model to create the computer image to video or TV models, such as NTSC, but also disallows some of the vivid colors that artists love to use.

HLS Specification

Another widely used color description system is the HLS (hue, lightness, saturation) system. The model used for this system is a cone with a second cone upside down on top of it. (See Color Plate 6.) *Hue* is measured in degrees starting with blue at zero degrees. *Lightness* is measured across the radius from very vivid at the outside edge to gray levels at the center. *Saturation* (amount of gray) is measured from the top (white) through shades of gray along the center axis to the bottom (black). The HSV and HLS systems are easier to understand intuitively than the RGB system, but our eyes do not perceive changes in hue in an even number of degrees, especially in the greens.

HVC Specification

A recently published specification, the Tektronix Hue, Value, Chroma (HVC) model, attempts to correct problems of nonlinearity and nonuniformity of models discussed in Taylor and Murch. This model is based on standard theories and a model of colorimetry, the CIELUV international color standard developed by the Commission Internationale de l'Eclairage (CIE). This means that any color specified in the CIE color system can be rendered on the display through its colorimetric values. In this system, *hues* are distributed uniformly around the vertical axis, which represents color *values* (lightness or darkness). The difference in this model lies in the representation of *chroma*, the level of color saturation. The HVC model, like the Munsell model, is irregularly shaped so that a different range of chroma is available for varying combinations of hue and value. (See Figure 8.2.)

The HVC model in Taylor, Murch and McManus incorporates three underlying principles. It is based on perceptually even color space, like the Munsell model. Unlike the Munsell model, which only deals with reflective surfaces, the HVC model provides a mechanism for transferring between media such as computer displays, video, and hard copy. Also unlike the Munsell model, the HVC model allows specification through an objective colorimetric standard, preferably the CIE color standard. There are algorithms to translate between HVC and other color models.

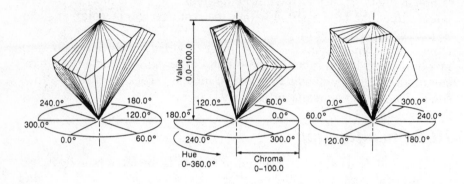

Figure 8.2   *The Tektronix HVC color solid from three perspectives*
Courtesy Tektronix, Inc.

CNS Specification

A Color Naming System (CNS) has been proposed that uses English color names (red, orange, brown, yellow, green, blue, purple, white, black, and gray) as described in Murch [1984c]. Other hue names are derived by specifying lightness, amount of gray, and color combination such as "dark, grayish, greenish blue." These are all familiar words, but they do not always have the same connotation for everyone.

Experiments and Studies

A 1982 experimental comparison of the CNS, HLS, and RGB color models by Berk et al. in the Schwartz, Cowan and Beatty article found that participants could most accurately name target colors with the proposed natural language naming system, followed by HLS coordinates, then by RGB coordinates.

A Tektronix study counted the number of steps it took subjects to match a panel of a particular color with an adjacent panel using the RGB and HLS systems and a variant of the Color Naming System, the Swedish Natural Color System. As expected, if subjects already knew one of the systems, they were more efficient with the known system. For inexperienced users, the HLS system was the easiest, followed by the Swedish Natural Color System. The RGB system was the most difficult according to Murch [1984c].

These experiments dealt with a discrete set of target colors and three specification systems. A recent color matching experiment by Schwartz, Cowan, and Beatty used five color models to match target colors on the CRT interactively with tablet-based input techniques. The models used were RGB, YIQ (a television broadcast standard), CIELAB (an international standard dealing with equal Euclidean distances in space), HSV, and opponent colors (a physiologically based color space). They found that the RGB system allowed fastest approximation to the target but was least accurate. There is an entire field of study based on color theory, and there are many unanswered questions. We refer you to readings at the end of this chapter if you wish to pursue this fascinating field further.

Duplicating a Color

In the experiment above, subjects were to match a target color by manipulating a second color patch. This resulted in some interesting results concerning the use of different color models. However, this experiment deals with a controlled situation where the subject matches colors on a single display with the same background color, with both target and control patches in a specific location on the display, with the same room lighting, and sitting the same distance from the display. All of these factors affect the color on the display.

We mentioned earlier that it is impossible to get exactly the same colors on a hard copy device from an image on the display. It is also very difficult, if not impossible, to get the same colors on two different displays. Different displays have different colors available. Color calibration differs from display to display. It is even difficult to duplicate colors on the same display at different times. Someone may readjust the color controls on a given display between the times you use it, and glare on the display and the type and location of lighting also affect the colors. Subtle color differentiations may not be noticeable on a different display or under different lighting conditions.

Color in Context with Other Colors

As a programmer, you cannot control every display or ambient lighting situation where your program might be used, but you can control the background or adjacent colors that also cause changes in perceived color. As discussed in Section 8.3, adjacent colors exert an influence on one another. If the background is dark, colors look lighter and brighter than they do if the background is light. Colors are perceived differently with a change in adjacent or background color. The size of the colored area also changes the appearance of the color. All of these can lead to misinformation if a particular color is to convey a specific meaning. Figure 8.3 outlines the best and worst color combinations according to a study where at least 25 percent of 16 subjects accepted or rejected each combination.

Best Color Combinations

(N=16)

Background	Thin Lines and Text	Thick Lines and Panels
White	Blue(94%), Black(63%), Red(25%)	Black(69%), Blue(63%), Red(31%)
Black	White(75%), Yellow(63%)	Yellow(69%), White(50%), Green(25%)
Red	Yellow(75%), White(56%), Black(44%)	Black(50%), Yellow(44%), White(44%), Cyan(31%)
Green	Black(100%), Blue(56%), Red(25%)	Black(69%), Red(63%), Blue(31%)
Blue	White(81%), Yellow(50%), Cyan(25%)	Yellow(38%), Magenta(38%), Black(31%), Cyan(31%), White(25%)
Cyan	Blue(69%), Black(56%), Red(37%)	Red(56%), Blue(50%), Black(44%), Magenta(25%)
Magenta	Black(63%), White(56%), Blue(44%)	Blue(50%), Black(44%), Yellow(25%)
Yellow	Red(63%), Blue(63%), Black(56%)	Red(75%), Blue(63%), Black(50%)

Worst Color Combinations

(N=16)

Background	Thin Lines and Text	Thick Lines and Panels
White	Yellow(100%), Cyan(94%)	Yellow(94%), Cyan(75%)
Black	Blue(87%), Red(37%), Magenta(25%)	Blue(81%), Magenta(31%)
Red	Magenta(81%), Blue(44%), Green(25%), Cyan(25%)	Magenta(69%), Blue(50%), Green(37%), Cyan(25%)
Green	Cyan(81%), Magenta(50%), Yellow(37%)	Cyan(81%), Magenta(44%), Yellow(44%)
Blue	Green(62%), Red(37%), Black(37%)	Green(44%), Red(31%), Black(31%)
Cyan	Green(81%), Yellow(75%), White(31%)	Yellow(69%), Green(62%), White(56%)
Magenta	Green(75%), Red(56%), Cyan(44%)	Cyan(81%), Green(69%), Red(44%)
Yellow	White(81%), Cyan(81%)	White(81%), Cyan(56%), Green(25%)

Figure 8.3   *Best and Worst Color Combinations from Murch [1984b]*

8.5   Principles of Effective Color Use

For centuries, artists have been able to evoke emotions and draw attention to specific details through the use of color. To obtain these skills, most artists have spent years studying and experimenting with color. If you are not trained in color theory, you would be wise to ask design artists about color selections, even before you test your screen designs on potential users for your software.

PRINCIPLE: Seek advice of professional artists in the use of color.

Elements of Color Combinations

Some colors are more effective in specific locations. Some colors are more effectively used for small areas or for large areas. Some color combinations may be disastrous. Some principles apply to color in general and are not changed by the fact that the display medium is a computer display instead of a canvas or piece of paper. Others are unique to the display medium.

Since it is difficult for a user to deal with more than five to seven elements at a time, the number of colors should be limited if they are to convey a specific meaning. The general application calls for a conservative use of colors unless there are reasons of aesthetics or realism that require more colors.

PRINCIPLE: Use no more than five to seven colors in a display.

Due to the physiological properties of the eye, some colors work better in certain locations and sizes. As we discuss in Section 8.2, cones are unevenly distributed on the retina. The cones containing the photopigments that allow us to perceive red and green are concentrated in the center of the retina. The cones containing the photopigment that allows us to see blue are evenly distributed across the retina. However, the cones containing "blue photopigment" make up only two percent of all the cones.

Because of these physiological properties, the eye is not sensitive to red and green if they are in the visual periphery, especially if they are used for text or small shapes. To see this for yourself, create a display using these colors both in the center and the edge of the screen, and notice how much more vivid the color appears when it is in the center of your vision.

PRINCIPLE: If you use red and green, place them in the center of the display, not in the periphery.

Since the eye is least sensitive to blue, blue is not easily perceived in small areas and is not good for text, thin lines or small shapes. However, since the eye is equally sensitive to blue whether it is in the middle or the periphery, blue makes an excellent background color. The inability to perceive blue increases in older viewers.

PRINCIPLE: Use blue for background or large areas.

Viewers will not be able to distinguish the edges between objects when the sole difference between adjacent colors is the amount, or brightness, of blue. Forms are distinguished both by shape and color. Since borders created only by the amount of blue appear fuzzy, they must be created by a hue and saturation difference, as well as by brightness.

PRINCIPLE: Avoid adjacent use of two colors that differ only in the brightness of blue.

As a general rule, it is better if color is not the only differentiating code, especially for small areas. For small areas, redundant coding such as a change in both shape and color, or brightness and color, will be discernible. For very fine detail, stick with black, white, and grays.

PRINCIPLE: Do not rely on color coding alone to distinguish small areas.

In order to discuss some color combinations, let us start with the "rainbow" or spectral order (red, orange, yellow, green, blue, indigo, and violet). This has been found to be a natural order for thinking about color. The choice of color combinations is very complex. Marcus [1986] warns against the use of bright color pairs such as red/green, red/blue, green/blue, or blue/yellow. Such colors create vibrations and afterimages at the adjoining edges. Wanda Smith [1987a] adds that it is very important to have brightness contrast on a display, in addition to color contrast. Without it, edges between a number of color pairs will be blurry. These pairs include blue/green and blue/yellow.

> PRINCIPLE: Do not use intense combinations of
> blue/yellow, red/green, red/blue or green/blue.

We see that even a two-color combination for a simple display is a complex issue. This reinforces the need for an artist on any software development team. Also, the ability to change the intensity as well as the color is an important need on a computer display.

Fatigue

It is commonly assumed that a monochromatic display is less fatiguing for extended use on such tasks as data entry or word processing. This is certainly true if you are comparing low-resolution color displays to the high-resolution monochromatic text displays such as those commonly in use with personal computers. On low-resolution color displays, the individual dots that make up the letters are evident, causing less distinct lettering. Also, colors are produced by lighting different colored phosphors with three electron guns, and misconvergence of these electron guns can result in colors side-by-side rather than together. For example, a yellow line may have red and green fringes on either side of it. High-resolution color displays with proper convergence of the electron guns alleviate these problems.

You still have fatigue problems if you use certain (or too many) color combinations. Since the wavelengths that produce specific colors are focused at different distances behind the lens of the eye, the eye must refocus to see each color sharply. Very vivid colors, especially color pairs such as red and blue, should be avoided because the constant refocusing to view them is visually fatiguing. However, Wanda Smith [1987a] found that proper use of color can reduce eye fatigue. Color can be used to guide the eye and to locate information. This decreases excessive eye movements and relieves muscle fatigue.

8.6   Color Lookup Tables

By far the most common color technology for computers is the raster screen display. This is a TV-based technology, creating the screen image from a matrix of small dots, called *pixels*. Each dot is created by the display controller based on the value of a unit of display memory. In a monochrome display, the memory required for each pixel is one bit (on or off, white or black); in a 16-color display, this memory is four bits; in a 256-color display, this memory is a full byte. There are two kinds of color

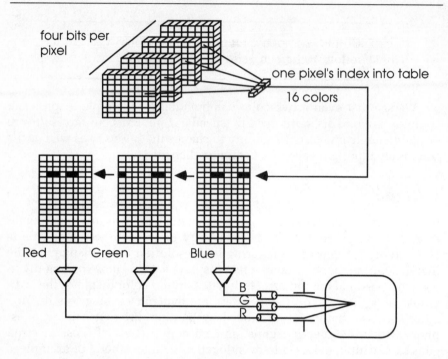

four bits per pixel

one pixel's index into table

16 colors

Red   Green   Blue

B
G
R

Figure 8.4   *Schematic lookup table translation*

storage. The memory for each pixel can store an integer which is an index into a color lookup table, giving a wide choice of actual colors for each of the color choices, or the memory for each pixel can hold the actual RGB representation for its color. We call the latter method "true color"; typically each pixel requires three bytes or more of memory.

Our use of color for user interfaces is somewhat different from its use in synthetic images in computer graphics. Our concern is to provide color as an information-enhancing addition to the display screen for our users. This can include coloring various screen components, such as icons or the various parts of windows discussed in Chapter 10, as well as using color in application programs to enhance the information the program gives the user.

The colors used for these purposes are "synthetic colors" as opposed to natural lifelike colors. We use the phrase "synthetic colors" to indicate that the choice of colors is completely arbitrary; for example, there is no "natural" color for a scroll bar. For these kinds of applications, the expensive "true color" technology is unnecessary, so we restrict our discussion to colors stored and managed in color lookup tables. Figure 8.4 illustrates how an index value is translated into an actual color on the screen. This translation is all done in the display driver hardware for the screen and is transparent to the user and programmer. However, you should note that all the colors in the table are specified by their RGB values, since raster CRT devices, the most common devices currently in use, have red, green, and blue guns providing their colors.

Figure 8.4 shows the schematic lookup table translation for each pixel in a 16-color display. Each pixel is represented by 4 bits of memory, which allows 16 options for color table entries. Each of these options points to an entry for each of the red, green, and blue values in the lookup table. For example, a pixel with binary memory representation 0011 points to the fourth entry in the lookup table where a particular value for each of the red, green, and blue intensities has been stored. At each of the 16 lookup table entries, we can set any of 256 reds, 256 greens, and 256 blues because they each have 8 bits and are independent. Thus our 16 colors are derived from 256 possible values for each of the red, green, and blue intensities, giving 16 simultaneous colors from a possible palette of 16 million colors.

Getting Color onto the Screen

Your first task is to get color onto the screen. As mentioned previously, each color is derived from a combination of varying intensities of red, green and blue. The user may not know, and should never need to know, that he or she is dealing with intensities of electron beams. The user's view of color depends only on the hardware and software being used. Most commercial software that allows the user to alter color contains one of the color models described in Section 8.4 or displays a color palette on the screen from which to select a color. Some hardware has color models built in as well. For example, Tektronix graphics terminals have contained the HLS (hue, lightness, saturation) model for a number of years, and now some of their high-end graphics systems contain the HVC (hue, value, chroma) model as a standard feature to aid in the selection of colors from among 16 million possibilities.

Interacting with Color

Lookup tables are useful only if you can change the color of any index. There are various interactive techniques to set values in lookup tables and control the color for any application, including the user interface. These techniques are applicable for any size of lookup table, from the 8 colors of a low-level graphics terminal to the 256, or more, colors of a full-function workstation. The latter device is, of course, a much more interesting and useful color tool since most applications needing color information in their output can be more effective if more colors are available. After we describe lookup table techniques, we give an example of their use in a real application: the ICARE color editor, designed by Donna Cox of the National Center for Supercomputing Applications, which is an outstanding example of many of the techniques we describe.

Building a Lookup Table

If we examine Figure 8.4, we see that the lookup table is really an array of RGB triples. Setting a value in a given index of the table is thus easily done by writing new RGB values into the array at the index's location. This leads us to the data definitions and SetColor function of Figure 8.5, which illustrate how this process could be defined in software. However, in a real system, the lookup table is in firmware on the display driver board, and the system provides you a function with the same results as this SetColor.

This SetColor function, or its system-provided equivalent, is the heart of any overall setting of the device color map or lookup table. It can be called repeatedly to set as many entries in the lookup table as need to be managed by the application or interface.

Selecting a Color or Colors to be Set

Now the focus of the color issue changes. It is no longer a question of how you change colors, but of how a user can specify what colors are to be changed, and also what the new colors are to be.

There are several ways one can specify a color or colors to be changed. Here we outline a few, but an interface designer may well come up with some new ideas for a particular application.

A *command* mode color choice can include both the color to be changed and the new RGB values it is to have. If the actual color storage is

```
typedef struct {
    unsigned char        Red, Green, Blue;  /* 8 bits for each color */
    }

color LUT[SIZE];

void SetColor( i, r, g, b )
    int i;
    unsigned char r, g, b;
{
    LUT[i].Red = r;
    LUT[i].Green = g;
    LUT[i].Blue = b;
}
```

Figure 8.5 *Example lookup table definition and code*

in integers in the range 0 to 255, as is sometimes the case for RGB colors, a command to set the color whose index is 49 to yellow might be setcolor 49 255 255 0. This could be useful for programmers, but we doubt that many users would be comfortable with it.

A *single-color menu* mode can have the user specify a color, and then the specified color and a method of changing the color come up on the screen. The color can be specified in several ways: by entering the color index, by choosing a color from a palette presented on the screen, or by choosing a pixel on the screen. This kind of color menu is useful for changing the color of an icon or other figure and is often used to set the colors on a low-end color graphics terminal.

A *multicolor menu* mode can have the user specify a range of color indices and set the colors for all these indices at once. The user might choose two indices, either by entering their numbers or by choosing two colors from an on-screen palette, set each of their colors by whatever means is desired, and then specify how the intermediate colors are to be determined from them (say, by linear interpolation in each of the red, green, and blue values). This can allow smooth color transitions in the screen display of numerical information.

A *global color* setting can be made by specifying a method to compute the color values for each of the available indices at once. This might be some functional operation that acts on each index and computes the color value as a function of the index. Each of the three color components can be set separately, leading to a rich choice of colors with significant variations across the indices. This technique needs to have some method of showing the user the effects of these global changes, and this is used very effectively by ICARE.

Finally, you can combine the ideas above for *mixed techniques*, in which various color choice methods can be used to determine colors. This might allow a global setting with a few special colors chosen for contrasting colors, to give emphasis to those few values. This is also used in ICARE with great success.

Any of these techniques can easily keep previous color values in an "undo buffer" so that an undo operation is available. This allows the user to experiment freely without fear that previously chosen color settings will be irretrievably lost.

Setting a Color

There are several techniques that can be used to define the color to be set for a specific index. The technique chosen for a particular application must fit the overall behavior of the program's user interface as well as the needs and expectations of the program's users. It is important to remember the subjectivity of colors. Whenever a color is adjusted, the new color should be displayed in a region that is large enough to see the color clearly and that has a neutral background.

A sampling of possible techniques follows. These emphasize RGB color but could easily be adapted to setting colors by adjusting HSV, HLS, or HVC specifications. Again, a designer might well be able to build additional techniques beyond these that match a specific need more closely.

A *dialog box* is a natural tool for changing a single color. As we point out in Chapter 7, a dialog box is designed for transitory information input from the user, and its contents are quite flexible. This box should contain a suitable area to display the current color, and can present the three values of the red, green, and blue color components as numbers. These numbers can be retyped, changing the color to fit the new numbers. As an alternative to the rather clumsy technique of typing individual color values, you can present three sliders for red, green, and blue. These sliders can show the intensity of the red, green, or blue hue being adjusted and can change as the sliders are adjusted. The box should also contain buttons for accepting the choice or canceling the change. An example of such a box is shown in Figure 8.6.

A global change operation should allow the user to see the entire color set and all the lookup table settings at once. In ICARE, this is done by allowing the user to set functions defining the value of each hue with a function. When the color editor comes up, three sine curves, slightly out of phase, are the default functions for the color map. These functions can

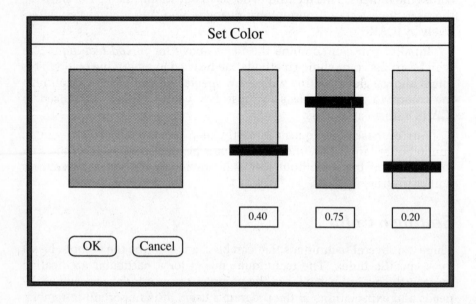

Figure 8.6   *A dialog box for setting colors*

be modified by changing their amplitude, phase, and frequency. Other kinds of functions are also possible, but the unit amplitude of the sine function makes it a natural choice for this application since the values of each hue are also unit values. The cover of this book shows how these functions are displayed in ICARE.

ICARE: Interactive Computer-Aided RGB Editor

This color editor program, written by Donna Cox of the National Center for Supercomputing Applications, allows scientists to visualize their research data and gain scientific insights from the vast amounts of data generated by complex simulations on the Cray supercomputer. The output from the simulation is downloaded to a workstation such as an IBM PC/AT or Sun, where the scientist can then apply different colors to convey information such as speed, temperature, or density.

This editor uses a computer memory array of numbers for each pixel on the screen. The numbers, from 0 to 255, are indices in a color lookup table of 256 colors. This lookup table can be customized by assigning to each table entry percentages of red, green, and blue, or intensity levels for each color. This allows the scientist to have continuous color regions or to have sharp disconnected regions of color. The ability to apply different coloring gives pictures new meaning and enables scientists to find errors in computations or to discover new information in their data. Figure 8.7 shows an ICARE screen that contains a scientific image in the lower-left

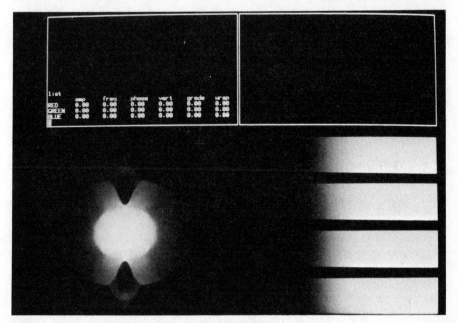

Figure 8.7 *Monochromatic ICARE display*

corner. This image is that of a neutron star collision generated from computations by scientist Charles Ross Evans III. Deriving information from this black and white image is similar to that of reading an X-ray. The cover of this book shows an ICARE screen containing the same scientific image with color added. Color Plate 7 shows how much more information can be derived from the neutron star collision image through the use of color. The image in Color Plate 7 was produced by the artist and scientist working together with ICARE.

ICARE divides the display into four windows, as illustrated on the cover of this book. The upper-right portion of the screen displays a waveform area where the x-axis represents indices (0 to 255) in the color lookup table, and the y-axis represents color intensity (0 to 100 percent) for each of the three sine waves for red, green, and blue. Corresponding to this waveform display is the color map in the lower-right area of the display. This color map represents the color defined at any point along the x-axis of the waveform display.

The scientist can define colors in the color table by controlling each of the sine curves independently. The scientist can control the amplitude to vary luminance from white (100 percent) through gray levels to black (0 percent), the frequency (number of sine curves), the phase (shifting the curve left or right), as well as the baseline, continuity, and beginning and end of each curve.

The user in this example enters choices through the keyboard, and the interactive keyboard session appears in the upper-left portion of the display, although this interaction could be accomplished through other kinds of input devices. The lower-left portion of the display shows how the scientific image looks with the current color selections.

This technique works effectively primarily because it is based on a visualization team. The artist works with the scientist to help make effective color choices to "visualize" the data produced by the computations.

8.7   The Meaning of Colors

You must be aware of what colors will mean to your intended users, or your displays will not convey the information you intend. In general, the warmer colors such as reds, oranges, and bright pinks, appear to be closer, especially on a neutral background. Artists use these color interpretations to add depth to paintings.

> PRINCIPLE: Use warm colors to bring objects closer to the viewer.

Color Plate 1: The same color appears different against different backgrounds. Albers, Plate IV-1, copyright 1963, Yale University Press, courtesy of the Josef Albers Foundation.

Color Plate 2: The same color appears different in different sized areas. Albers, Plate XVI-4, copyright 1963, Yale University Press, courtesy of the Josef Albers Foundation.

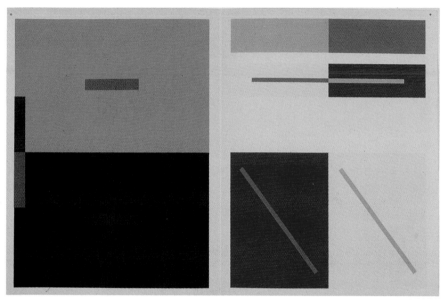

Color Plate 3: Two colors look the same. Albers, Plate VII-5, copyright 1963, Yale University Press, courtesy of the Josef Albers Foundation.

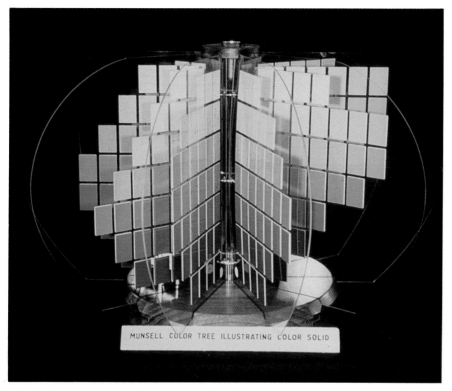

Color Plate 4: Compliments of Munsell Color, 2441 N. Calvert St., Baltimore, MD 21218.

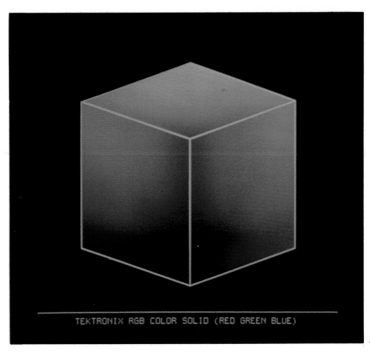

Color Plate 5: Courtesy of Tektronix, Inc.

Color Plate 6: Courtesy of Tektronix, Inc.

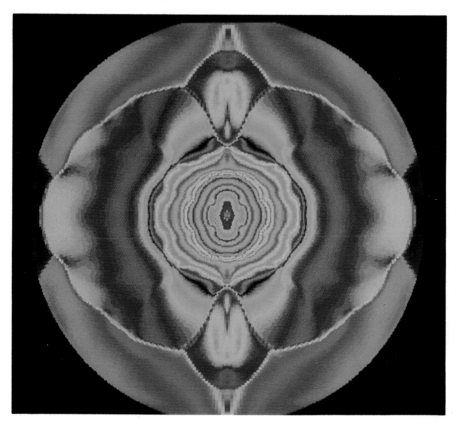

Color Plate 7: Neutron star collision. Courtesy of the National Center for Supercomputing Applications.

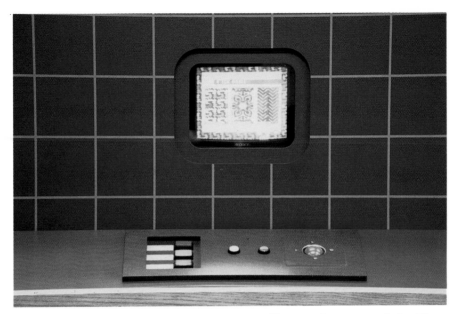

Color Plate 8: An Interactive Image installation. Courtesy of the Electronic Visualization Laboratory.

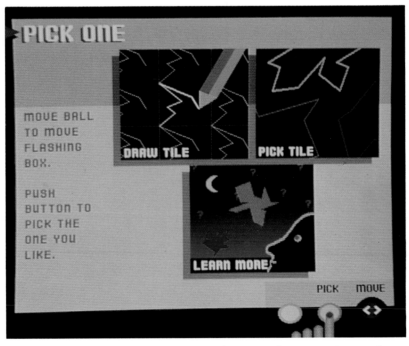

Color Plate 9: An Interactive Image educational screen. Copyright 1987 Debra Weisblum Herschmann, courtesy of the Electronic Visualization Laboratory.

Color Plate 10:   Noobie with a child. Courtesy of Allison Druin.

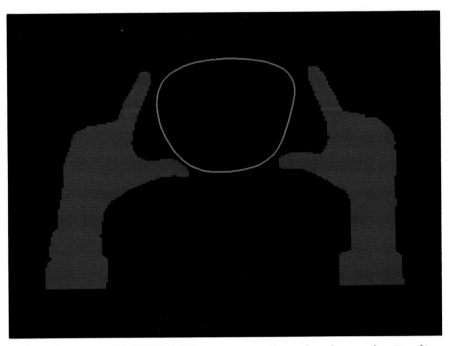

Color Plate 11: VIDEOPLACE user controlling the shape of a B-spline curve. Courtesy of Myron W. Kreuger, Artificial Reality Corporation.

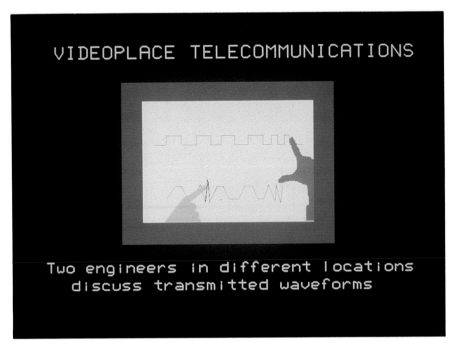

Color Plate 12: A VIDEOPLACE image combined from two sources. Courtesy of Myron W. Kreuger, Artificial Reality Corporation.

You must also think about what specific colors might mean to your viewers. We traditionally consider that red means "stop" or "danger," yellow means "caution," and green means "go" or "all safe." In other cultures, these associations may not have been learned, and these colors may mean something else. Even in our culture, computer displays of CAT scans often use green or purple to indicate dangerous areas and red or yellow for normal conditions. Some of the usual associations in our western culture are that white signifies purity, red signifies love, and purple denotes royalty. In some cultures, different colors have male and female connotations.

> PRINCIPLE: Use familiar color codings appropriately.

There is not a general consensus on the emotional effects of color, but it is generally accepted that colors can and do affect our moods and emotions. When it was suggested that pink has a sedentary effect, prisons painted cells pink, and one Big Ten university painted the locker room for the opposing football team pink. (Opposing teams came in and papered the walls with newspapers to cover the pink.) Orange and yellow are considered to be hunger-producing colors; have you noticed how many fast food restaurants are decorated in orange and yellow? The emotional impact of a color cannot always be predicted. As mentioned earlier, the color is affected by adjacent and background colors, the size of the color area, and the ambient lighting. The color's meaning also varies with the user's experiences.

8.8   Compatibility with Monochromatic Displays

You may want your program to be usable on a monochromatic display. (See Chapter 13 for a discussion of adapting programs to various devices.) Although color in a display has been shown to increase productivity, and people prefer color, there are still homes and offices where the budget does not allow for a new color display. If you want to write two display drivers so that you use crosshatching or varying intensities instead of varying colors, that will work fine. However, you can achieve nearly the same compatibility if you choose your adjacent colors carefully, so that dark colors are always adjacent to pale colors.

For example, on a black and white display, pale red appears to be the same shade of gray as pale green. If you make sure that adjacent colors vary in intensity, as well as hue, they will be more easily differentiable. You can select a bright red to place next to a pale green.

PRINCIPLE: Put light colors next to dark colors to remain black and white compatible.

You should always check your color choices on a monochromatic display to assure that they still have the desired effect. Your program may check for output device and write to a color or monochrome device as discussed in Chapter 13. However, projection devices such as the Kodak DataShow are becoming popular for presentation use. These devices take the image from a color display and project it in black and white.

8.9   Readings

For general information about color theory, we refer you to the Albers book for insight into the exciting ways colors interact, to Varley for a delightful book on color in a variety of contexts, and to the essay by Marcus in Greenberg et al.

Many of the human factors discussed in this chapter are discussed in more details in a series of articles presented by Murch [1987], Wanda Smith [1987a], [1987b], and Smith and Farrell at the 1987 ACM SIGGRAPH conference in a tutorial on *Color in Computer Graphics*.

For more information about the science of color, color models, and laboratory tests involving color selection, we refer you to a series of articles by Murch in the Tektronix publication, *Tekniques*, and an article by Taylor and Murch and a comprehensive discussion of the HVC model by Taylor, Murch, and McManus. A comparison of color models is discussed in Schwartz Cowan, and Beatty. Also, standards for video are discussed in Mathias and Patterson.

General applications of color are covered in articles by Marcus, [1987] and [1986], and by Utz, and further details on ICARE, the RGB Color Editor, are provided in Maxine Brown's article [1987].

Chapter 9

DIRECT MANIPULATION SYSTEMS AND SPECIAL ENVIRONMENTS

This chapter discusses two items vital to current software. Direct manipulation is the basis of much of the best new interface techniques and must be understood to program applications for the Macintosh or for many window systems or User Interface Management Systems. Moreover, this direct manipulation can be used to support novel and exciting ideas in user interfaces. A few examples of these creative implementations are given in this chapter, giving us some insight into a realm of new, exciting possibilities.

9.1   Direct Manipulation Concepts

The PLATO educational software system, from Control Data Corporation, was one of the first systems based on direct manipulation. It presented screens on which a student could select, move, and combine figures on a touch-sensitive screen. PLATO was the subject of considerable research and study, but in the end it proved to be too expensive (it required special host computers and terminals) for widespread educational use. It disappeared a few years ago, but it is a good example of pioneering work and has influenced direct manipulation since.

Direct manipulation is the key for many current systems that are based on the work in the 1970's at Xerox PARC that resulted in the development of the iconic interface and the Smalltalk language system. The Apple Lisa and Macintosh, the Sun and Apollo workstations, and Microsoft Windows all use this approach extensively. The Smalltalk language system usually requires bitmapped graphics and direct manipulation support, though it does not use icons. A Smalltalk screen is shown in Figure 9.1.

A new application of direct manipulation is the Macintosh HyperCard system. This allows a user to create very personal ways to define information with rich interactions and complex linkages to organize, store, and retrieve the information. HyperCard may be the first instance of a whole new way to see computers as information tools. It is illustrated in Figure 9.2.

Techniques for direct manipulation are found in a number of computer graphics texts such as Foley and van Dam. These techniques may be based on standards such as GKS, but the most efficient ones are those specially designed for particular systems.

As we suggest in Chapter 2, direct manipulation is based on an entirely different mode of operation from either menus or commands. Both menus and commands operate by allowing the user a specific set of options at any given point in a program, and these options will change, often dramatically, from point to point within the program. This change of options is one of the things that makes software difficult for users. The strength of menus is that they make these options visible. The strength of

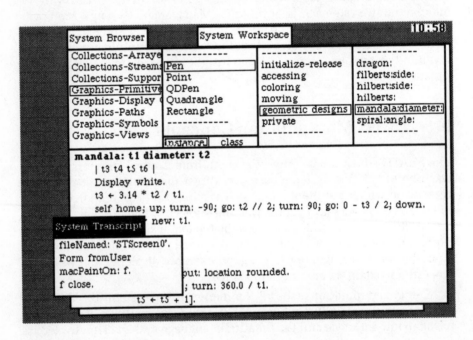

Figure 9.1 *A Smalltalk screen from the Macintosh.*

Figure 9.2 *A HyperCard screen from the Macintosh.*
Copyright Apple Computer, Inc., used by permission

commands is that they let the user choose an option quickly. On the other hand, in a direct manipulation system most options are available at all times on any visible object. This reduces potential user confusion. Moreover, the options are chosen by operations directly linked to the objects on which they operate. This is the strength of direct manipulation and the reason that the major thrust of user interface development is now directed towards direct manipulation techniques.

Probably the most important aspect of a direct manipulation system is the main event loop with user feedback for each user-initiated event. Each user action must be echoed with an appropriate screen action, and this echo must be seen by the user as essentially instantaneous. The most important actions on which an application should provide feedback are cursor tracking and making selections. The aspects of feedback that we emphasize are the cursor, to indicate the point of a selection on the screen; the revealed structure of the object chosen so the user can see how to manipulate it; and the manipulable screen objects built to support the user's work.

The cursor is the image that indicates the position of the mouse or other selector on the screen. The cursor contains a "hot spot," the actual point returned by the selector event. This point must be easily identified by the user so detailed selections can be made. When using the program,

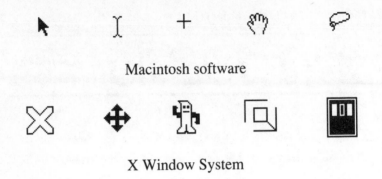

Macintosh software

X Window System

Figure 9.3   *Various cursors*

the user's attention is focused on the cursor, so this is a good place to give user feedback. By changing the cursor's shape, the program can inform the user of the current mode or the action that will happen at the cursor's point. Several different cursors from both Macintosh programs and the X Window System are shown in Figure 9.3. Whatever the cursor's shape, it must be visible against any possible background on the screen. This is often done by outlining a dark cursor with a light line or building a light cursor with a dark outline.

Once one or more objects have been chosen (and it is important to allow the choice of multiple objects for parallel operations) the user must be given visual information on what can be done to the selected objects. Revealing the structure of the objects to the user provides visual information, as is illustrated by some examples from the Macintosh. In *Aldus PageMaker*, text blocks come with handles at the top and bottom and with margin bars, all of which can be moved. In *Microsoft Word*, the "Show ¶" option under the Edit menu shows spaces, paragraph breaks, and linefeeds which are invisible when a document is printed. In *MacDraw*, selected objects have a bounding box with handle squares that can be used to resize the object, while a "reshape polygon" operation on a spline curve (a "smoothed" polygon) shows all the spline knots and allows them to be moved to reshape the curve. These are shown in Figure 9.4. This revealed structure makes the system more predictable and easier to use.

Users need genuinely manipulable objects to enhance the reality of the application. The ARK system, described in Section 9.4, uses the model of physical objects and gravity to reinforce the user's work with the system's objects. Virtual environments, also described in Section 9.4, can carry this concept further to tie the behavior of screen objects to the actions of remote robotic devices. Manipulable objects are probably best

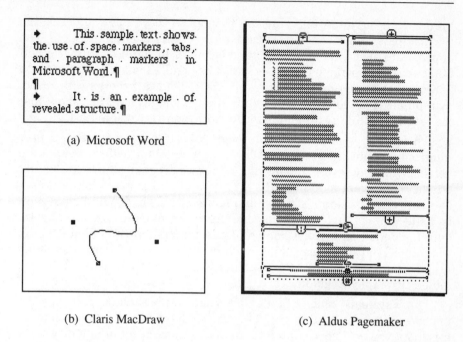

(a) Microsoft Word

(b) Claris MacDraw

(c) Aldus Pagemaker

Figure 9.4   *Revealed structure examples*

modeled on objects the user can physically handle. However, along with the objects, the user must be given the tools to perform the manipulations natural to the objects, and the tools must have the effects the user expects.

9.2   Programming Direct Manipulation

The activities and commands in a direct manipulation system are handled as *events*, so these systems are *event-driven* instead of being command-driven. The event model views the user interface as comprised of events, usually generated by the user, and event handlers, selected by the event to invoke the appropriate user interface or application action. The main program runs as an event loop, handling events and passing them on to the appropriate event handler. If you write this *main event loop* with no toolkit support, you must use the computer's architecture to detect events and decide how to handle them.

Some events, such as button presses, may generate hardware interrupts to indicate occurrence, while other events, such as mouse or cursor motion, may leave their location or displacement in known memory addresses. A getEvent procedure, then, might be invoked by an interrupt to read both the interrupt value and the mouse coordinates to determine the nature of the event and what is under the event's location. The appropriate event handler is then called with location coordinates and other necessary parameters. Events must be handled quickly. If a user is to believe that an action and its result are related, a necessity for direct manipulation as noted above, standard psychological studies show that the result must follow the action by no more than 1/10 of a second.

This description of the main event loop is echoed in several user interface systems. In Microsoft Windows, window functions handle the details. Omitting several details of a Windows program shown in Chapter 10, the main event loop polls the event queue and dispatches the associated message. The loop is shown in Figure 9.5(a). The X Window System is quite similar, but event dispatching is even more explicit. Again, omitting details shown in Chapter 10, this loop is shown in Figure 9.5(b). The same kind of programming is characteristic of standard Macintosh programming using only the Macintosh toolbox, as illustrated by the toolbox example in Chapter 10.

Other systems, such as Sun's NeWS and Apple's MacApp, handle the main event loop quite differently. If you search their applications' code for this loop, you will never find it. Both of these are object-oriented systems and create an object whose function is to manage events. Details of object-oriented programming are outside the scope of this book (though we have some references in the Readings section of this chapter). However, an object-oriented system is characterized by Schmucker [1988] as:

- the encapsulation of data and the programs that run on that data,
- the run-time dynamic binding of the messages sent to an object and the programs encapsulated with it, and
- the inheritance of both data and programs from one class of object to another.

Object-oriented techniques separate the user interface code (usually set up as methods for interface objects) from the computations of the application, and they package user interface styles (how the interface looks and acts) for the programmer. Other advantages of these techniques include using data objects instead of data types, packaging the object's functionality along with the data and allowing the application problem-solving to occur at higher levels of abstraction; differential programming, or programming by changing only small amounts of code to achieve small differences in function; and greatly reducing the volume of code for an application.

Any application program based on direct manipulation begins with an *initialization* step and is followed by a *run* step containing the event loop. For example, the main program code for the MacApp example in Chapter 10 simply involves a Run method and is shown in Figure 9.5(c). All

MacApp main programs, in fact, look essentially like this. The Run method for the application object takes care of all the event handling and dispatching with no further programmer intervention.

Another object-oriented system, Sun's NeWS, hides the main event loop in a different way. This system has the program (client) create and manage processes within the NeWS server on the workstation. These processes share a common memory and can be accessed by the client or workstation easily with event messages. These processes can "express an interest" in certain classes of events. Any event on the workstation is distributed to processes in a well-defined order according to the processes' interest, and the receiving processes handle each event independently. This kind of abstraction is difficult to describe and to understand, but the further description of NeWS in Chapter 10 should be helpful.

Cursor tracking is a special kind of event handling. Whenever the event handler is not dealing with another event, it can check the cursor location and update the cursor's position. Indeed, this continual updating

```
while (GetMessage((LPMSG)&message,NULL,0,0)) {
    TranslateMessage((LPMSG)&message);
    DispatchMessage((LPMSG)&message);
}
```

(a)

```
while ( !done ) {
    XNextEvent( mydisplay, &myevent );
    switch (myevent.type ) {
        case Expose: ...
        case MappingNotify: ...
        case ButtonPress: ...
        case KeyPress: ... }
}
```

(b)

```
BEGIN
    InitToolbox(8);
    InitUDialog;
    New( TTwoDialogsApplication );
    gTwoDialogsApplication.ITwoDialogsApplication;   {initialize}
    gTwoDialogsApplication.Run;
End.
```

(c)

Figure 9.5 (a) Microsoft Windows main event loop, (b) X main event loop, (c) MacApp main program

is the main feature of cursor-based direct manipulation, since the object that is selected is the one indicated by the cursor's location. In MacApp, cursor (mouse) tracking is done by the TApplication.Trackcursor method of the application object; in particular, it is called by the TApplication.Idle method, since mouse tracking is only done when the rest of the application is idle.

Having mentioned object-oriented programming, it is worth noting the natural relationship between objects and a direct manipulation system. Since direct manipulation is the manipulation of objects on the screen, the encapsulation of data and function allows the object itself to respond to the events it receives. Smalltalk-80, NeWS, and MacApp offer both object orientation and user interface support, while other object-oriented languages such as C++, Objective-C, Object Pascal, Flavors (LISP), and Object Logo offer object support for user interface development.

Object-oriented programming is particularly important in dealing with server-based systems. Servers are basically a product of networking and are introduced in the context of windows and window systems in Chapter 10. However, here we need to make a distinction between the terminology of servers for window systems and other uses of the term. For window systems, a *server* is software that runs on the user's workstation, and it maintains a part of a program's function at the user's end of the network, while the program itself runs on a remote host. A server manages the display of interface objects, the details of cursor tracking and user selections, and all user feedback. A server is linked by a network to one or more *clients*, programs running on (possibly remote) host computers. The client controls the interface on the user's workstation by sending the server appropriate messages. This relationship is shown in Figure 10.2.

Jon Meads points out two distinct types of objects that a program can manipulate in a server. *Visual objects* are the objects that carry the program's function. They can be stock objects available in the server or, if the server is programmable, they can be new objects programmed into the server by the application. They are displayable objects that recognize events and whose methods contain their own semantics, and that can change their display properties to show their program context. Note that the client application itself may not know the details of the current program, which are sometimes maintained in the server until an event occurs that sends them back to the remote client.

Alternately, *interaction objects* are the objects that carry the user interaction for the program. These are high-level objects that manage user interactions and construct input from the user to the remote client. These objects present prompts, accept and manage input, generate feedback, and manage input constraints and syntax. They are most likely stock objects, though again a programmable server gives the option of constructing special interaction objects. An interaction object must contain several components. These include:

- an initial state and value,
- the prompt or visual cue offered to the user,
- a current state and value,
- an echo of the current state to the user,
- a condition (called a trigger) to return the object's value as input to the client application, and
- an acknowledgement to the user that the trigger has fired.

9.3 Direct Manipulation Techniques for Data Input

Using direct manipulation techniques, you can design a variety of input methods for a program. These methods usually present a virtual screen model of some sort of control panel, on which direct manipulation is used to adjust or set the controls. The control panel model of input gives you a variety of simulated controls with which to work, as shown in Figure 9.6. You should carefully consider how real control panels are designed for your application before designing your virtual controls. These controls should be handled the same way a person would use the real controls; sliders slide, dials are rotated, and buttons are pushed. To slide a slider, the user should select the slider control and move it in the desired direction; to rotate a dial, the user should select the dial pointer and move it, with the dial control rotating around the dial's center; buttons are handled like any radio button set. In any case, remember the principle of giving the user feedback and include a display of the current value beside the device being manipulated. This display should also show the current or default values when the panel is first presented.

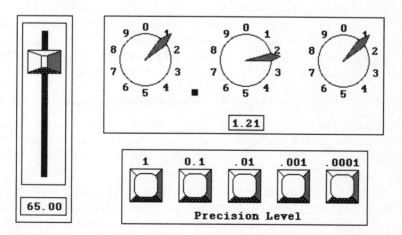

Figure 9.6 *Some possible onscreen controls*

As discussed so far, this numeric control is rather coarse. Since real control panels also have this problem, you can use similar onscreen solutions such as vernier scales or multi-level controls. These controls set more and more detailed accuracy in the input value.

Implementing direct manipulation controls can be based on graphics primitives as discussed in Chapter 2 or can be based on predefined types of controls provided by windowing systems or User Interface Management Systems, as discussed in Chapter 10. The former requires a fairly detailed set of programming operations using selectable graphics segments, while the latter usually requires only creation of instances of predefined objects with special properties as required by the application.

9.4   Experimental and Advanced Environments

This book concentrates on conventional user interfaces for standard computer software, using a range of conventional tools. However, there have been many interesting computing advancements for which an experimental or novel user interface has been important. This section describes a few of these innovations. We believe that they are both interesting and instructive, and that a creative use of the computer and the user interface can be important in making software that users both enjoy and find more comfortable and productive.

We start with relatively straightforward screen use and work toward less familiar work, ending with examples that involve neither keyboard nor mouse, and where a computer does not even seem to be involved. We are very excited by the kind of work represented here and hope you will see the possibilities that are available through imagination and creativity.

Our first example, the Alternate Reality Kit, uses a standard display and keyboard in an innovative programming environment. The Interactive Image uses a familiar display, but the museum environment for which it was built requires a sturdy replacement for the keyboard and an equally sturdy user interface. The voice recognition systems discussed use standard displays and some degree of artificial intelligence to allow users to control both ordinary software and robots through verbal commands.

Noobie, the "furry computer," is in a class by himself, a computer you can hug. Designed as an experimental play station, children squeeze parts of Noobie to build fantasy animals on a Macintosh display built into Noobie's body.

Our other examples use the hands or body to manipulate synthetic creatures or other graphic objects on the display. This use of the body is called *gestural input*. In some cases, this gestural input is accomplished by touching the screen, which is sensitive to the position, pressure and shear force of the finger on the screen.

VIDEOPLACE also uses gestural input, but with no contact with the screen. The participant moves his or her hand or body in front of a video camera. When the video image of the participant touches a graphic image on the display, the computer responds, leading to the term Responsive Environment.

Other research projects deal with what is called a virtual environment. The user wears some special equipment such as NASA's three-dimensional head mount for a three-dimensional view, or the DataGlove or DataSuit which records the position and gesture of the hand or body, respectively, as input to a program allowing the user to manipulate a synthetic tool or world. In this case, "gesture" refers to body posture or the shape and location of the hand, as opposed to body or hand movement.

Several of these environments, such as voice recognition, VIDEO-PLACE, and DataSuit, can be used to control physical devices. This kind of control is known as *telerobotics*. Research in this area is continuing in the area of force feedback, where the user physically feels the effect of touching a synthetic object. For example, to move the cursor from one end of a jagged line on the display to the other end with a joystick, the joystick would have to trace the jagged line back and forth, and the user would feel the shape of the line through the joystick.

ARK—The Alternate Reality Kit

ARK, the Alternate Reality Kit, is a visual programming environment for experimenting with the fundamental laws of physical objects and their interaction, and is implemented with the Xerox Smalltalk system. The primary motivation of ARK is a desire to make the abstractions of physics more concrete for university-level students. This is done by allowing the user to build "microworlds" in which both physical objects and theoretical abstractions take concrete form and manifest themselves in interactive, animated simulations.

Since ARK programming is constructive, syntax errors and variable assignment errors are impossible, and success depends on the user's familiarity with physical objects, their behaviors, and how to manipulate them. Once a microworld (called an "artificial reality" in ARK) has been built, its objects can be set in motion to show the laws of nature in this reality. Modifying the physical laws changes the motion, of course, allowing the user to experience the effects of the laws on the objects directly. Two ARK experimental realities have been built: "Bubble Chamber" simulates classical bubble chamber experiments, while "Collision World" allows students to learn about the laws of conservation. They are being used to study how students learn about physics and physical laws.

In ARK, "programming" is taken in the sense of visual programming: the use of visual techniques to control the computer. This programming in ARK is not the construction of instruction sequences but the selection of objects, determination of their interactions, and setting of physical laws that make up the basic level of system building and control for the user. This allows the user to pick up and change physical laws as easily as manipulating physical objects. Other kinds of user construction, or programming, are available and are being developed. Thus ARK is both concrete and extensible. ARK has some difficulties with some of the nonphysical data types, such as matrices, equations, or chemical formulas, and its developers are working to support them.

Figure 9.7 shows a screen from the ARK system. It shows several objects that should be understood to appreciate ARK. The screen shows the hand, interactors, a slider switch, and the warehouse. Each of these, as well as the button and message box objects, is described below.

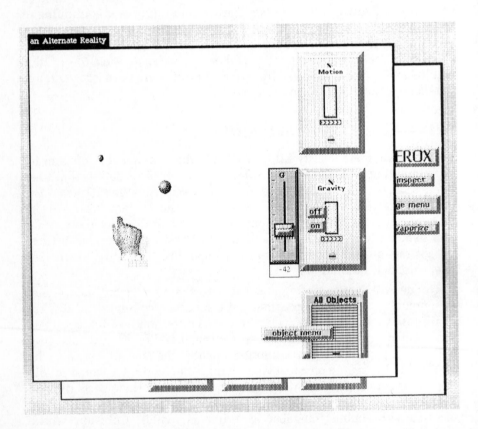

Figure 9.7   *An ARK screen*

Courtesy of Randall B. Smith, Xerox Palo Alto Research Center

- *The Hand*: this is the user's means of interacting with the system; it activates buttons, carries objects, and imparts initial velocity to thrown objects.

- *Interactor*: the screen shows both Motion and Gravity interactors. These are physical manifestations of the rules of nature, allowing the user to interact with these values.

- *Slider Switch*: this is a way to specify numbers. When it is attached to an interactor it can set a value for the rule of nature.

- *Warehouse*: this contains prototypes of all the objects the user can make in the system. Pressing the "object menu" button presents a list of prototypes, and choosing a prototype emits a copy of it from the warehouse into the reality of this simulation.

- *Button*: a user's means of communicating with an object. A button can be moved to and dropped on the surface of any object and will stick on the surface of any object that understands the button's message.

- *Message Box*: a more general means of sending Smalltalk messages to objects. The message is built in the box and is attached to its receiver by a plug.

ARK is very literal. It is based on the behavior of objects in a real world. This is critical to its mission. However, the author of ARK, Randall B. Smith [1987], uses the term "magic" to describe the connection of objects to the system and the intuition it gives the user. This concept of magic in the system is what gives ARK much of its appeal and makes it a tool for exploring artificial realities. Attaching a button or property to an object by dropping the button on the object establishes a magical connection between them. The magic carries over to all aspects of the system: manipulators because they concretely control an abstraction; the screen (as a window on a microworld) because objects can leave the window and still keep their behavior, possibly reappearing at some future time; and multiple realities (multiple simultaneous windows) because simultaneous realities can be compared, each with its own version of its physical laws. Thus ARK contains the power of magic and the learnability of literalism, a combination that multiplies the power of the system.

The Interactive Image

The Interactive Image is an exhibition of state-of-the art computer graphics and imaging technology that premiered at Chicago's Museum of Science and Industry in 1987 and has become a permanent exhibit at the Computer Museum in Boston. As a pilot study of the use of interactive digital television as a medium for learning, the Interactive Image uses technology to teach technology. The interactive installations encourage visitors to explore scientific and mathematical concepts in a setting where they do not have to worry about making mistakes or breaking anything.

The museum environment requires special interface considerations, both in hardware and software. Since the purpose of the exhibit is for both adults and children to interact with the installation and explore possibilities, a special means of input is necessary. An ordinary keyboard would be too complex for young children and too fragile for the pounding it would receive. Furthermore, a loosely attached keyboard would likely disappear. The problem is to design an input device that is simple, sturdy, and built-in. The result, in this exhibit, is the button box positioned below the display, as shown in Color Plate 8. On the left are three color coded buttons for making selections, on the right is a track ball to move the graphics cursor and manipulate the image, and there are two buttons in the center for interacting with the software. This design held up reliably, and using the same design at all the interactive installations allows visitors to interact with every program in a consistent manner.

For this environment, reliability and consistency of the software, as well as user feedback and reinforcement, are very important. Since you are dealing with all levels of technical expertise, the software cannot break no matter what choice the user makes. Feedback to the user about the selection made is important. Color Plate 9 shows one of the educational screens in the ERIC: Tesselations, Kaleidoscope, Animation installation. (ERIC is short for Escher-like Reflective Interactive Computer.) This image screen shows how the user is instructed to move the cursor and make a selection and also illustrates the image of a hand on the screen showing which button is being pushed.

The Interactive Image was developed at the Electronic Visualization Laboratory, University of Illinois at Chicago, under codirectors Tom De-Fanti and Dan Sandin. Engineering and art students worked together in teams to develop the interactive components using RT/1 (Real Time/One) graphics programming language developed by Tom DeFanti.

Voice Recognition

Chapter 14 discusses the importance of voice recognition as an input device for persons with disabilities. Interest in this technology continues to grow for many kinds of applications. In order for computers to understand speech, very sophisticated software algorithms are being developed to permit the computer to distinguish between spoken words. A scientist at Kurzweil AI is shown in Figure 9.8 studying a spectrographic image, a frozen visual representation of a word on the computer screen. Such studies are necessary for the development of voice recognition algorithms and have resulted in applications such as medical dictation systems.

The Kurzweil VoiceEM system for Emergency Medicine and the VoiceRAD system for Radiology both allow physicians to dictate, edit, and print accurate patient records in seconds. Each system uses built-in phrases appropriate to the application. Such systems allow medical

Figure 9.8 *Kurzweil AI scientist studies spectrographic image of a word*

dictation to be accomplished faster and more accurately than through traditional means. In addition, with an increased market for voice recognition systems, the prices will likely decrease, making them more affordable for persons with disabilities.

Quadriplegics can use voice recognition systems to replace traditional input devices such as the keyboard, or to control a robot as illustrated in Figures 9.9 and 9.10. The voice-controlled robot shown in Figure 9.9 can perform everyday tasks in home settings. Speaking into a headset microphone in Figure 9.10, quadriplegic Bob Yee asks the Advanced Robotic Aid to pass him a mug. The Kurzweil Voicesystem translates his spoken commands into computer code that controls the robot's arm movements. When the robot is sent into an adjoining room to fetch an object, Yee can track the robot's movements on the monitor in front of him.

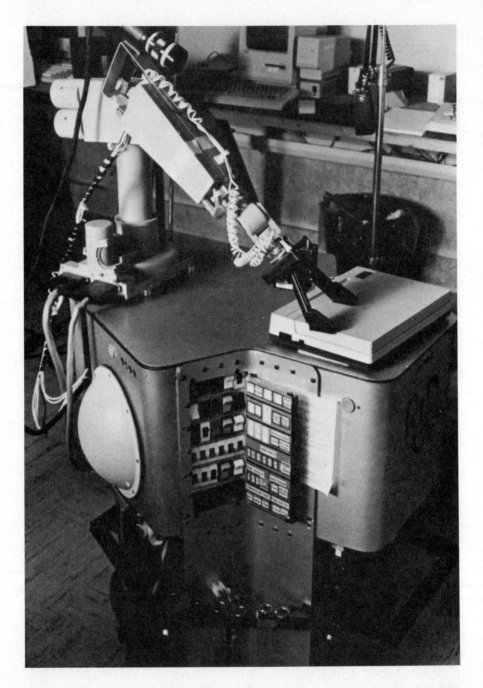

Figure 9.9 *Advanced Voice-Controlled Robotic Aid designed by engineers at Stanford University and the Veterans Administration Medical Center in Palo Alto, CA, under the VA Rehabilitation R & D service*

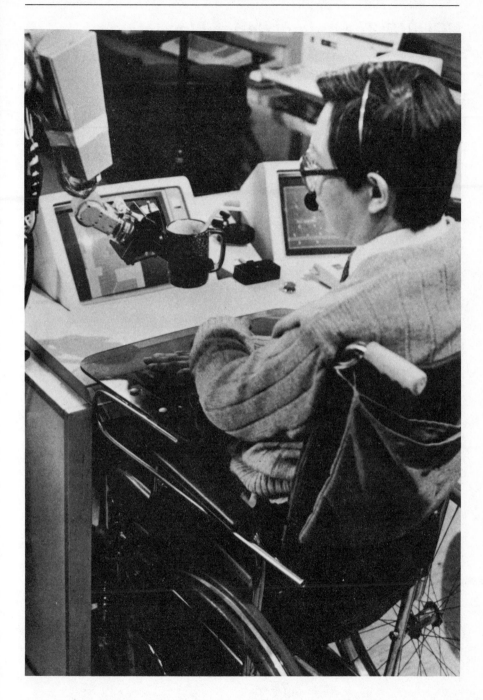

Figure 9.10   *Quadriplegic Bob Yee uses Kurzweil Voicesystem to control robot*

NOOBIE: The Animal Design Playstation

Noobie, or "New Beast," is an alternative to the traditional design workstation with keyboard and mouse. Noobie is made from puppetry, animation, imagination, and Apple Computer electronics. Noobie has fur, feathers, and an iridescent fish tail, and children can stand or sit on Noobie's lap while they build their own fantasy animals on the Macintosh screen contained in Noobie's stomach.

When the computer is switched on, a startup movie uses music and animation to show what kind of animals can be made from the animal parts in the database, and an animal (Noobie, Jr.) remains on the screen, as shown in Figure 9.11.

The parts that can change on Noobie, Jr. include eyes, ears, nose, antennae, horns, mouth, arms, hands, legs, feet, and tail. When a child squeezes one of these parts on Noobie, a particular sound is heard, and a new animal part appears on Noobie, Jr. Figure 9.12 shows some of the animals that Noobie, Jr. can be, and Color Plate 10 shows a child selecting a new tail on Noobie.

Noobie was constructed with the VideoWorks animation driver from Macromind, Inc., LightSpeed C for the application programming, and an Apple Macintosh Plus with a hard disk, wired to a Yamaha synthesizer and amplifier. The hardware was placed in Noobie's softsculpture belly, and the keyboard keys were replaced with microswitches embedded in each of Noobie's parts.

This research was part of the Vivarium, a five-year project funded by

Figure 9.11 *Noobie, Jr.*

Figure 9.12   *Some of the forms of Noobie, Jr.*

Apple Computer at the MIT Media Lab. Allison Druin led a group of MIT researchers in building this alternative workstation for children. The design team included Doug Miliken, structural hardware design; Margaret Minsky, hardware consultant; Tom Trobough, music synthesis; Larry Singer, electrical hardware design; Gwen Gordon, soft sculpture design; and Hans Peter Brandmo, software design.

VIDEOPLACE

VIDEOPLACE is the Responsive Environment in which the computer responds in real time to a participant's physical movements and displays the response graphically. This vision of an artificial world in which you can physically participate and use your body to control computers is a vision that has been pursued for over 20 years by Myron W. Kreuger of the Artificial Reality Corporation.

The human-machine interaction in VIDEOPLACE is accomplished by aiming a video camera at the user. A silhouette of the user appears on the display along with whatever graphic objects the user is to manipulate, and the computer responds whenever the video image of the user touches a graphic object. Hence, the user can do anything he or she could with an ordinary device, such as typing or menu selection, by simply pointing at the appropriate graphic object. Nothing else needs to be learned to use the system. A user can even draw on the screen by moving his or her hand through space.

Besides providing a general purpose input, VIDEOPLACE techniques open up new possibilities. If the video camera is placed above the VIDEODESK, the user's hands are shown in silhouette on the desktop. This can offer unique advantages for mechanical designers as shown in Color Plate 11. Here, the user is manipulating a B-spline curve, commonly used in the design of objects with curved surfaces, such as airplane wings or car bodies. With VIDEOPLACE, the user can control four points simultaneously, while traditional devices allow only one control point to be positioned at a time.

VIDEOPLACE is also valuable for telecommunication and telerobotics. Two people in different places can share a common video experience. Color Plate 12 shows the image seen by two engineers in different cities, a combined image of their hands and their individual graphic data. They can point to features in the data as if they were at the same table. Similarly, a user can control a robot some distance away by moving his or her hands on the VIDEODESK.

Three-Dimensional Virtual Environments

Several research projects have dealt with constructing and using virtual environments. These are systems in which the program presents a synthetic visual environment and allows the user to manipulate it by the computer. These visual environments have been used for animating synthetic creatures, manipulating virtual tools or virtual controls, and controlling remote physical devices. This latter kind of environment goes by the name of telerobotics. The components of these virtual environments are a high-capacity input device and some sort of display.

Virtual environment displays are often standard, though high-quality, screens. This is the case for synthetic animation and for most virtual tools and controls, such as the screen controls described earlier in this chapter. However, some work, principally at NASA, has used a head-mounted display to give the wearer a completely synthetic world containing either virtual objects to be manipulated or virtual control panels to control the program. These head-mounted displays are fully three-dimensional, but are limited to wireframe images. Advances in display technology should allow high-quality color in them in the near future.

Input devices for virtual environments are more specialized. Typical needs for these devices include several degrees of freedom, three-dimensional control, a relationship between the device and the actions needed in the environment, and some kind of feedback to the user through the device. There are a few high-function three-dimensional joysticks that offer several degrees of freedom, and a device containing a handle mounted on several strings in a box meets all these criteria. However, using these devices for an interface requires that the user learn device-based manipulation techniques. Much more natural control is allowed by the DataGlove and more recently the DataSuit, both from VPL Research. These devices, shown in Figure 9.13 (a) and (b), instrument the human hand and human body, respectively, to capture the exact positions and actions of a hand or body and treat them as input to a program. They allow the user to behave naturally, grasping or pointing to a control, or reaching and moving about in space. The computer can echo these actions in the virtual environment as animation input, as input to affect virtual controls, or as direct handling of virtual tools. Force feedback is not yet available on these devices, but it is being developed.

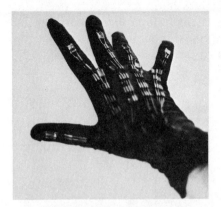

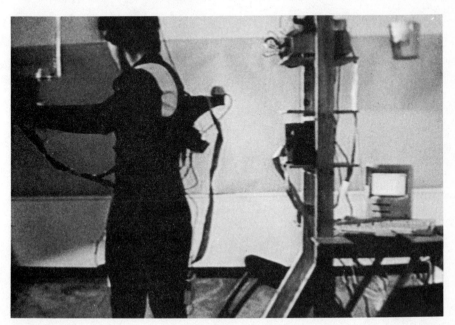

Figure 9.13   *(a) The DataGlove and (b) the DataSuit*
Courtesy of VPL Research

An additional use of these devices is to develop a vocabulary of gestures to serve as command input to a program. Chapter 4 shows how to have user-defined commands for a program, and the abbreviations discussed there can be extended to gesture abbreviations made with the hand or body.

The extraordinarily direct link between the user's actions and the computer function establishes a powerful metaphor for such varying applications as robotic functions in space and delicate microsurgery. Here the user can work to an arbitrary, comfortable scale and have his or her actions echoed by an external device with the appropriate force and scale needed for the application. This concept is outlined visually in Figure 9.14. More generally, this kind of visual technique for controlling the environment is one aspect of the field of visual programming, an emerging technology that supports some applications and interfaces very well.

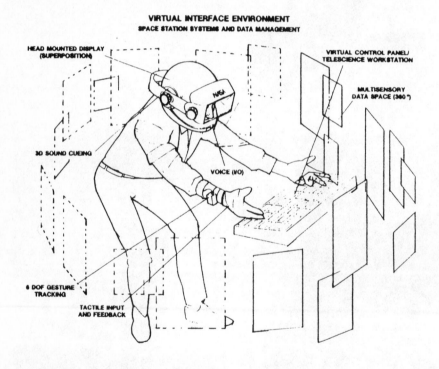

Figure 9.14 *The NASA design for telerobotics*

9.5 Readings

There has been little written directly about direct manipulation techniques. Much of it can be extrapolated from general graphics interaction as noted above. Details of event handling and direct manipulation for a particular system must be sought in manuals such as Apple's MacApp Manual, *Inside Macintosh* for the Macintosh toolbox, or books such as Jamsa or Petzold for Microsoft Windows. More references for window systems and user interface management systems are given in Chapter 10.

Object-oriented programming is a relatively new software technology. There are few books on the subject, most of which are tied to specific languages or systems. Smalltalk is described in Goldberg, C++ in Stoustroup, and Object Pascal for the Macintosh (in the context of MacApp) in Schmucker [1986]. An extensive tutorial on object-oriented programming has been written by Patterson , while the Cox book describes Objective-C in a general context. Interested persons should also attend the annual ACM OOPSLA (Object-Oriented Programming, Systems, and Languages) conferences.

Some of the user interface management systems and window systems discussed in Chapter 10 are also object-oriented. That chapter and its Readings section give you further information on the subject.

The special environments that we discuss in this chapter are described in various places in the current literature. ARK is described in two papers by Randall B. Smith. The Interactive Image is described more fully in two articles by Maxine Brown [1988] and DeFanti. The paper by Druin describes Noobie's concept and design. The concepts behind VIDEO-PLACE are described by Kreuger [1983]; this book is out of print but might be available in libraries. Other sources on VIDEOPLACE are articles by Kreuger [1985] and Peterson. More information on manipulation by force and position sensitive screens can be found in an article by Minsky. Virtual environments and DataGlove applications are described by Foley and by Williams, while the virtual environment aspect of visual programming is discussed in Shu.

Chapter 10

WINDOWS AND USER INTERFACE MANAGEMENT SYSTEMS

M ore and more, software is being built with a user interface implemented on a windowing system or a user interface management system. This chapter gives an overview of these systems and describes a number of them.

The range of system services and philosophies represented in this chapter is very broad, but the discussions indicate on a case-by-case basis what kind of tools each has. One service needed for any application is a consistent "look and feel"—the overall design of the screen and its components, the way the user performs operations, and the way the system responds. Some systems provide no particular interface style but let the programmer implement whatever type of interaction is desired; we call these *anarchist* systems. Other systems define the interface almost completely, allowing you only to choose which predefined components to use; we call these systems *dictatorial*. Most systems fall somewhere between these extremes, of course, and we describe the kind of options you would have in building an interface with each of the systems we discuss.

This chapter considers two separate, but closely related, kinds of systems: window systems and user interface management systems (UIMS's). Window systems are more fundamental in concept, dealing with the mechanics of input, output, events, and window management. A UIMS is usually built on top of a window system and provides more complete interface support, often including look and feel definition as well as assistance with undo operations, cut and paste, and help.

10.1 Window Systems Concepts

A window system is minimally a set of tools for managing program input and output through a restricted part of a display screen. Some of the systems we describe here operate at this level, and they have their uses. However, other window systems go far beyond this, providing extensive support for networking, multitasking, and advanced interaction techniques.

These advanced window systems involve managing multiple applications sharing common devices. In this, they have much in common with modern operating systems. They must provide access to resources and must share these among appropriate clients. Where an operating system's primary resources are memory and input/output devices, a window system's resources are windows, events, text input, text and graphic output, and various object attributes. The scheduling concept for a window system is much more like that of a real-time operating system than a time-shared operating system. Where a time-shared operating system is scheduled by algorithm and by I/O blockage, a window system is scheduled by user-generated events that are essentially interrupts to be handled immediately.

From the user's point of view, the most evident management function of a window system is managing onscreen windows. The collection of windows on the screen is managed as a tree, as shown in Figure 10.1. Whenever a window event requires that the screen be updated, this tree is traversed in a depth-first fashion, with special ordering for the children (subwindows) of each window, and the appropriate windows are notified of their individual need to be updated. Different systems handle this differently, depending on the capabilities of the window system itself and of the window toolkit being used.

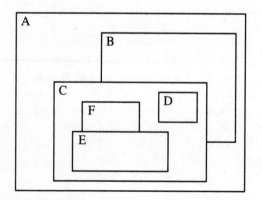
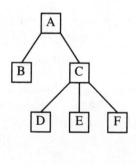

Figure 10.1   *Several windows on a screen and the window tree*

The complexity of the task of managing extensive windowing is so daunting that nobody really manages it from scratch. There are several systems of varying power that can be used to ease the task of handling windows in programs. A brief list of some representative windowing systems follows.

- *Curses*: a text-only window library on Unix systems, using the basic character-handling capabilities of termcap, the Unix terminal database described in Section 3.2. This is somewhat quirky and under-documented but usable. It is not often used for large-scale projects, however. Curses is controlled entirely from an application and assumes that the terminal is owned by that single application. There is almost no resource management and no window multitasking in the system.

- *Microsoft Windows*: an environment for running MS-DOS applications in windows and developing software with a graphical user interface. Multiple applications can be resident at once, control can be switched among them, and data can be moved from one to another. This is the basis of the OS/2 Presentation Manager interface and is designed to be compatible with the user interface portion of IBM's System Application Architecture.

- *Macintosh Toolbox:* an extensive collection of window, text, and graphics tools built into the ROM on Macintosh systems. These tools are accessible from a number of systems and languages, most notably the Macintosh Programmer's Workshop (MPW) through assembler, C, and Pascal language systems. These tools cover a much broader range of function than just user interaction operations. Their use requires a thorough, careful knowledge of the ROM tools through the *Inside Macintosh* books. Since the Macintosh is not a multitasking machine, the Macintosh Toolbox does not support the usual multitasking part of a window system.

- *NeWS*: a network-oriented, server-based windowing system designed for Sun workstations but potentially available on other systems. Sun has now implemented this in a combined X11/NeWS server system. NeWS is based on object-oriented PostScript, and since it is built on a programming language, its window operations are programmable. NeWS is device- and resolution-independent because it uses the PostScript stencil concept for painting the screen. It supports multiple input devices, multiple simultaneous processes, and an easy integration of display and printing. It provides standard user interface objects such as windows and menus but allows the designer and programmer to customize them extensively.

- *The X Window System*: a network-oriented, server-based windowing system developed at MIT and supported by most vendors of Unix-based workstations, it is becoming a standard in this environment. X servers communicate with their client applications by device-independent messages that are interpreted in the server. Applications will usually use the Xlib toolkit and widgets, software tools that include text, a text editor, menus, valuators, scroll bars, and command buttons. Further interface tools can be written on top of X.

Other window systems are available from various vendors, but we limit ourselves to these major examples since most major software development is expected to use these in the near future.

The architecture of window systems also presents several options. Some systems, such as the Macintosh Toolbox, support windows in the operating system kernel, and all window operations are made by direct system calls. This is an example of a *kernel-based* window system. A second model is the *windows library*, such as curses or Microsoft Windows. This adds a layer of window support on top of the operating system. Again, this is not very portable, and it suffers the overhead of function calls. It is more flexible than kernel-based systems, however, because you can add additional window functions by adding your own programming. Both these window architectures have the application process handling all window operations.

To take this load off the application process and to work with the networking environment, a third window architecture has been developed—the *window server*. This is the architecture of NeWS and the X Window System. A window server is a process or program running on a display device, whose function is to take window messages from the *client* application and return messages from screen interactions to the client. The server may be running on the same processor as the client (as in the case of a workstation or personal computer with its own processor) or on a different processor (as in the case of a networked environment). This is shown in Figure 10.2. The problems with this model are the high volume of message traffic, which may strain the capacity of a network, and the need to provide synchronous interaction when the network is naturally asynchronous.

The client views the server as an abstract device that encapsulates all the functions of the display. Thus, the server is explicitly very device-dependent, and each kind of display device will have to have its own server written. This model is clearly oriented to networks, and an application using a given server model will work on any device with this server. Not only workstations can run servers; servers for X and NeWS are starting to be available on personal computers and even terminals.

User interface style is a somewhat separate issue from window systems themselves. The degree to which the windowing system dictates the user interface style varies considerably. Both the Macintosh Toolbox and Microsoft Windows offer certain standard appearances and interface behaviors that cannot easily be overridden. Such dictatorial systems offer

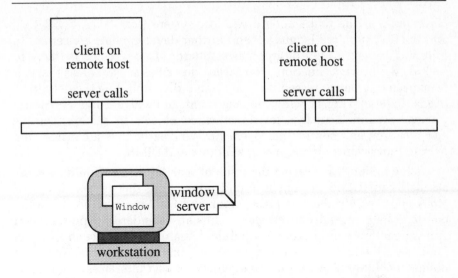

Figure 10.2 *Clients and server on a network*

few choices, as compared with more flexible systems, such as X and NeWS, which offer a range of possibilities but no predefined look. However, dictatorial systems have major advantages to the user, since they offer quicker learning and similar operation across a range of applications. They are also easier for the developer, since they neither need nor allow low-level interface design. When a window system does not offer a predetermined look (or even if it does, if it is difficult to use), it is possible to use a User Interface Management System (UIMS) to achieve a uniform interface. These kinds of systems are discussed in Section 10.4 with examples from some commercial UIMS's.

One aspect of style provided by window systems is found in *widgets*. The term widget comes from the X Window System; a widget provides on-screen access to a user interface function. Examples include close boxes, zoom boxes, resize boxes, scroll bars, cursors, and strings. They are usually available through toolkits that accompany a window system. Widget terminology seems loaded with neologisms; a widget is *pickled* if it is interpreted (say, from a file) at runtime or *embellished* if it started as a standard widget to which styles, images, or text has been added. Widgets are available as objects, if the toolkit is object-oriented, or as procedures, and they are very specific to their individual window system.

The question of standards in window systems and eventually User Interface Management Systems is quite new and the results are uncertain. Version 11 of the X Window System is now being taken as an informal standard by many vendors and is being developed as a formal standard.

However, it is the first standard window system (recall that FORTRAN was the first standard language!) and further developments are certain to follow. The next round of graphics standards in the 1990's is likely to include windowing functions. Jon Meads describes several areas that can be expected to be addressed in future standards, including the definition of a basic set of widgets, widget management, and widget communication; procedures and languages for downloaded objects in servers; context specification; and conflict management. We clearly have a considerable learning curve ahead in the area of windows and UIMS's.

Some people have raised the issue of whether there should be some standards for UIMS presentation and interaction, that is, standards for "look and feel." In the first place, "look and feel" has been found in the courts to be potentially proprietary. Thus any standard for presentation and interaction would require a public-domain approach such as Open Look, described later in this chapter. Even if this were possible, we would not be in favor of it. A continuing openness of user interfaces, even if it is only a growing collection of UIMS's beginning with the Macintosh, Microsoft Windows, and Open Look, is desirable to allow and encourage innovation. We see presentation and interaction styles as analogous to programming languages, where some common ones are standardized, but the opportunity for new development is always there.

There are also smaller issues in windows that affect developers but are much less visible to the user. The first is the question of how the window system writes to the screen. Most window systems, such as Microsoft Windows and X, use a pixel model of the screen and use raster operations to draw objects on the screen. NeWS, however, draws by applying a stencil-and-paint operation to the screen based on PostScript. The stencil model is scaleable and eliminates problems with overlaying and removing objects, especially in color. The Macintosh Toolbox uses both pixel (MoveTo, DrawTo) and stencil (ClipPath) operations.

Another issue is the behavior of window contents when the window is resized. As more (or less) area is shown in the window, what happens to the image in the window? If the window grows horizontally, the extra space can be added at the right, the left, or equally on both sides; similar options are possible for vertical growth and for window shrinkage. The Macintosh, and most window systems, hold the upper-left corner of the screen fixed through all resizing operations. The X window system, however, allows all nine combinations of the options above for screen behavior. Each is called a "gravity"; for example, "center gravity" forces the center of the original window to remain at the center of the resized window.

The final question concerns input focus and window activation. Input focus determines which window gets keystrokes from the workstation. Focus often goes to the active window but would not go to an error box or other window that would not take keystrokes. In this case, keystrokes may be ignored altogether. The question of input focus, then, is related to the question of which window is active. In some computers, such as the Macintosh, the active window is chosen by an event such as a mouse click in the window, and often the active window is moved to the top of the window set. On other systems such as X, a window is active precisely when the cursor is in it; the window can be partly covered by other windows and still get keystrokes, although their echo can be hidden by the covering windows. Other kinds of focus are possible, such as the focus of selections, while some events, such as mouse events, must always be available over the entire display.

10.2   Windows and Window Systems

To get a general overview of the process of using windows in programs, we show some examples of window applications in several different systems. For most of these, we take two straightforward (and simple) window applications and show how they can be implemented in the windowing environment. The windows we implement are a warning alert box, to be located in the middle of the screen, and/or a dialog box in which the user will enter a single line of text, to be placed at the top center of the screen. These dialog boxes are simpler than general program windows, but this simplicity allows us to present their code. For some of the more sophisticated (and less widely known) window systems, however, we show more general examples that illustrate details of the system better than these simple examples can.

The main function of the examples below that relate to actual systems is to provide a quick overview of the system and a small example of its operation. Entire books have been written about each windowing system; we restrict ourselves to giving you a quick look at each and a way to compare them. A more extensive comparison of window systems based on their architecture and features is found in Meyer. This includes several of the less widely known window systems that are not discussed here.

Character-Mapped Windows

The techniques we present here are available on any system that allows direct-access screen writing to text screens. They are not based on any commercial software, but rather on standard ways to handle characters that are fairly widely used in this environment. We will end up managing every character on the screen manually. This can make for painful code, but it works—and with good communication design, it can work quite well. Our implementations do not assume that the current screen is held in physical memory, but they can adapt easily to this situation.

The first approach we present is for error or warning boxes and dialog boxes. The procedures for this purpose are relatively straightforward, since we are not optimizing them for speed. We have two corresponding procedures whose designs are in Figures 10.3 and 10.4; that each window is immediately removed when the user is finished with it. With these designs, each window requires a separate procedure since the window's data are part of the procedure's data. We will see a more general approach later. When working with a window, it is necessary to know what your coordinate system is. This can easily cause some confusion; the entire screen has a coordinate system, but it is natural to view the upper-left corner of the window as the first row and first column. We will use the convention that the coordinates of a window character refer to its position in the window itself, and compute the coordinates of that character on the actual screen as the sum of the character's coordinates in the window and the location of the window on the screen.

```
PROCEDURE:  WarnWindow

INPUT:  none

PROCESSING:
    Constants:
        W_Rows, W_Cols    { rows and columns }
        CorRows, CorCols  { row and column of top left corner }
        StrRow, StrCol    { row and column of string beginning }
    Local Variables:
        string : array[nChars] of char
                = "...."
        backup:  array[W_Rows,W_Cols] of char

    for i = 1 to W_Rows
        for j = 1 to W_Cols    { back up window }
            backup[i,j] = SCREEN[CorRow-1+i,CorCol-1+j]
            SCREEN[CorRow-1+i,CorCol-1+j] = blank
    for i = 1 to nChars         { put up string }
        SCREEN[StrRow,StrCol-1+i] = string[i]
    update
    readln        { wait until RETURN key is pressed }
    for i = 1 to W_Rows
        for j = 1 to W_Cols
            SCREEN[CorRow-1+i,CorCol-1+j] = backup[i,j]
    update
```

Figure 10.3   WarnWindow *pseudocode*

PROCEDURE: `DialogWindow`

INPUT: `none`

PROCESSING:
```
local variables and constants as above, with the addition of
    a screen position where user input is to be placed

Save window as shown in the design above
Blank out the window space and present prompt information
GotoXY( input position )
handle input as in Section 4.5 until RETURN is received,
    building LINE
Replace window as in the design above
```

RETURN: `LINE`

Figure 10.4 DialogWindow *pseudocode*

We are next interested in a more general transient window. This is presented in the discussion of interactive screens in Chapter 7, where we showed how a stack of windows can be maintained. The area covered by a new window is pushed onto the stack and the screen refreshed from the stack after the window is removed. This approach will work well for multiple windows with two assumptions: the windows are always presented and removed in a last in/first out fashion, that is, the windows form a stack, and each window's size and location is fixed.

As discussed in the general window approach in Chapter 3, we make a major improvement in a window system if we separate the data in a window from the code used to put up the window on the screen. This leads again to the concept of a resource, this time a window (or a dialog box) resource. A window resource would specify the window's location and size, the tools associated with the window (scroll bars, zoom box, resize box, drag box, etc.), and the window's contents and their locations. Of course, most of these tools are not applicable in this section, but examples of resources for windows are found in the sections on Microsoft Windows and MacApp later in this chapter (Figures 10.10 and 10.19, respectively).

Using these resource concepts, a general windows procedure is called with the window name as the parameter. That name is looked up in the resource file and the window's resource data is retrieved. This resource data is then interpreted and the resulting display is produced. The kind of windows we discuss here need the components shown in Figure 10.5.

```
name
        location
        tools list
        list of window items:  for each item
                type of item
                location of item
                attributes of item
                default value of item (if applicable)
```

Figure 10.5   *Window resource components*

If the window is used for actual program operation, this simple kind of resource is not adequate. Such a window operation is associated with a program's data, often called a document (text file, graphics page, spreadsheet, etc.), and the window needs to specify information about the part of the document it will display.

There is another design possibility for text windows that is much more flexible, though it may be slower and require more memory. Consider each window as its full screen image, with the space not covered by the window containing a "transparent" character, a character that is to generate a one-space cursor move without changing the screen contents. These windows are to be arranged in a list, with the bottom window at the front of the list and the topmost window at the end of the list. For each position on the screen, the corresponding position on each window image also forms a list; to determine what character to show at that position, traverse the list and display the topmost nontransparent character you found. This design allows you to rearrange, move, or resize any window very flexibly.

```
...execute code
if (warning) {
    initialize the window
    display the window
    when any key is pressed
        remove the window }
proceed with application
```

Figure 10.6   *Pseudocode invoking a warning window*

Curses

Curses is a Unix library that allows for direct screen manipulation and windowing. It is most commonly found on Berkeley Unix and its derivatives and is based on the *termcap* terminal database described in Section 3.2. Its name derives from cursor manipulation. It is not well documented, is somewhat quirky, and is generally regarded as a hacker's system. Still, it can be a useful tool for the right environment: Unix, C language, and text-only programming.

As far as windows are concerned, curses offers an adequate set of tools for its environment. Windows can be constructed in the background and made visible as needed. Multiple windows can exist on the screen, and they can overlap. The windows can be layered and rearranged in any order. They can have highlighted text, and input or output can be handled through any window. Its model follows the "list of screens" concept above to a certain extent.

Curses is used much like any other Unix library called from C. Code using it must start with the include statement #include <curses.h> and compilation must include the appropriate libraries such as the curses and termcap libraries as in the example

cc [options] myfile.c -lcurses -ltermcap...

The code body, then, can use any of the curses functions as described in the on-line Unix manuals.

The coding for our two window examples is straightforward. The output-only warning window would be used in such a manner as shown in Figure 10.6, and the code and output for this is shown in Figure 10.7.

The second window example calls for putting up a window to get a single input string from the user. This is very much like the first example but requires a somewhat wider window and some input handling. Since curses includes input routines that extend the standard C string input, we can use them. For example, wgetstr(win,str) extends the normal scanf("%s",str) where str is of type *char. Alternately, we can use our own input-handling techniques, modifying them to act through the window with curses tools. We choose the former here to keep our code short.

Of course, curses allows windows to be used for input as well as output. The code in Figure 10.8 shows a window used for text entry. It is modified from an example in the manual for Utek, Tektronix' implementation of bsd 4.2 Unix.

Microsoft Windows

Microsoft Windows, often called simply "Windows" in this section, is a window system for machines running 8086, 80286, or 80386 processors. It uses MS-DOS and requires a graphics adaptor, since it does all its work via

```
#include <curses.h>
#define HOR '='
#define VER '|'
#define LEN 11
#define WTH 31
#define INY 6
#define INX 25

main()
{
    WINDOW *win, *bkg;
    char *msg = "WARNING", ch = 'a';
    int col, row = 0;

    initscr();                  /* initialize curses environment */
    bkg = newwin( 24, 80, 0, 0 ); /* create new background window */
    /*
     *  do whatever processing is desired with output to
     *  the "background window" bkg
     */
    wrefresh( bkg );            /* display the background window */
    win = newwin( LEN, WTH, INY, INX );  /* create new warning window */
    wstandout( win );           /* all text in window is emphasized */
    for ( row = 0; row <= 9; row++ ) {
        wmove( win, row, 1 );    /* direct access in window */
            waddstr( win, "                        " );
            /* write string in win*/
    }
    box( win, VER, HOR );       /* draw box around window */
    wmove( win, 5, 12 );
    waddstr( win, msg );
    wrefresh ( win );           /* display warning window */
    ch = wgetch( win );         /* get input character through window */
    wstandend( win );           /* end emphasized (standout) mode */
    wrefresh( bkg );            /* restore the original background */
    endwin();                   /* end curses environment (required!) */
}
```

Figure 10.7 *Code and output for warning window with curses*

```
#include <curses.h>

WINDOW *cmdwin;

main()
{
    int i, c;
    char buf[120];

    initscr();
    nonl();
    noecho();
    cbreak();

    cmdwin = newwin(3,COLS,0,0);           /* window definition */
    for (i=0; i<LINES; i++ )
        mvprintw(i,0,"This is line %d of stdscr", i);

    for (;;) {                             /* continue until break */
        refresh();
        c = getch();
        switch (c) {
            case 'c':                      /* enter command */
                werase(cmdwin);
                wprintw(cmdwin,"Enter command:");
                wmove(cmdwin,2,0);
                for (i=0; i<COLS,i++)
                    waddch(cmdwin,'-');
                wmove(cmdwin);
                touchwin(cmdwin,1,0);
                wrefresh(cmdwin);
                wgetstr(cmdwin,buf);
                touchwin(stdscr);
                /* input is now in buf and can be processed */
                break;
            case 'q':                          /* quit */
                endwin();
                exit(0);
        }
    }
}
```

Figure 10.8   *A string-input window in curses*

the bitmapped screen; EGA or VGA graphics are recommended. At this writing, it is available in release 2.0 for the 8086/80286 and as Windows/386 for the 80386. It conforms to the Common User Interface (CUA) part of IBM's Systems Application Architecture (SAA), which will underlie the next generation of IBM systems and is the basis for the Presentation Manager in IBM/Microsoft's OS/2. Windows has a fixed style to its windows but, in our opinion, does not package enough functionality to be called a UIMS. An example of a Microsoft Windows window is in Figure 10.9.

Both Microsoft Windows 2.0 and Windows/386 offer a multitasking operating environment, but Windows/386 also offers true program multitasking. Windows 2.0 shows several programs simultaneously, but only one is actually running. Its model of simultaneous programs is a coroutine model, with the user acting as the scheduler. Since this seems to be the main difference between the two versions of Microsoft Windows, we concentrate on Windows 2.0 in our discussion.

To support the multitasking environment, Windows includes a virtual memory manager. This is a segmentation facility that allows inactive programs to be swapped out and large active programs to run in a physical memory much smaller than their address space. The memory overhead of Windows itself is said to be only 70K, allowing many nonsegmented programs to run without modification.

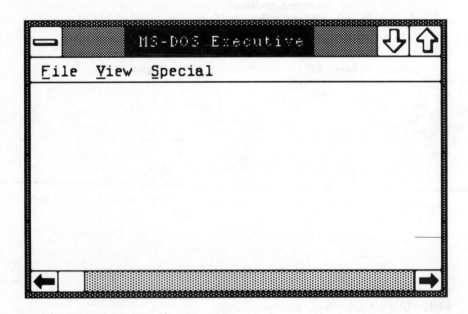

Figure 10.9   *A Microsoft Windows window*

Courtesy of Microsoft Corporation

Windows is somewhat object-oriented. It is based on the concept of a window as an object, with information passed among windows by messages. Any window may have one or more child windows, and there are functions for retrieving the parent or any child of a given window. Windows has good capabilities for manipulating the window tree generally.

To use a window, you must first register the window class; in our example this is done in the GetNameInit function. You can then make instances of this window with the CreateWindow function, and can have a number of instances of this window class. Certain window properties, such as the colors of the window components, belong to the window class and are shared by all its instances.

Messages are created, directly or indirectly, by events. These events can come from the keyboard, where the input focus determines which window gets the message; from the mouse, where the window under the mouse point gets the message; or from the system clock via a timer, where the program setting the timer gets the message. Events are handled in a system queue and in individual program queues. In our example program, messages are picked up by GetMessage, sent back to the system queue in Windows by TranslateMessage, and parsed and sent to the individual window by DistributeMessage. At that point, the individual window's message handler, such as DlgGetNameBox in the example, will decypher the message identifier and act on it according to its parameters. The message parsing and passing are determined by the message data structure, which contains several fields:

- msg->hwnd   handle to window to get the message,
- msg->message   message identifier,
- msg->wParam   one-word (16-bit) parameter,
- msg->lParam   long (32-bit) parameter,
- msg->time   time message structure placed in queue, and
- msg->pt   mouse coordinates at the time message was placed in queue.

Many of Windows' operations are handled by child windows. Child windows are declared by the CreateWindow function including window style parameter WS_CHILD, and must lie entirely within their parent. There are five predefined child window classes:

- listbox class: selects items in a list contained in the box, such as the directory list in a FILE window,
- edit class: types and edits text in one or multiple lines,
- scrollbar class: presents a scroll bar,
- static class: presents a box and text only, with no messages returned from this window,
- button class: presents any one of eleven different kinds of buttons, including pushbuttons, checkboxes, and radio buttons.

As predefined window classes, the user must simple create instances of these windows and define their contents.

In common with other window systems, Windows uses the concept of resources with a resource compiler and resources included in the program linkage. Windows includes nine kinds of resources: icons, cursors, bitmaps, character strings, user-defined resources, menus, keyboard accelerators, dialog boxes, and fonts. Two of these, dialog boxes and icons, can be built interactively by programs named DLGBOX and ICONEDIT, respectively, and icons, cursors, and fonts are built from bitmaps. Dialog boxes can also be built by using a pointer to a template in memory, so you need not use a precompiled resource box. Many of these resources are self-explanatory, but two of them bear some discussion.

- Character strings allow you to define as resources the text your program will use. This allows you to change the text to another language without recompiling the program and so move to international or special-use markets.

- Keyboard accelerators map special keys or key combinations to commands. Unfortunately, this reinforces one of MS-DOS's user interface problems, the proliferation of combination key presses to shortcut commands. At least, if accelerators are used, it is very important to use Windows mouse functions to allow equivalent input from a mouse or other special device. See Chapter 14 for more background on the problem of combination key presses for users with disabilities.

Windows uses a unified model for all its text and graphics, the bitmapped screen. Text is painted on from text fonts while graphics primitives such as lines, ovals, and rectangles are painted on as well. This contrasts with the stencil-and-paint model of NeWS and some of the Macintosh graphics. It also makes graphics operations hardcoded in pixels vulnerable to systems having different screen resolutions. Colors are managed by lookup tables and lists of color constants, and are stored in 32-bit RGB triples defined by $0 | (((R<<8) | G)<<8) | B)$.

We note a few aspects of our Windows code example in Figure 10.10. This is adapted from Jamsa with a few additions to fit Windows 2.0. Note that this example includes several files, including a header file, resource script file, module definition file, and application code file. We think this example is illustrative of the nature of Windows programming.

Macintosh Toolbox

One of the features of the Macintosh design is an extensive library of supporting routines in ROM. The functions this provides are standard across all Macintoshes, but the ROM has grown and increased in function as this system line has matured. The original Macintosh ROM was 64K,

```
/*  Code for text entry window, pp. 323-327 in [Jamsa] */
/*  modified to account for some changes in Windows 2.0 */
```

```
/*  Contents of getname.h  */

#define OK_PUSH 1
#define NAME 2
```

```
/*  Contents of resource script file  */

#include "windows.h"
#include "getname.h"

GETNAME ICON GETDRIVE.ICO

GETNAME_MENU menu
begin
   MENUITEM "Change name", 1
end

GETNAME_DLG DIALOG 10, 10, 200, 80
STYLE WS_BORDER | WS_POPUP
CAPTION "Get name"
begin
   CTEXT "Enter your name",        1, 15, 10, 100, 12
   EDITTEXT NAME,                  15, 35, 100, 12
   DEFPUSHBUTTON "Ok",             OK_PUSH, 15, 60, 100, 12
                                   WS_GROUP
end
```

```
/*  Contents of module definition file */

NAME              GETNAME

DESCRIPTION       'Windows Dialog Edit Application'

STUB              'WINSTUB.EXE.'

CODE              MOVEABLE
DATA              MOVEABLE MULTIPLE

HEAPSIZE          512
STACKSIZE         4096

EXPORTS
   GetNameWndProc @1
```

```
/*  Contents of application code file */

#include "windows.h"
#include "getname.h"
```

continued

```
#define APPLICATION_NAME "GETNAME"
#define ICON_NAME "GETNAME_ICO"

FARPROC lpprocGetName;

long FAR PASCAL GetNameWndProc(HWND, unsigned, WORD, LONG);

static HANDLE hInst;
char   name_buffer[255];

BOOL FAR PASCAL DlgGetNameBox(hDlg, message, wParam, lParam)
  HWND hDlg;
  unsigned message;
  WORD wParam;
  LONG lParam;
{
  switch (message) {
    case WM_COMMAND:
      if (wParam == OK_PUSH) {
        GetDlgItemText(hDlg, NAME, (LPSTR) name_buffer, 255);
        EndDialog(hDlg, TRUE); }
      return(TRUE); break;
    case WM_INITDIALOG:
      SetDlgItemText(hDlg, NAME, (LPSTR) name_buffer);
      return(TRUE); break;
    default:
      return(FALSE); break;
} }

BOOL GetNameInit(hInstance)
  HANDLE hInstance;
{
  WNDCLASS  pClass;

  pClass = (NPWNDCLASS) LocalAlloc(LPTR, sizeof(WNDCLASS));
  pClass->hCursor        = LoadCursor(NULL, IDC_ARROW);
  pClass->hIcon          = LoadIcon(hInstance, (LPSTR) ICON_NAME);
  pClass->cbClsExtra     = 0;
  pClass->cbWndExtra     = 0;
  pClass->lpszClassName  = (LPSTR) APPLICATION_NAME;
  pClass->lpszMenuName   = (LPSTR) "GETNAME_MENU";
  pClass->hbrBackground  = (HBRUSH) GetStockObject(WHITE_BRUSH);
  pClass->hInstance      = hInstance;
  pClass->style          = CS_HREDRAW | CS_VREDRAW;
  pClass->lpfnWndProc    = GetNameWndProc;

  if (!RegisterClass((LPWNDCLASS) pClass)) return FALSE;

  LocalFree((HANDLE) pClass);       /* return space to heap */
  return TRUE;                   /* registration successful */
}

int PASCAL WinMain(hInstance, hPrevInstance, lpszCmdLine, cmdShow)
  HANDLE  hInstance, hPrevInstance;
  LPSTR   lpszCmdLine;
  int     cmdShow;
{
```

continued

```
MSG     message;
HWND    hWnd;

if (!hPrevInstance)  /* initialize if this is first instance */
    if (!GetNameInit(hInstance))
        return FALSE;    /* initialize failed - return to Windows */

hWnd = CreateWindow((LPSTR) APPLICATION_NAME,
                    (LPSTR) APPLICATION_NAME,
                    WS_TILEDWINDOW;
                    0,    /* x position - ignored for tiled windows */
                    0,    /* y position - ignored for tiled windows */
                    0,    /* cx size - ignored for tiled windows */
                    0,    /* cy size - ignored for tiled windows */
                    (HWND) NULL,    /* no parent */
                    (HWND) NULL,    /* use class menu */
                    (HANDLE) hInstance,
                                /* handle to window instance */
                    (LPSTR) NULL );  /* no parameters to pass */

lpprocGetName = MakeProcInstance(
                        (FARPROC) DlgGetNameBox, hInstance);
hInst = hInstance;
ShowWindow(hWnd, cmdShow);           /* make window visible */
UpdateWindow(hWnd);

/* Poll messages from the event queue and dispatch them */
while (GetMessage((LPMSG) &message, NULL, 0, 0)) {
    TranslateMessage((LPMSG) &message);
    DispatchMessage((LPMSG) &message); }

return (int) message.wParam;    /* return control to Windows */
}

long FAR PASCAL GetNameWndProc(hWnd, message, wParam, lParam)
    HWND hWnd;
    unsigned message;
    WORD wParam;
    LONG lParam;
{
    switch (message) {
      case WM_COMMAND:
        DialogBox(hInst, (LPSTR) "GETNAME_DLG",hWnd,lpprocGetName);
        break;
      case WM_DESTROY:
        PostQuitMessage(0);    /* tell Windows ready to terminate */
        break;
      default:    /* let Windows process the message */
        return DefWindowProc(hWnd, message, wParam, lParam);
        break;
    }
    return(0L);
}
```

Figure 10.10 *Microsoft Windows code example*

tightly packed, but now the Macintosh Plus ROM is 128K and the Macintosh SE and Macintosh II ROMs are 256K. The toolbox ROM contains library procedures for operating systems functions (memory manager, event manager), graphics (QuickDraw), and user interface operations.

The user interface components of the toolbox are the Window Manager, Dialog Manager, Menu Manager, Control Manager, and TextEdit routines. These are collectively called the "user interface toolbox," and we concentrate on them here.

TextEdit deals with small amounts of text, certainly less than would be needed in a word processor. It supports general text entry points, character and word selection, style changes, and cut and paste. Text is entered in the *destination rectangle*, while only the text in the *view rectangle* is actually shown on the screen. TextEdit manages the scrolling of text in the view rectangle. TextEdit can be used for text input in dialog boxes.

The *Control Manager* handles the various controls in a window. These include buttons and the parts of scroll bars. The Control Manager checks to see if events occur within controls and also handles all the relocation of controls that are required by window operations such as moving or resizing, as well as control events such as scrolling.

The *Menu Manager* handles the main menu bar in a Macintosh application, as well as all the menus that pull down from it. Menus are generally defined in an application's resource file. An example of this file is given in the MacApp section later in this chapter. Menu items, in the main menu or in submenus, can be deactivated and reactivated to maintain a consistent menu look, even when some choices are not appropriate at a given point in the program.

The *Dialog Manager* is responsible for some of the window functions we discussed earlier in this chapter. It puts up dialog and alert boxes for the application. Dialogs can be read from a resource file or be created by the program as it runs. They can include their own text handling, supplementing that provided by TextEdit. The Macintosh recognizes two types of dialogs: *modal dialogs* and *modeless dialogs*. A modal dialog is one which requires the user to take some definite action before the application can continue; it generally does not have a close, or "go away," box. A modeless dialog provides optional information to the user; it usually has a close box so the user can dismiss it without any other action.

Finally, the *Window Manager* creates, manages, and manipulates windows on the Macintosh screen. It manages the window tree and handles redrawing the screen as needed when windows are moved, resized, closed, or activated. Windows managed by the Window Manager include a content region and (optionally) one or more additional regions, including a close box, the drag region, and the grow region (resize box). Figure 10.11 shows these regions; other regions that you might expect to see, such as scroll bars, are controls managed by the Control Manager.

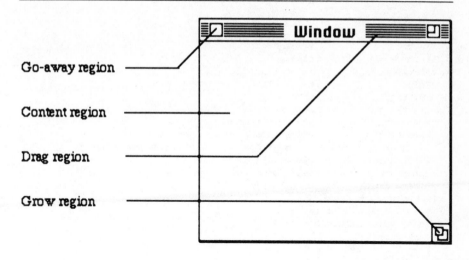

Go-away region

Content region

Drag region

Grow region

Figure 10.11   *Components of a Window Manager window*

A window is active immediately after it is opened or when it gets a mouse click event in its structure region, which is the entire window. The active window on the screen is always the top window and has the input focus for the application.

In Figure 10.12 is the Macintosh Programmers' Workshop (MPW) C code for the Macintosh sample application distributed with MPW, which opens a small window for TextEdit text entry. Note the structure of the example program; the main( ) function does initialization and handles the main event loop, the showAboutMeDialog( ) function handles the About choice under the Apple menu item, and the doCommand(mResult) function handles mouse events in the menu bar. This is a simple application, but it does show how many details must be mastered to use the Toolbox.

A lot of code is required to manage all the Macintosh Toolbox functions, and it takes programmers a good deal of work to understand the necessary sequencing and interaction between these functions. This was a problem in the early days of the Macintosh, but there is now a pool of programmers and shops with Macintosh expertise. There are also a number of development environments that allow full toolbox access from several languages. Nevertheless, this is still enough of a problem to make development systems such as MacApp very attractive, especially to small developers. MacApp is described in some depth in Section 10.4.

```
int main()
{
    Rect                    screenRect;
    Rect                    dragRect;
    Rect                    txRect;
    Point                   mousePt;
    CursHandle              ibeamHdl;
    EventRecord             myEvent;
    WindowPtr               theActiveWindow;
    WindowPtr               whichWindow;
    register    WindowPtr   myWindow;       /* Referenced often */
    WindowRecord            wRecord;
    extern void             setupMenus();
    extern void             doCommand();
/* Initialization traps */
    UnloadSeg(_DataInit);
    InitGraf(&qd.thePort);
    InitFonts();
    FlushEvents(everyEvent, 0);
    InitWindows();
    InitMenus();
    TEInit();
    InitDialogs(nil);
    InitCursor();
/* setupMenus is execute-once code, so we can unload it now. */
    setupMenus();                /* Local procedure, below */
    UnloadSeg(setupMenus);
    /*
     * Calculate the drag rectangle in advance.
     * This will be used when dragging a window frame around.
     * It constrains the area to within 4 pixels from the screen edge
     * and below the menu bar, which is 20 pixels high.
     */
    screenRect = qd.screenBits.bounds;
    SETRECT(&dragRect,4,20+4,screenRect.right-4,screenRect.bottom-4);
    /*
     * Create our one and only window from the WIND resource.
     * If the WIND resource isn't there, we die.
     */
    myWindow = GetNewWindow(windowID, &wRecord, (WindowPtr) -1);
    SetPort(myWindow);
    /*
     * Create a TextEdit record with the destRect and viewRect set
     * to my window's portRect (offset by 4 pixels on the left and right
     * sides so that text doesn't jam up against the window frame).
     */
    txRect = myWindow->portRect;
    InsetRect(&txRect, 4, 0);
    TextH = TENew(&txRect, &txRect);
            /* Not growable, so destRect==viewRect */
    ibeamHdl = GetCursor(iBeamCursor);          /* Grab this for use later */
    /*
     * Ready to go.
     * Start with a clean event slate, and cycle the main event loop
     * until the File/Quit menu item sets DoneFlag.
```

continued

```
*
 * It would not be good practice for the doCommand() routine to
 * simply ExitToShell() when it saw the QuitItem — to ensure
 * orderly shutdown, satellite routines should set global state,
 * and let the main event loop handle program control.
 */
DoneFlag = false;
for ( ;; ) {
    if (DoneFlag) {
        /*
         * Quit has been requested, by the File/Quit menu, or
         * perhaps by a fatal error somewhere else (missing
         * resource, etc. Here we could put up a Save Changes? DLOG,
         * which would also allow the Cancel button to set DoneFlag
         * to false
         */
        break;          /* from main event loop */
    }
    /*
     * Main Event tasks:
     */
    SystemTask();
    theActiveWindow = FrontWindow();
            /* Used often, avoid repeated calls */
    /*
     * Things to do on each pass throught the event loop
     * when we are the active window:
     * [1] Track the mouse, and set the cursor appropriately:
     * (IBeam if in content region, Arrow if outside)
     * [2] TEIdle our textedit window, so the insertion bar blinks.
     */
    if (myWindow == theActiveWindow) {
        GetMouse(&mousePt);
        SetCursor(PtInRect(&mousePt,&myWindow->portRect) ?
                                        *ibeamHdl : &qd.arrow);
        TEIdle(TextH);
    }
    /*
     * Handle the next event.
     * In a more complex application, this switch statement
     * would probably call satellite routines to handle the
     * major cases (mouseDown, keyDown, etc), but our actions
     * are simple here and it suffices to perform the code in-line.
     */
    if (!GetNextEvent(everyEvent, &myEvent)) {
        /*
         * A null or system event, not for me.
         * Here is a good place for heap cleanup and/or
         * segment unloading if I want to.
         */
        continue;
    }
    /*
     * In the unlikely case that the active desk accessory does not
```

continued

```
 * handle mouseDown, keyDown, or other events, GetNextEvent()
 * will give them to us!  So before we perform actions on some
 * events we check to see that the affected window in question
 * is really our window.
 */
switch (myEvent.what) {
    case mouseDown:
        switch (FindWindow(&myEvent.where, &whichWindow)) {
            case inSysWindow:
                SystemClick(&myEvent, whichWindow);
                break;

            case inMenuBar:
                doCommand(MenuSelect(&myEvent.where));
                break;

            case inDrag:
                DragWindow(whichWindow,&myEvent.where,&dragRect);
                break;

            case inGrow:
                /* There is no grow box. (Fall through) */

            case inContent:
                if (whichWindow != theActiveWindow) {
                    SelectWindow(whichWindow);
                } else if (whichWindow == myWindow) {
                    GlobalToLocal(&myEvent.where);
                    TEClick(&myEvent.where,
                        (myEvent.modifiers & shiftKey)!= 0,TextH);
                }
                break;

            default:
                break;
        }/*endsw FindWindow*/
        break;

    case keyDown:
    case autoKey:
        if (myWindow == theActiveWindow) {
            if (myEvent.modifiers & cmdKey) {
                doCommand(MenuKey(myEvent.message&charCodeMask));
            } else {
                TEKey((char)(myEvent.message&charCodeMask),TextH);
            }
        }
        break;

    case activateEvt:
        if ((WindowPtr) myEvent.message == myWindow) {
            if (myEvent.modifiers & activeFlag) {
                TEActivate(TextH);
                DisableItem(MyMenus[editMenu], undoCommand);
            } else {
                TEDeactivate(TextH);
```

continued

```
                        EnableItem(MyMenus[editMenu], undoCommand);
                    }
                }
                break;

            case updateEvt:
                if ((WindowPtr) myEvent.message == myWindow) {
                    BeginUpdate(myWindow);
                    EraseRect(&myWindow->portRect);
                    TEUpdate(&myWindow->portRect, TextH);
                    EndUpdate(myWindow);
                }
                break;

            default:
                break;

        }/*endsw myEvent.what*/

    }/*endfor Main Event loop*/
    /*
     * Cleanup here.
     */
    CloseWindow(myWindow);

    return 0;          /* Return from main() to allow C runtime cleanup */
}
/*—————————————————————————————————————*/
/*
 * Display the Sample Application dialog.
 * We insert two static text items in the DLOG:
 *      The author name
 *      The source language
 * Then wait until the OK button is clicked before returning.
 */
void showAboutMeDialog()
{
    GrafPtr savePort;
    DialogPtr   theDialog;
    short       itemType;
    Handle      itemHdl;
    Rect        itemRect;
    short       itemHit;

    GetPort(&savePort);
    theDialog = GetNewDialog(aboutMeDLOG, nil, (WindowPtr) -1);
    SetPort(theDialog);

    GetDItem(theDialog, authorItem, &itemType, &itemHdl, &itemRect);
    SetIText(itemHdl, "Flash Bazbo");
    GetDItem(theDialog, languageItem, &itemType, &itemHdl, &itemRect);
    SetIText(itemHdl, "C");

    do {
        ModalDialog(nil, &itemHit);
    } while (itemHit != okButton);
```

continued

```
    CloseDialog(theDialog);

    SetPort(savePort);
    return;
}
/* Process mouse clicks in menu bar */
void doCommand(mResult)
    long      mResult;
{
    int                  theMenu, theItem;
    char                 daName[256];
    GrafPtr              savePort;
    extern MenuHandle    MyMenus[];
    extern Boolean       DoneFlag;
    extern TEHandle      TextH;
    extern void          showAboutMeDialog();

    theItem = LOWORD(mResult);
    theMenu = HIWORD(mResult);          /* This is the resource ID */

    switch (theMenu) {
        case appleID:
            if (theItem == aboutMeCommand) showAboutMeDialog();
            else {
                GetItem(MyMenus[appleMenu], theItem, daName);
                GetPort(&savePort);
                (void) OpenDeskAcc(daName);
                SetPort(savePort);
            }
            break;

        case fileID:
            switch (theItem) {
                case quitCommand:
                    DoneFlag = true; break;
                default: break;
            }
            break;

        case editID:
            /*
             * If this is for a 'standard' edit item,
             * run it through SystemEdit first.
             * SystemEdit will return FALSE if it's not a system window.
             */
            if ((theItem <= clearCommand) && SystemEdit(theItem-1)) {
                break;
            }
            /*
             * Otherwise, it's my window.
             * Handle Cut/Copy/Paste properly
             * between the TEScrap and the Clipboard.
             */
            switch (theItem) {
                                case undoCommand:
                                    /* can't undo */
                                    break;
```

continued

```
                              case cutCommand:
                              case copyCommand:
                                      if (theItem == cutCommand) {
                                              TECut (TextH) ;
                                      } else {
                                              TECopy (TextH) ;
                                      }
                                      ZeroScrap () ;
                                      TEToScrap () ;
                                      break;
                              case pasteCommand:
                                      TEFromScrap () ;
                                      TEPaste (TextH) ;
                                      break;
                              case clearCommand:
                                      TEDelete (TextH) ;
                                      break;
                              default:
                                      break;
                      } /*endsw theItem*/
                      break;

              default:
                      break;

      }/*endsw theMenu*/

      HiliteMenu (0) ;

      return;
}
```

Figure 10.12 *Macintosh sample application code*
Copyright Apple Computer, Inc., used by permission

Sun NeWS

NeWS, the Network Extendable Window System, is a window system developed by Sun Microsystems based on PostScript, a standard in page description languages. NeWS is based on the server model of window systems described in Section 10.1, with the window system on the server side of the client/server connection. Even though NeWS was developed by Sun, it is not restricted to their workstations; NeWS servers are also available for the Macintosh, for example.

The PostScript basis for NeWS makes this window system quite different from all others, especially since NeWS extends PostScript to an object-oriented language. Chapter 9 gives reasons why object-oriented languages and systems are particularly well suited for direct manipulation. Object-oriented systems appear frequently in our discussions and clearly represent a critical trend in user interfaces. The extension of PostScript to an object-oriented language is managed through PostScript's dictionary stack mechanism. More information on PostScript is pointed out in the Readings at the end of the chapter.

The use of PostScript has two major implications for NeWS. The simpler and more obvious one is that NeWS uses PostScript to manage its screen output, putting information on the screen through PostScript's stencil-and-paint mechanism. This means that NeWS is device- and resolution-independent, has a complete integration of text and graphics, and has a natural ability to print its screen output. NeWS's color model is 24-bit true color, with the server providing the color requested as best it can.

The second implication is that PostScript is much more subtle as an imaging model, and it is critical to understand this model in order to understand the nature of NeWS. All communication between a NeWS client and its server is carried out in PostScript. This means that a client or any other process, such as an initialization routine, can send new definitions to the server's definition stack, creating new objects, creating subclasses of existing objects, or changing methods on existing objects. NeWS is thus a *programmable* window system.

While NeWS is inherently flexible and does not commit to any particular user interface style, programmability allows a user interface style to be defined within NeWS. For example, NeWS comes with a predefined "lite" toolkit for user interaction functions. This contains the class *Object* with the subclasses:

- *Window*, managing *FrameCanvas*, *ClientCanvas*, and *IconCanvas*,
- *Menu*, associating a string with an action, and
- *Item*, containing the subclass *LabeledItem*, which are user-definable, graphic, interactive, input/output objects; predefined instances of LabeledItem include buttons, sliders, scroll bars, dials, text fields, and message areas.

A client can manage its own user interface or can move user interface functions into the server to whatever extent it desires. A User Interface Management System can also be built that functions entirely in the server and is downloaded to the server by either a remote host or the server's local host. In Figure 10.13 is an example of a small "Hello, World" program in NeWS, courtesy of Jerry Farrell of Sun, which illustrates the nature of the window system. This program puts up a default window on the screen and writes "Hello World" in the window. This default window offers the standard NeWS window handling functions. Both this and a later example are written entirely in PostScript.

NeWS is built on the concept of a *canvas*. A canvas is a single screen area differentiated from others in its input and output; it is the fundamental entity of a screen from the implementor's point of view. The user, however, sees a screen as made up of windows, where each window contains many canvases. There is one canvas for each control or information area in the window, as shown in Figure 10.14.

A NeWS server manages all these canvases and the events that happen through them. Most of the actual work of the server is done by a very large

```
#! /usr/NeWS/bin/psh
% A hello_world with windows & menus.

/TextColor 0 def
/FillColor 1 def
/PaintText {
    FillColor setgray clippath fill
    TextColor setgray 10 10 moveto
    /Times-Bold findfont
        24 scalefont setfont
    (Hello World) show
} def
/SetColors { % txtcolor fillcolor => -
    /FillColor exch store
    /TextColor exch store
    /paintclient win send
} def

/win framebuffer
    /new DefaultWindow send def
{   /FrameLabel (LiteWindow!) def
    /PaintClient {PaintText} def
    /ClientMenu [
    (Black on White)    {0 1 SetColors}
    (White on Black)    {1 0 SetColors}
    (Gray on White)     {.5 1 SetColors}
    (White on Gray)     {1 .5 SetColors}
    ] /new DefaultMenu send def
} win send
/reshapefromuser win send
/map win send
```

Figure 10.13   *The NeWS Hello World*

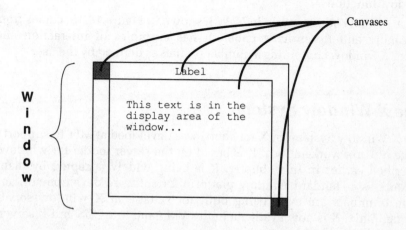

Figure 10.14   *Canvases in a NeWS window*

number of *lightweight processes*, processes that run in a single address space in the server and manage all the server's events and activities. Overall, the server has many of the properties of an operating system, since it contains the window system. It must manage a number of processes per canvas, the window tree (or, more properly for NeWS, the canvas tree), a serialized event queue, and all cut and paste selection data. Each event goes to the topmost window in which the event occurs. If this window has "expressed an interest" in events of this type, the event is handled by the window's processes; if not, the event is passed up the tree to the next window containing the event point. Events are processed from the event queue in lockstep order; any client handling an event is able to lock out all other event handling until it is finished with the current event. Thus, for example, when a window is being moved or resized, other events and activities are held back since they might be confused by having an uncertain image of the screen.

Since NeWS operates with PostScript communication, it might be natural to assume that an application programmer using NeWS must know PostScript. However, this is not the case. For example, the macro capability of C allows a C programmer to use a header file that translates C to PostScript. This header, named *cps*, can completely hide PostScript, but the programmer can move into PostScript as much as is desired. From other languages, NeWS is accessible by preparing a small compiler that translates the language into PostScript.

Sun's current implementation of NeWS is in a merged server, named X11/NeWS, that supports both NeWS and version 11 of the X Window System. While X will probably be a Window System standard, NeWS is healthy and will remain viable. The choice of NeWS or X has something of the status of a religious discussion with few windows programmers being neutral, but both NeWS and X are capable and provide a good set of window functions.

A second code example in NeWS, shown in Figure 10.15, comes from Densmore and Rosenthal's paper. It has examples of interaction and builds a window containing a number of lines as defined by the user.

The X Window System

The X Window System (or X for short) was developed at MIT to support a range of Unix workstations. It is based on the server model for windows described earlier in this chapter. It is being widely accepted by many vendors as a standard window platform for software development, and some terminals are even being built to contain an X window server. Besides Unix, X is now available under VMS and MS-DOS and X servers are available for the Macintosh.

X provides the lowest level of functions on which higher layers of tools and applications are built. It provides window mechanisms, not user

```
#! /usr/NeWS/bin/psh
/fillcanvaswithlines {                                  % linesperside => -
    gsave
    1 fillcanvas                                        % paint the background
    0 setgray                                           % default color is black
    clippath pathbox
    scale pop pop                                       % make coords 0 to 1
    0 1 3 -1 roll div 1 {        % 0 delta 1 {..} for
        ColorDisplay? {dup 1 1 sethsbcolor } if         % change color if needed
        0 0 moveto 1 1 index lineto stroke              % draw line to top
        0 0 moveto 1 lineto stroke                      % draw line to side
        pause                                           % let others on
    } for
    grestore
} def

/main {
    /linesperside 10 def                                % start with 10 lines
    /setlinesfromuser {                                 % value => -
        /linesperside exch store                        % set new value
        /paintclient win send                           % make window repaint
    } def

    /LinesWindow DefaultWindow                          % new subclass of DefaultWindow
    [/LinesCanvas]                                      % instance var: the subwindow
    classbegin                                          % override two methods
        /CreateClientCanvas {                           % this one creates the canvas
            /CreateClientCanvas super send              % do super's create
            /LinesCanvas ClientCanvas
            newcanvas store                             % create a subcanvas
            LinesCanvas /Mapped true put                % map it in
        } def
        /ShapeClientCanvas {                            % this one (re)-shapes it
            /ShapeClientCanvas super send               % do super's shape
            gsave
            ClientCanvas setcanvas clippath             % make path and
            LinesCanvas reshapecanvas                   % reshape lines canvas
            grestore
        } def
    classend def                                        % call new class LinesWindow

    /win framebuffer /new LinesWindow send def          % make a new LinesWindow
    {
        /FrameLabel (Lines) def                         % Label it Lines
        /PaintClient {                                  % PaintClient method
            LinesCanvas setcanvas                       % fills LinesCanvas
            linesperside fillcanvaswithlines             %  with linesperside lines
            FrameBorderColor strokecanvas               % and draws a box
        } def
        /PaintIcon {                                    % PaintIcon method
            10 fillcanvaswithlines 0 strokecanvas       % uses 10 lines
        } def
        /ClientMenu                                     % the menu sets linesperside
        [(10) (20) (100) (250) (500)]
        [{currentkey cvi setlinesfromuser}]
        /new DefaultMenu send def
    } win s                                             % override the methods
    /reshapefromuser win send                           % shape the window
    /map win send                                       % Map it in
} def

main
```

Figure 10.15 *NeWS interaction code example*

interface policy. The team developing X formulated several requirements for a base window system that are met by X, given in Schiefler and Gettys. These requirements are listed below.

- The system should be implementable on a variety of displays. For X, this means bitmapped displays with a pointer device, though support for additional input devices is being developed.
- Applications must be device independent. It should be unnecessary to touch application code to use a new hardware display.
- The system must be network transparent. An application running on one machine must be able to use a display on another machine with a different operating system or architecture.
- The system must support multiple applications displaying concurrently. It must be truly multitasking.
- The system should be capable of supporting many different applications and management interfaces. It should allow different interfaces for different tasks and should support the evolution of user interface capabilities.
- The system must support overlapping windows, including output to partially obscured windows.
- The system should support a hierarchy of resizable windows, and an application should be able to use many windows at once. Subwindows provide an important mechanism for exporting basic system information back to the application.
- The system should provide high-performance, high-quality support for text, two-dimensional synthetic graphics, and imaging. The application must describe the image precisely, and the system does not try to second-guess the application.
- The system should be extendable. For example, it should be possible to extend the system to support three-dimensional graphics.

In its basic form, the X Window System with the standard Xlib library is not an easy system for building applications. It has been called the Unix of window systems, built by hackers for hackers. An application at this level must manage the entire X system. This includes explicitly creating all the windows necessary, communicating with the system for all events, and handling them in a main event loop. This particularly involves handling "expose" events caused by any change in the way windows are displayed on the screen. These events require repainting one or more screen areas, as shown in Figure 10.16.

An example of a minimal application at this level is given by the "Hello, World" program in Figure 10.17 from Jones and Hersch. This application sets up a connection to the workstation, creates a top-level window, sets standard properties for window managers, creates X resources as graphics contexts (GC's), selects input events, maps the window, reads and interprets input events, generates graphical output, and shuts down when the application is complete.

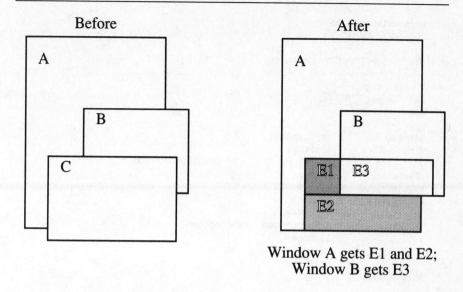

Window A gets E1 and E2;
Window B gets E3

Figure 10.16 *Areas exposed by a window removal*

X is a complex system with many details and concepts to be mastered. A brief summary of some of these serves to introduce some X ideas. First, when we speak of a window in X, we do not mean only the relatively large screen area including the output area, title, scroll bars, and other special areas. Each special area is actually a separate window to X, a subwindow of the main area, and the way X detects window control events is to recognize which subwindow the event occurs in. It is not unusual for a screen to contain over 100 windows at one time.

Second, windows in X can select the events they will recognize, passing along other events to the window below them on the screen. This mechanism supports the one-window-per-control concept above. It also allows a window to specify whether it will accept a "cursor enters the window" event to assert its ownership of the text input focus, or whether it requires a more explicit event such as a "mouse button press in window" to take the focus. This allows X to support both *real-estate* focus (focus is wherever the cursor is) and *listener* focus (focus is in the last window to take a mouse button click), respectively.

Third, all screen output is bitmapped. All output goes to the graphics context (GC) that is created for the window. Text is output via bitmapped fonts, of which there are a wide variety, and graphics is supported by fairly standard kinds of line, curve, and area primitives that are translated into bitmapped operations. Bitmaps (or, in color, pixmaps) are available for several functions, including drawing primitives, window backgrounds and borders, clip masks, and cursor sources. X uses RGB colors as in Chapter 8, but its color output model depends on the workstations capabilities; both true color and color lookup tables are supported.

```
#include <X11/Xlib.h>
#include <X11/Xutil.h>

char hello[] = {"Hello, World."}, hi[] = {"Hi!"};

main( argc, argv )
    int   argc;
    char  **argv;
{
    Display         *mydisplay;
    Window          mywindow;
    GC              mygc;                 /* graphics context */
    XEvent          myevent;
    KeySym          mykey;
    XSizeHints      myhint;
    int             myscreen;
    unsigned long   myforeground, mybackground;
    int             i, done;
    char            text[10];
/*
 *  initialization
 */
    mydisplay = XOpenDisplay("");
    myscreen = DefaultScreen( mydisplay );
    mybackground = WhitePixel( mydisplay, myscreen );
    myforeground = BlackPixel( mydisplay, myscreen );
    myhint.x = 200;              /* values are in pixels */
    myhint.y = 300;
    myhint.width = 350;
    myhint.height = 250;
    myhint.flags = PPosition | PSize;
    mywindow = XCreateSimpleWindow(mydisplay,
              DefaultRootWindow(mydisplay),myhint.x,myhint.y,
              myhint.width,myhint.height,5,mybackground,myforeground);
              /* 5 is the pixel width of the window border */
    XSetStandardProperties(mydisplay,mywindow,hello,hello,None,
    argv,argc,&myhint);
    mygc = XCreateGC(mydisplay,mywindow,0,0);
    /*window created here*/
    XSetForeground(mydisplay,mygc,mybackground);
    XSetBackground(mydisplay,mygc,myforeground);
    XSelectInput(mydisplay,mywindow,
              ButtonPressMask|KeyPressMask|ExposureMask);
    XMapWindow(mydisplay,mywindow);       /* makes the window visible */
/*
 *  Main event-reading loop
 */
    done = 0;
    while (done == 0) {
        XNextEvent(mydisplay, &myevent);
        switch (myevent.type) {
            case Expose:                 /* repaint window on expose events */
                if (myevent.xexpose.count == 0)
                    XDrawImageString(mydisplay,mywindow,
                        mygc,50,50,hello,strlen(hello));
                break;
```

continued

```
            case MappingNotify:        /* process kbd mapping changes */
                XRefreshKeyboardMapping( &myevent );
                break;
            case ButtonPress:          /* process mouse-button presses */
                XDrawImageString(mydisplay,mywindow,mygc,
                        myevent.xbutton.x,myevent.xbutton.y,hi,
                        strlen(hi));
                break;
            case KeyPress:             /* process keyboard input */
                i = XLookupString(&myevent,text,10,&mykey,0);
                if ((i==1) && (text[0]=='q')) done = 1;
                break;
        }   /* switch */
    }       /* while */
/*
 *   Terminate
 */
    XFreeGC(mywindow,mygc);
    XDestroyWindow(mydisplay,mywindow);
    XCloseDisplay(mydisplay);
    exit(0);
}
```

Figure 10.17   *An X "Hello, World"*

Finally, X manages much of its operations through *resources*. These include windows, graphics contexts, pixmaps, cursors, fonts, and the like. They are created in the server and, when created, return a 29-bit resource identifier to the client. A resource is ephemeral and inexpensive and can be shared by several different clients.

As we noted above, few application programmers using X are expected to work with the basic system. Instead, X supports a number of toolkits and window managers. These two ideas need to be distinguished. A *window manager* is essentially a client program that handles resources and window adornments; at this time, the *uwm* manager is most widely used. On the other hand, a *window toolkit* is a library of prebuilt window operations that can be used by the programmer to implement an application's user interface; it can also support a given look and feel for an application. At this writing, Xtk (the standard X toolkit), Andrew, and Open Dialogue are available toolkits for X, and Open Look implements specific look and feel models for X. Figure 10.18, from Rosenthal, shows the code for a "Hello, World" application written using Xtk.

```
#include <stdio.h>
#include <X11/Xlib.h>
#include <X11/Intrinsic.h>
#include <X11/Atoms.h>
#include <X11/Label.h>

#define STRING   "Hello, World"

Arg wargs[] = {
    XtNlabel, (XtArgVal) STRING,
};

main(argc,argv)
    int argc;
    char **argv;
{

    Widget   toplevel, label;

    /*
     *  Create the Widget that represents the window.
     */
    toplevel = XtInitialize(argv[0],"Xlabel",NULL,0,&argc,argv);

    /*
     *  Create a Widget to display the string, using wargs to set
     *  the string as its value.
     */
    label = XtCreateWidget(argv[0],labelWidgetClass,toplevel,wargs,
                                           XtNumber(wargs));

    /*
     *  Tell the toplevel widget to display the label.
     */
    XtManageChild(label);

    /*
     *  Create the windows, and set their attributes according to the
     *  Widget data.
     */
    XtRealizeWidget(toplevel);

    /*
     *  Now process the events.
     */
    XtMainLoop();
}
```

Figure 10.18   *An X "Hello, World" with the Xtk toolkit*

Copyright Sun Microsystems, Inc., used by permission

The Xtk toolkit is object-oriented, is written in C, and provides the basic definition of a widget, or user interface abstraction object. It is designed to promote user interface innovation, to facilitate the sharing of user interface ideas, and to separate the form of a user interface from its function.

It is clear that X will be the basis for many applications' user interfaces, but it itself is going through further development. The graphics model is being extended in several ways, including three-dimensional graphics support. A leading candidate for future three-dimensional graphics in X is PEX, PHIGS Extensions to X, and two-dimensional graphics using Display PostScript is also being developed. Additional toolkits are also being developed and will probably continue to do so as new things are learned about the ways computers and people work together.

10.3   User Interface Management Systems

A great deal of development effort in the user interface area has gone into developing and building user interface management systems. While these have a wide range of functions and operations, we use the following as a working definition of a UIMS:

> *A UIMS provides prepackaged interaction support allowing a designer to build the presentation and interaction for an application along consistent lines. It usually passes its details to lower-level software such as a windowing system to carry out the display and event handling it requires.*

Since the UIMS carries the presentation and interaction for the application, it is responsible for the "look and feel" of the application. It thus allows designers to create a consistent interface across a range of applications. It also allows the programmer to separate the user interface function from the application code for a program, to change the user interface design easily in the development process, and to support the training process for the user.

One very important function of a UIMS is to implement the dialog structure, or syntax, of the interface. It analyzes user actions, calls the appropriate application routines, displays the application output, and displays the user interaction options available for the application at any time. As its name implies, it manages the user interface as it is defined by the designer and implemented by the programmer.

A UIMS is usually presented as a software toolkit with functions that can be called by the programmer, keyed to a particular language and often to a particular computing system or family. One problem with these systems traditionally has been strong system-dependence. Future UIMS's will give the system designer an expanded range of support functions. This will include an expanded widget toolbox with an extensive collection of powerful widgets, improved image generation support well beyond the level of the GKS standard, support for very general cut and paste and UNDO, context-sensitive help, and the ability to maintain user profiles and tailor the user interface presentation to the user's preferences.

With all the tools provided by a full-function UIMS, it is possible to bring a real multidisciplinary team to the process of building software. We suggest the importance of this team in Chapter 1, but it is imperative here. This team includes an application specialist, who understands the application area thoroughly, who knows something of computers' capabilities, and who defines what the interface is to do, though possibly not how to do it. It also includes a graphic designer, who understands the use of line, color, shape, pattern, and the like, who may know very little of computers, and who designs the visual aspects of the interface. The team must include an applications programmer, who knows something of the application and has computational skills in the area, and who implements the noninterface parts of the application programming. All this is pulled together by the interface programmer, who is skilled in the tools of interface design and prototyping, understands how to present the model and metaphor of the application to the user, can direct the testing of prototypes with end user groups, and who implements the actual software interface with the tools available.

In the sections below we describe some commercial UIMS's, describing (as applicable) the kinds of presentation and interaction they support, their platforms and languages, and the kind of screens they present. These systems vary widely in both style and function, since the role of UIMS is not so well defined as that of a programming language. Some code examples are included so you can get an idea of working with the system. Our inclusion of the UIMS's in this section is not in any way an endorsement of these products nor a statement of their suitability for any particular project. This is certainly far from a complete list. As much as anything else, these UIMS selections are here to help the reader get a feeling for the high-function user interface tools now available to support the software developer. Many of these UIMS's are in a state of flux; their final look has not yet been defined or they are still being ported to new systems.

MacApp

There are many ways to write programs for the Macintosh; many languages and programming environments have been developed for it. Yet, the Macintosh retains the reputation of requiring unusual effort to develop software. This is largely due to the complexity of writing for a system that includes so much functionality in its kernel and so many details in its interface specification. The main event loop presented in the discussion of the Macintosh toolbox above is an indication of the complexity of managing all your own events.

Fortunately, there is a Macintosh programming and development system that makes it unnecessary for a programmer to deal with most of the Macintosh toolbox routines for fundamental program operations, such as the main event loop, and for user interface operations, such as menus, windows, and dialog boxes. This system is named MacApp, "The Expandable Macintosh Application." MacApp is written in Object Pascal, an extension of standard Pascal to an object-oriented language that requires the Macintosh Programmer's Workshop (MPW) system for programming support. MacApp is also accessible from the MPW assembler and is expected to have C++ and Smalltalk support as well. Object-oriented systems are mentioned briefly in Chapter 3, at more length in Chapter 9, and in the discussion of Microsoft Windows. See the Readings section at the end of Chapter 9 for more pointers.

MacApp is a user interface management system since it is responsible for packaging interaction and presentation for its applications. It is built directly on the Macintosh toolbox ROM routines. MacApp rigorously enforces the standard style of Macintosh user interface presentation and communication. In this, it clearly belongs in the dictatorial group of user interface systems, but Macintosh users want consistency more than innovation in their program interfaces.

Programming with the MacApp application is somewhat unusual. It has, in fact, two main features: programming by cut-and-paste and programming by example. The application comes with a number of sample programs from which you can assemble interface operations and the beginning of your function, and in which you can find many examples of working code similar to what you need. You need write from scratch only the code specific to your application. Besides providing so much function so easily, the MacApp examples have a startling effect on a programmer's learning curve; the initial lag is dramatically shortened. It seems as though MacApp reinforces the idea of recognition memory being much more powerful than recall memory.

The example presented in this section presents two dialog boxes. It has many of the features you expect to have in a Macintosh application: a working menu bar with pulldown windows, an "About" box, proper handling of desk accessories, and the text entry function to allow standard editing. However, since it presents only dialog boxes instead of full windows, it does not have window moving, sizing, scrolling, closing, or zooming. Windows with these functions are not much more difficult, and examples of these operations are included with the MacApp package.

The example code is shown in Figure 10.19. It includes five files:

- TwoDialogs.make   the make file for the application
- TwoDialogs.r   the resource file for the application
- TwoDialogs.p   the entire (five lines!) main program for the application
- UTwoDialogs.inc1.p   the implementation part of the application library unit, spelling out the application's special methods
- UTwoDialogs.p   the interface part of the application library unit

```
File TwoDialogs.make

AppName = TwoDialogs
Creator = 'RSC1'
NeededSysLibs =  ∂
            "{Libraries}RunTime.o"  ∂
            "{Libraries}Interface.o"  ∂
            "{PLibraries}PasLib.o"
BuildingBlockIntf = "{SrcMacApp}UDialog.p"
BuildingBlockObjs = "{SrcMacApp}UDialog.p.o"
OtherInterfaces =
OtherLinkFiles =
OtherSegMappings =
OtherRezFiles =
OtherRsrcFiles = "{RezMacApp}Dialog.rsrc"
```

```
File TwoDialogs.r

/* Modified from MacApp's DemoDialogs sample program. */

include MacAppRFiles"MacApp.rsrc";
include MacAppRFiles"Dialog.rsrc";

include "TwoDialogs" 'CODE';

resource 'DLOG' (1501, purgeable) {
    {100, 150, 200, 350},
    dBoxProc, invisible, noGoAway, 0x0, 1501, "" };

resource 'DLOG' (1502, purgeable) {
    {50, 70, 210, 432},
    dBoxProc, invisible, noGoAway, 0x0, 1502, "" };

resource 'DITL' (201, purgeable) {          /* About box */
    { /* array DITLarray: 3 elements */
        /* [1] */ {130, 182, 150, 262},
        Button { enabled, "OK" };
        /* [2] */ {10, 80, 110, 270},
        StaticText { disabled,
            "Demonstration of two simple dial"
            "og boxes for Brown and Cunningha"
            "m, Programming the User Interfac"
            "e: Principles and Examples"    };
        /* [3] */ {10, 20, 42, 52},
        Icon { disabled, 1 }
    }
};

resource 'DITL' (1501, purgeable) {          /* warning dialog */
    { /* array DITLarray: 3 elements */
        /* [1] */ {60, 60, 80, 140},
        Button { enabled, "OK" };
```

continued

```
        /* [2] */ {15, 70, 30, 130},
        StaticText { disabled, "Warning Text" };
        /* [3] */ {0, 0, 0, 0},
        UserItem { disabled }
    }
};

resource 'DITL' (1502, purgeable) {          /* text dialog */
    {  /* array DITLarray: 5 elements */
        /* [1] */ {120, 60, 140, 140},
        Button { enabled, "OK" };
        /* [2] */ {120, 190, 140, 270},
        Button { enabled, "Cancel" };
        /* [3] */ {16, 60, 30, 140},
        StaticText { disabled, "Prompt:" };
        /* [4] */ {16, 150, 30, 270},
        EditText { enabled, "Default value" };
        /* [5] */ {0, 0, 0, 0},
        UserItem { disabled }
    }
};

resource 'ALRT' (201, purgeable) {
    {90, 100, 250, 412},
    201, {
        OK, visible, silent;
        OK, visible, silent;
        OK, visible, silent;
        OK, visible, silent      }
};

resource 'SIZE' (-1) {
    saveScreen, acceptSuspendResumeEvents, doOwnActivate,
    128 * 1024, 96 * 1024
};

resource 'cmnu' (1) {               /* apple symbol pulldown menu */
    1, textMenuProc, 0x7FFFFFFD, enabled, apple,
    {   /* array: 2 elements */
        /* [1] */ "About TwoDialogs…",
                    noIcon, noKey, noMark, plain, cAboutApp;
        /* [2] */ "-", noIcon, noKey, noMark, plain, nocommand
    }
};

resource 'cmnu' (2) {               /* File pulldown menu */
    2, textMenuProc, allEnabled, enabled, "File",
    {   /* array: 2 elements */
        /* [1] */ "Close", noIcon, noKey, noMark, plain, cClose;
        /* [2] */ "Quit", noIcon, `Q`, noMark, plain, cQuit
    }
};

resource 'cmnu' (3) {               /* Edit pulldown menu */
```

continued

```
    3, textMenuProc, 0x7FFFFEBD, enabled, "Edit",
    {    /* array: 10 elements */
         /* [1] */ "Undo", noIcon, "Z", noMark, plain, cUndo;
         /* [2] */ "-", noIcon, noKey, noMark, plain, nocommand;
         /* [3] */ "Cut", noIcon, "X", noMark, plain, cCut;
         /* [4] */ "Copy", noIcon, "C", noMark, plain, cCopy;
         /* [5] */ "Paste", noIcon, "V", noMark, plain, cPaste;
         /* [6] */ "Clear", noIcon, noKey, noMark, plain, cClear;
         /* [7] */ "-", noIcon, noKey, noMark, plain, nocommand;
         /* [8] */ "Select All", noIcon, "A", noMark, plain, cSelectAll;
         /* [9] */ "-", noIcon, noKey, noMark, plain, nocommand;
         /* [10] */ "Show Clipboard", noIcon, noKey, noMark, plain,
                          cShowClipboard
    }
};

resource 'cmnu' (4) {                    /* Dialogs pulldown menu */
    4, textMenuProc, allEnabled, enabled, "Dialogs",
     {   /* array: 2 elements */
         /* [1] */ "Warning Dialog", noIcon, "1", noMark, plain, 1501;
         /* [2] */ "Text Entry Dialog", noIcon, "2", noMark, plain, 1502
     }
};

resource 'MBAR' (128) {                  /* menu bar */
    {1; 2; 3; 4}
};
```

```
File MTwoDialogs.p

{ Modified from MacApp's DemoDialogs sample program }

PROGRAM TwoDialogs;

USES
    {$LOAD MacIntf.LOAD}
        MemTypes, QuickDraw, OSIntf, ToolIntf, PackIntf,
    {$LOAD UMacApp.LOAD}
        UObject, UList, UMacApp,
    {$LOAD}

    UDialog,
    UTwoDialogs;

VAR
    gTwoDialogsApplication: TTwoDialogsApplication;

BEGIN
    InitToolbox(8);
    InitUDialog;
    New(gTwoDialogsApplication);
    gTwoDialogsApplication.ITwoDialogsApplication;
    gTwoDialogsApplication.Run;
END.
```

---

continued

```
File UTwoDialogs.incl.p

{ Modified from MacApp's DemoDialogs sample program }

CONST
    kStaggerAmount      = 16;

VAR
    {Global variables used with the test Dialogs}
        gMarginSetting, gStaggerCount:      INTEGER;
        gDialogRecord: DialogRecord;
        {Global modal-dialog storage; only one of these is needed}

    PROCEDURE  TTwoDialogsApplication.ITwoDialogsApplication;
    BEGIN
        IApplication('RSC1');

        {Initialize global variables used in the demonstration dialogs}
        gMarginSetting := 6;
        gStaggerCount := 0;
    END;

    PROCEDURE  TTwoDialogsApplication.PoseDialog(aCmdNumber:CmdNumber);
        CONST   kStartTxtItem   =   4;
        VAR aDialogView: TDialogView;
            aRadioCluster:    TRadioCluster;
            hitItem:          INTEGER;
            someText:         Str255;
            inputItem:        TNumberText;

    BEGIN
        New(aDialogView);
        FailNIL(aDialogView);    { Handle failure if unable to allocate }

        IF aCmdNumber = cDialog1 THEN BEGIN
            aDialogView.IDialogView(NIL, @gDialogRecord,
                aCmdNumber, 3 {hookItem}, 1 {dfltButton}, TRUE);
            {initialize it from resource file}
                { 3 is the 'hook item' the user provides in the dialog
                    item list
                  1 is the item number of the Default Button ("OK") in
                    the dialog item list}
            {display dialog and interact with user}
            aDialogView.TalkToUser(hitItem, StdItemHandling);
                {This puts up the modal dialog which interacts with the
                    user; control does not return until the user has
                    dismissed the dialog}
            { IF hitItem = ok THEN; User hit "OK" button; finish}
            END
        ELSE {cDialog2} BEGIN
            aDialogView.IDialogView(NIL, @gDialogRecord,
                aCmdNumber, 5 {hookItem}, 1 {dflt button}, TRUE);
                {initialize it from resource file}
                { 5 is the 'hook item' the user provides in the dialog
                    item list
```

continued

```
                    1 is the item number of the Default Button in the dialog
                        item list}
            aDialogView.SetEditSelection(kStartTxtItem);
                    {results in a SELECT ALL on item number kStartTxtItem
                        as the initial condition}
            aDialogView.TalkToUser(hitItem, StdItemHandling);
                {This puts up the modal dialog which interacts with the
                    user; control does not return until the user has
                    dismissed the dialog}
            IF hitItem = ok THEN {User dismissed the dialog by hitting
                    the OK button; report results}
                aDialogView.RetrieveText(kStartTxtItem, someText);
            END;
        aDialogView.Free;
    END;


    FUNCTION TTwoDialogsApplication.DoMenuCommand(aCmdNumber:CmdNumber):
        TCommand;
    BEGIN
        DoMenuCommand := gNoChanges;
        IF (aCmdNumber = cDialog1) OR (aCmdNumber = cDialog2) THEN
            PoseDialog(aCmdNumber)
        ELSE
            DoMenuCommand := INHERITED DoMenuCommand(aCmdNumber);
    END;


    PROCEDURE TTwoDialogsApplication.DoSetupMenus;
    BEGIN
        INHERITED DoSetupMenus;

        Enable(cDialog1, TRUE);
        Enable(cDialog2, TRUE);
    END;


    PROCEDURE TTwoDialogsApplication.HandleFinderRequest; OVERRIDE;
    BEGIN
        {We override this with an empty method since we want to do NOTHING,
            rather than launch a blank document, when the application is
            opened}
    END;
```

```
File UTwoDialogs.p

{ Modified from MacApp's DemoDialogs sample program }

UNIT UTwoDialogs;

INTERFACE

USES
    {$LOAD MacIntf.LOAD}
        MemTypes, QuickDraw, OSIntf, ToolIntf, PackIntf,
    {$LOAD UMacApp.LOAD}
        UObject, UList, UMacApp,
    {$LOAD}
    UDialog;
```

continued

```
CONST

    {Command numbers — one for each of the two kinds of dialogs that can be
      requested by the user in the "Dialogs" menu}

      cDialog1          = 1501; {the command to put up the Warning dialog}
      cDialog2          = 1502; {the command to put up the Text Entry dialog}

TYPE

    TTwoDialogsApplication = OBJECT(TApplication)

      PROCEDURE TTwoDialogsApplication.ITwoDialogsApplication;
          {Initialize the application}

      PROCEDURE TTwoDialogsApplication.HandleFinderRequest; OVERRIDE;
          {Since this application has no documents, the generic
              HandleFinderRequest is overridden by this empty method,
              in order that no attempt be made to launch a blank
              document when the application's icon is opened}

      FUNCTION  TTwoDialogsApplication.DoMenuCommand
              (aCmdNumber: CmdNumber):   TCommand; OVERRIDE;
          {The menu commands are the 2 requests for dialogs in the
              'Dialogs' menu}

      PROCEDURE TTwoDialogsApplication.DoSetupMenus; OVERRIDE;
          {Arms the menu commands handled by DoMenuCommand}

      PROCEDURE TTwoDialogsApplication.PoseDialog
              (aCmdNumber: CmdNumber);
          {Put up modal dialogs on request}

      END;

IMPLEMENTATION

{$I UTwoDialogs.incl.p}

END.
```

Figure 10.19 *MacApp TwoDialogs code*

It is worth noting that this program was created in only a couple of hours from a sample MacApp program by a programmer with no previous Macintosh programming experience.

The windows put up by this program are standard-style Macintosh windows, handled from a standard menu bar by standard mouse techniques. These windows are shown in Figure 10.20.

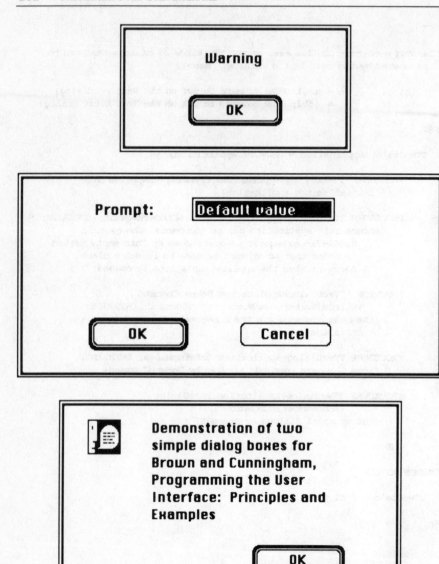

Figure 10.20   *The Warning, Text, and About windows*

It is beyond the scope of this book to do much more with MacApp. However, a summary of the way MacApp organizes program windows is appropriate.

MacApp builds a hierarchy of objects in its environment, as shown in Figure 10.21. The responsibility of handling various event and program functions are as follows:

- The *View* draws a representation of the document and responds to certain mouse gestures.
- The *Frame* handles scroll bars, mouse tracking, zooming and reducing, and the like.
- The *Window* manages moving, scaling, and closing, and contains frames.
- The *Document* handles its menus and windows, handles disk I/O, and handles changes to data.
- The *Application* handles the main event loop, manages windows and documents, and handles printing.

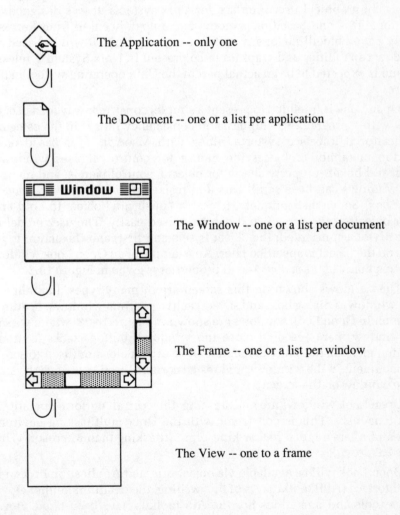

The Application -- only one

The Document -- one or a list per application

The Window -- one or a list per document

The Frame -- one or a list per window

The View -- one to a frame

Figure 10.21 *The MacApp hierarchy*

Since all these are represented by formal MacApp objects with built-in methods, the programmer need only specify actions that differ from or are not among the standard ones. For some objects such as windows, the exact nature of tools available for the object is specified in the resource file. The main things for a programmer to define are the structure of a document, the layout of frames, the way the document is to be presented in a view, and editing methods on the document's data. Indeed, even editing procedures are supported in MacApp, including Undo/Redo, probably the hardest user interface problem in general.

Open Look

Open Look is a new user interface technology designed to present a consistent graphical user interface for Unix systems. It was designed by Sun for AT&T and based on window technology licensed from Xerox—surely a good bloodline for any system involving Unix. It will be based on window capabilities and graphics to be present in Unix System V release 4.0 and is expected to be an actual part of the Unix operating system in the future.

Open Look is intended to present a simple, consistent way for a user to work with a program. Its emphasis on consistency puts it in the category of dictatorial interface systems, along with MacApp. It is based on a desktop metaphor and uses the mouse for control. It uses windows, command boxes, property sheets for objects, control panels, and menus. The windows can have scroll bars and resize boxes; they always have a close box. Somewhat uniquely, it uses a "push pin" object to hold any other object on the screen so it can be reused easily. The user model is basically object-oriented; the object is selected first, and the action to be done on the object is specified later. An example of an Open Look window showing many of these objects and properties is given in Figure 10.22.

The windows shown on this screen are of many types, including a help window, a dialog box, and several active program windows. Features common in Open Look windows are shown in Figure 10.23, where we see the window mark (used to close the window), button stacks (buttons opening menus), buttons (no menu is present), an elevator (used to scroll the document in the window), and resize corners (used to change the size of the window on the screen).

Open Look windows are multitasking; they can all perform operations simultaneously. This is consistent with the Unix multitasking environment and offers a much higher kind of multitasking than Microsoft Windows 2.0 provides.

Open Look will be available via object-oriented Application Programmer Interface (API) toolkits. As of this writing, the details of neither Open Look's tools and operations nor the API toolkits have been fixed. However, two toolkits will be provided initially, one based on the X Window System and one on the Sun X11/NeWS system.

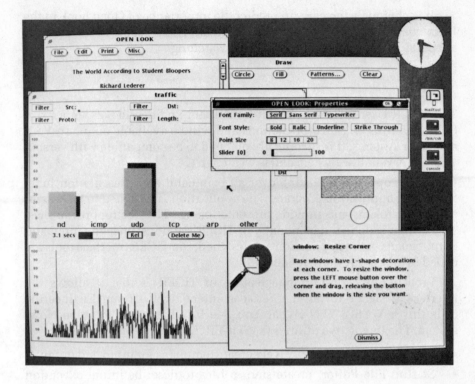

Figure 10.22   *An Open Look screen*

Courtesy of AT&T and Sun Microsystems, Inc.

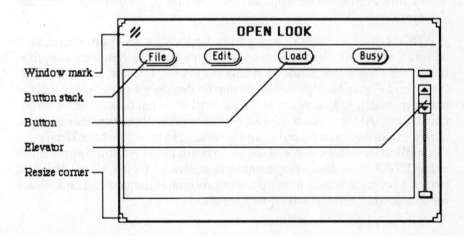

Figure 10.23   *The parts of an Open Look window*

It is obviously too early to predict the importance of Open Look in the Unix community, but its potential is great. There seems to be industry support for this system, and it will bear watching.

TIGER

The TIGER User Interface Toolkit from Team Engineering of Santa Cruz, California runs on Sun workstations and will be available on micro-VAX and other systems. It is specifically planned to be compatible with version 11 of the X Window System and is written in C.

TIGER operates by taking over all command and presentation functions of an application program. The application is designed to take input as a list of tokens and provide presentation via TIGER support routines. This design is done independently of TIGER's actions; once the input and output needs of the application are designed, the TIGER interface tools are called in to provide these functions.

Probably the most unique feature of TIGER is that it allows the interface designer to build interfaces interactively. Team Engineering calls this a WYSIWYPN (What You See Is What You Prototype Now) system. The interactive utilities that TIGER includes are as follows:

- Template Editor: interactively create templates for input and output,
- Startup File Editor: create startup files to describe initial execution environment,
- Icon Editor: create or modify icons,
- Font Editor: create or modify fonts,
- Symbol Definition Editor: draw a symbol and define its macros, and
- Picture Editor: create and edit picture files to be displayed and manipulated.

TIGER does not enforce any particular look for its applications, so it offers a flexible interface look as opposed to a uniform look across applications. It manages five kinds of events: KeyPress, Locator, Menu, Symbol Input, and Figure Manipulation, giving the designer a sound set of tools to use in interaction. Events are buffered until an event occurs which terminates input. At this time the input is processed with history substitution, macro expansion, and scanning and screening to produce the token list for the application. An example of the main event loop for a small application using TIGER from Team Engineering is shown in Figure 10.24. This is a part of a program which puts up a window containing a menu and allows menu selection and the subsequent action.

```
# include "tiger.h"
#define KADD     400
#define KDELETE  401
#define KPRINT   402
#define KFIND    403
#define KQUIT    404

static int tupleLib = 0;

void main()
{
    token   tokList, lastTok;
    char    *s;
    char    mesg[MAX_STRING_LEN];

    /* Initialize tiger, keywords, dictionaries, windows */
    TigStartupTiger["tuple.startup"];
    /* Initialize local data for this program */
    InitDatabase();
    while ( 1 == 1 ) {
        s = AwaitInput(&tokList,&lastTok);/* wait for processed user input*/
        switch( tokList->type ) {
            case KADD:      DoAddCommand( tokList ); break;
            case KDELETE:   DoDeleteCommand( tokList ); break;
            case KPRINT:    DoPrintCommand(); break;
            case KFIND:     DoFindCommand( tokList ); break;
            case KQUIT:     exit(0);
            default:        sprintf( mesg,"Unknown Command: %s",tokList->str);
                            ErrorMesg( mesg );
                            break;
        }
        /* deallocate sortage allocated by AwaitInput */
        free( s );
        DisposeTokList( &tokList );
    }
}
```

Figure 10.24   *A TIGER main event loop*

Courtesy of Team Engineering, Inc.

Overall, the TIGER input management routines support a good collection of user input routines, including graphic menus, dialogue template management, macro expansion, graphic symbol macros, figure manipulation, program input history, input redirection, macro dictionaries, and input command separation. The result is a flexible, usable UIMS with an emphasis on going from interactive prototyping to the running application quickly and easily.

iCpak 201

iCpak 201 is a collection of objects in Objective-C, an object-oriented version of the C language. These objects allow programmers to add an iconic multi-window user interface to applications written for various workstations, including Sun, Apollo, DEC VAX, and Hewlett-Packard 9000. They are implemented either directly on low-level graphics routines or on a windowing system.

iCpak 201 does not provide a fixed look for applications. Instead, its building blocks can be assembled as the programmer wants. The warning window we describe for other systems is a simple instance of the Prompter class in iCpak 201, and the text input window is an instance of the StringEdit class. Menus are as easy; to create a File menu with two choices, New and Open, and make it a popup window, you need only the four lines of code in Figure 10.25.

The object orientation of the system makes it easy to define the features of objects such as windows; for example, to add vertical and horizontal scroll bars to a window takes only the four lines of code in Figure 10.26. Of course, it is easy to see how you can place window features wherever you should like. Moreover, an iCpak 201 window can easily have a familiar look, as shown by the StdSysLayer window shown in Figure 10.27 with a title, close box, vertical and horizontal scroll bars, and a resize box.

```
menuModel = [Menu str: "File"];
[menuModel append: [Menu str:"New" selector: @selector(new)]];
[menuModel append: [Menu str:"Open" selector: @selector(open)]];
myPopUpMenu = [PopUpMenu createInterfaceFor:menuModel];
```

Figure 10.25   *iCpak 201 popup window definition*
Courtesy of Stepstone Corporation

```
vScrollBar = [ScrollBar verticalInterfaceFor: aWindow];
[vScrollBar attachTo: aWindow at: topRightCorner];
hScrollBar = [ScrollBar horizontalInterfaceFor: aWindow];
[hScrollBar attachTo: aWindow at: lowerLeftCorner];
```

Figure 10.26   *Adding scroll bars to a window*
Courtesy of Stepstone Corporation

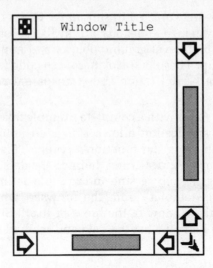

Figure 10.27   *A StdSysLayer window in iCpak 201*

Courtesy of Stepstone Corporation

Actor

Actor is an object-oriented language for MS-DOS systems that uses Microsoft Windows for its windowing functions. Its syntax is based on Pascal and C. Actor combines the two most important user interface advances of the late 1980's: object-oriented programming and window systems. This combination makes it an important and unique tool for software development in the MS-DOS world.

The Actor system, however, is more than just a language. It includes the concept of a system workspace with a browser and inspector similar to those in Smalltalk. It also includes automatic memory management and garbage collection, as well as an application profiler. Actor also offers incremental compilation as its code is written, as well as when information is entered at runtime. This shows the language author's roots in Forth, though the Actor language itself shows no trace of Forth syntax or semantics.

Actor's object structures are not precisely the same as Microsoft Windows', although Actor can call Windows functions (Call) and send Windows messages directly. Standard Actor objects include dialog boxes, controls, and several pre-defined kinds of windows. In the example of Figure 10.28, the GraphWindow class is a descendent of the standard class Window, while the dialog box in which a function is entered is an instance of the InputDialog window class.

On an MS-DOS machine, Actor requires 640K of memory, a mouse, a graphics display, and a hard disk. Actor 1.2 supports LIM extended memory, which gives the user up to 500K for an application. Future versions of Actor are expected to run under OS/2, Unix, and the Macintosh operating system. Extensions are available or planned in several areas, including high-level graphic objects and application frameworks, similar to MacApp. These will isolate source code from specific window managers and make application code transparent across a range of systems.

We illustrate Actor with a complete example taken from the Whitewater Group. This application allows a user to enter a function of one variable and then plots the function's graph. This involves creating a subclass of the class Windows and defining the data and methods for this subclass. In Actor, the subclassing and variable definition are made in the "Class Definition" template from the browser, while the methods are entered in the edit window of the browser itself. Since we cannot illustrate this process here, we list the data and method definitions in Figure 10.28.

```
/*  Data definitions for the class GraphWindow */

    start,          /* starting axis value for both X and Y axes */
    stop            /* ending axis value for both X and Y axes */
    increment,      /* step level for evaluation by function */
    precision,      /* scale factor used for converting values to integers
                                                     for plotting */
    X,              /* variable to hold value to be evaluated */
    last_FX,        /* last value of the evaluated expression */
    border,         /* value which inflates window to put border around the
                                                               graph */
    hdc,            /* handle to a MS-Windows display context */
    cBuf,           /* buffer to hold the evaluated expression */
    aParser,        /* the parser which evaluates the expression */
    txt             /* hold expression to be drawn */

/*  Methods for the Graph Window application */

Def init(self)  /* set initial parameters of size and scale */
{   start        := -5;
    stop         := 5;
    increment    := 0.02;
    border       := 1.04;
    last_FX      := 0;
    X            := 0;
    txt          := "5*sin(X)";
    cBuf         := new(Function, 200);
    aParser      := copy(Parser);
    aParser.lex  := new(ActorAnalyzer);
    init(aParser);
    createMenu(self);
    changeMenuItem(self, "SelectFunction!",  GRAF_FUNC, 0, MF_APPEND);
}
```

continued

```
Def command(self, wP, lP)   /* create a dialog box to get the function to
                                                          be drawn. */
{   if (wP == GRAF_FUNC)
    then
        if (tempText := new(InputDialog, self, "Graph Function",
            "Enter formula for graph as a function of X:", txt))
        then txt := tempText;
        draw(self, parseFunction(self));
        endif;
    endif;
}


/* parses an expression and returns BlockContext to be evaluated later */
Def parseFunction(self | temp, aBlk)
{   new(GraphWindow);
    temp                    := CStream.collection;
    CStream.collection      := cBuf;
    aParser.lex.collection  := asciiz("{" + txt + "}");
    aBlk                    := parse(aParser, self);
    CStream.collection      := temp;
    ^aBlk
}


Def draw(self, aBlk | longStr, new_FX)   /* this is the workhorse of the
                                                          application */
{   hdc := getContext(self);
    eval(aBlk);
    X := start;
    precision := MaxPositiveInteger/((stop-start)*border);
    setMode(self);
    repaint(self);
    axes(self, 0.0, start, 0.0, stop);
    axes(self, start, 0.0, stop, 0.0);
    do (over(start, stop+1)
        {using(idx)
         tick(self, -0.24, idx, 0.48, 0.0);
        });
    do (over(start, stop+1)
        {using(idx)
         tick(self, idx, -0.30, 0.0, 0.60);
        });
    X := start;
    moveTo(point(upScale(self, X),
                    last_FX := upScale(self, eval(aBlk))), hdc);
                    do(overBy(upScale(self,start)), upScale(self, stop),
                    upScale(self,increment),
        {using(idx)
         X := downScale(self, idx);
         newFX := upScale(self, eval(aBlk);
         if (abs(last_FX - new_FX) >= MaxIntegerRange)
         then moveTo(point(upScale(self,X), new_FX), hdc);
         else lineTo(point(upScale(self,X), new_FX, hdc);
         endif;
         last_FX := new_FX;
        });
    releaseContext(self, hdc);
}
```

continued

```
/* set the MS Windows mode to make the origin the center of the screen */
Def setMode(self, wd, hi, aRect)
{   Call SetMapMode(hdc, MM_ANISOTROPIC);
    aRect := clientRect(self);
    wd := width(aRect);
    ht := height(aRect);
    Call SetWindowExt(hdc, upScale(self,border*(stop-start)),
        upScale(self,border*(start-stop)));
    Call SetViewportExt(hdc, wd, ht);
    Call SetViewportOrg(hdc, wd/2, ht/2)
}

Def axes(self,x_from,y_from,x_to,y_to)   /* draw the axes of the graph */
{   moveTo(point(upScale(self,x_from),upScale(self,y_from)),hdc);
    lineTo(point(upScale(self,x_to),upScale(self,y_to)),hdc);
}

Def tick(self,x_org,y_org,x_direct,y_direct)
/* draw a tick mark on an axis */
{   moveTo(point(upScale(self,x_org),upScale(self,y_org)),hdc);
    lineTo(point(upScale(self,x_org+x_direct),
            upScale(self,y_org+y-direct)),hdc);
}

Def upScale(self, x | temp)  /* convert value to coordinate system */
{   temp := x * precision;
    if (temp > 0)
    then ^asInt(min(MaxPositiveInteger, temp));
    else ^asInt(max(MaxNegativeInteger, temp));
    endif;
}

Def downScale(self, x)
/* convert coordinate system value to actual value */
{   ^x/precision;
}
```

Figure 10.28   *Actor code for a graphing application*

The GraphWindow class definition is not complete. To make it operate, we must create an instance of GraphWindow and send it the message show. The two lines below, typed in the Actor workspace, cause the GraphFunction dialog box to be displayed, as shown in Figure 10.29. The function graph is then plotted in a very standard fashion in a separate window, as shown in Figure 10.30.

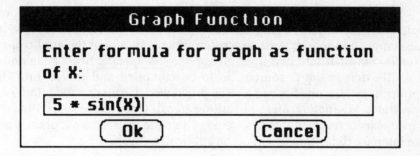

Figure 10.29 *The command function and the dialog box it produces*

Courtesy of The Whitewater Group, Inc., used by permission

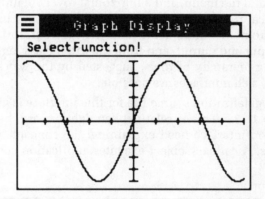

Figure 10.30 Graph Display *window*

Courtesy of The Whitewater Group, Inc., used by permission

Open Dialogue

Open Dialogue is a UIMS designed by Apollo Computers to run under the X Window System. It has a fundamental object-oriented basis and separates the user interface function from the application. While Open Dialogue is available from C, C++, Pascal, and FORTRAN, we describe the C version here.

The programmer has two ways to use Open Dialogue for an application. A separate dialog definition source file (called a .dds file because its name must end in .dds) can be written independently of the application. This is compiled into two files: an application-specific header file and a stub file that is the C source file to be compiled and linked into the application. The .dds file can also be previewed to examine the interface's operation. Alternately, an application can call Open Dialogue routines to create objects itself. In this case, Open Dialogue is used as a toolkit, since the interface definition is part of the application itself.

Open Dialogue is illustrated with an example from Apollo Computer. Figure 10.31 shows a menu interface built with this system. This illustrates some of the components of its user interfaces. There is an unusual limitation in Open Dialogue: no window can contain more than one "row," although that row can be vertical or horizontal and can be made up of various kinds of objects. In this example, there is a vertical row containing the label and the menu, and a horizontal row containing the Exit icon and the vertical row; each row is enclosed by a heavy black line. These objects are from the field, icon, sub_window, menu, and scrollbar classes for input and output, and from the label class for output only. By constructing a hierarchy of rows, suggested by the way this example is built, suitably rich interfaces are possible.

The dialog definition source file for this interface is given by the .dds file in Figure 10.32. This is relatively straightforward, but two things in the application interface need explaining: the concepts of *callback* and *return* classes. A callback object executes application code by calling an

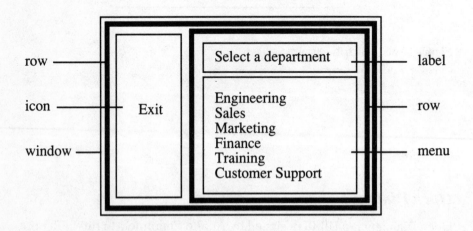

Figure 10.31 *A sample Open Dialogue screen with its parts*

Courtesy Apollo Computer

```
(
// VISUAL PARTS OF INTERFACE

// title for menu
    menuTitle : label
    {
        border_width    = 3 ;
        congtents       = "Select a department" ;
        exports         = true;
    };

// menu with entries
    departmentMenu : menu;
    {
        mark_style      = outline ;
        highlight_gap   = true ;
        entries         = (          // surround list with parentheses
                            "Engineering" ;
                            "Sales" ;
                            "Marketing" ;
                            "Finance" ;
                            "Training" ;
                            "Customer Support" ;
                          )
        selection_dst   = dst {
                            object  = departmentMenuCallback ;
                            id      = trigger ;
                            };
        export          = true ;
    };

// icon for exiting
    exitIcon : icon
    {
        contents        = "Exit" ;
        corners         = round ;
        highlight_gap   = true ;
        outline_width   = 1 ;
        selection_dst   = dst {
                            object  = exitIconReturn ;
                            id      = trigger ;
                            }
        export          = true ;
    };

// LAYOUT

// row to put label on top of menu
    menuRow : row
    {
        orientation     = vertical ;    // no quotes around vertical
        outline_width   = 1 ;           // because it's a symbolic name
```

continued

```
        contents         = (
                                menuTitle ;
                                departmentMenu ;
                            ) ;
        export           = true ;
    } ;

// row to put menuRow next to icon
    finalRow : row
    {
        orientation      = horizontal ;
        division_width   = 3 ;
        border_width     = 3 ;
        outline_width    = 2 ;
        edge_gap         = true ;
        contents         = (
                                exitIcon ;
                                menuRow ;
                            ) ;
        export           = true ;
    } ;

//APPLICATION INTERFACE
    departmentMenuCallback : callback
    {
        routine = "makereport" ;  // subroutine in application
        export = true ;
    } ;
    exitIconReturn : return
    {
        export = true ;
    } ;
)
```

Figure 10.32   *A dialog definition source (.dds) file*

Courtesy Apollo Computer

application subroutine; when the subroutine terminates, control returns to the interface directly. A return object passes control to the application, but control returns to the line after the dlg_event_wait statement, so the application must deal with the Open Dialog interface directly at that point. The example uses a callback, departmentMenuCallback, to manage the menu, and only uses a return, exitIconReturn, to exit the application. This separates the user interface from the application better, and is the recommended Open Dialogue style.

Finally, the application code that uses the .dds file is given in Figure 10.33.

```
/*  select_dept.
    Source code for a program that uses interface in select_dept.dds
*/
#include <stdio.h>
#include <string.h>
#include "dlg.h"
#include "select_dept.h"

/*  global definitions */
dlg_status  st;

/*  makereport callback routine; body not included  */
void makereport()
    ...

/*  main part of application */
main( argc, argv )
    int   argc;
    char *argv[];
{
    dlg_event         event;
    dlg_id            id;
    dlg_obj           returnObj;
    /* a .dds file is compiled into a .ddb file before use  */
    static dlg_string    fileName = "select_dept.ddb";
    ldg_string_len       fileNameLen;

/*  load interface, wait for return, and terminate  */

        fileNameLen = strlen( fileName );
        id = dlg_load_select_dept_file( fileName, fileNameLen,
                                   dlg_select_dept_key, &st );
        returnObj = dlg_event_wait( NULL, &st );
        dlg_terminate( id, &st );
}       /* end of main */
```

Figure 10.33   *Application code using the dialog definition*

Courtesy of Apollo Computer

NewWave

NewWave is a software environment developed by Hewlett-Packard to
support software development for systems built on Intel's 80286 and
80386 processors. It is built on top of Microsoft Windows, from which it
inherits much of its fundamental operations. The look of NewWave's
interface is shown in Figure 10.34 and clearly shows its Windows background. NewWave will be available for OS/2 with the Presentation Manager and for Unix System V with the Interface Definition 2.

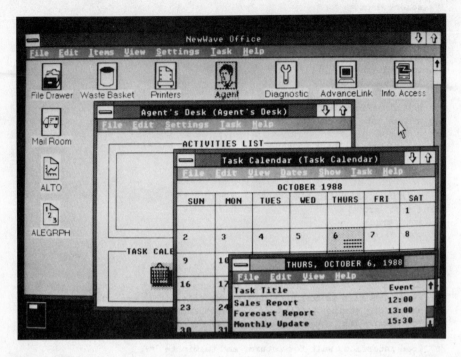

Figure 10.34 *A sample NewWave screen*

Courtesy of Hewlett-Packard Co.

NewWave's functional relation to Microsoft Windows, MS-DOS, a user, and the user's program is shown in Figure 10.35. NewWave uses Windows for interaction with the user and for MS-DOS system calls. NewWave itself has two other components, the Object Management Facility (OMF) and the Application Program Interface (API).

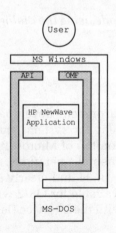

Figure 10.35 *Functional diagram of NewWave*

The Object Management Facility extends Windows' message-passing, somewhat object-oriented approach to a more conventional object/method/message model, though it is still not fully an object-oriented system in the sense of Chapter 9. A key addition to object structures in NewWave is the "information link." In a compound object, an object that contains several subobjects, these subobjects may be physically present or may be linked from other objects and be included by applying a method to the external object. There are two kinds of information links: data passing links and visual links. Data passing links pass the data from one object into another object and manipulate that data in the receiving object. For example, a data passing link to a spreadsheet from a charting program will import the spreadsheet data and chart it in the charting program. A visual link, however, passes a graphic from one object into another object, where it can be displayed. A visual link from a text document file to a charting file would include a chart in the text. In both cases, however, changes in the spreadsheet would be reflected immediately in the chart and in the text document; the linkage relation is dynamic and is much more powerful than cut-and-paste.

The Application Program Interface gives the programmer access to three specific capabilities: an Agent facility, context-sensitive help, and computer-based training. The structure of these API capabilities is shown in Figure 10.36. The Agent facility allows the user or developer to automate application processes. An Agent task is a series of commands to be executed automatically, and a single task can be used by different applications. Tasks can be created by entering commands through an editor or by recording application operations while working with the application. This is an instance of the user-defined command concept from Chapter 4. Tasks can be bound to keystrokes or menu commands, can be scheduled for specific times, or can be invoked by a program or system event. The

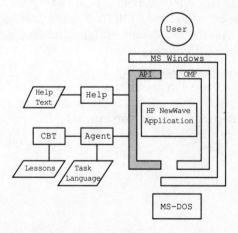

Figure 10.36 *The structure of the API facility*

Agent facility is expected to be the foundation for future Artificial Intelligence capabilities in NewWave. Computer Based Training is implemented through the Agent facility, and uses the actual application for its own training. Again, this is an instance of the learning aids concept from Chapter 11. Sample application operations can be recorded and replayed as examples, or sample runs can have explanations or other information edited into them.

Context-sensitive help is provided by having the API intercept Windows events and pass help events to the help system instead of to the application. These events then call up specific text from a help text file and present it to the user. These help texts can be built separately and linked to objects, and when an event refers to an object, its help text is retrieved. This technique is similar to the context-sensitive help we suggest in Chapter 12, though it is much more sophisticated and highly automated.

NewWave is a good example of a second-level development system. While using a base window system for its screen look and events, in this case Microsoft Windows, it adds a more sophisticated object orientation and support for important user functions.

10.4   Readings

Window systems, and especially user interface management systems, are very new. There are few books about them, though an overview of implementation issues in window systems is found in Hopgood *et al* [1986b]. Most of the information we have used is from papers, notes from short courses such as the Farrel and Schwartz course at SIGCHI and the Steinhart course at SIGGRAPH, and materials from vendors.

Of the systems in this chapter, the Macintosh toolbox is the most fully documented, being described in depth in Apple's *Inside Macintosh* volumes. In addition, the overall Macintosh look and feel is documented in Apple's *User Interface Guidelines*.

Microsoft Windows is also widely documented but, like most products for the IBM PC, this is largely by trade books. Jamsa covers Windows version 1; Petzold gives a very full description of version 2; and Townsend describes details of programming version 2 in C. More books on this system will doubtless appear.

Both NeWS and the X Window System are quite new and have little material published about them yet. Arden *et al* have written a book on NeWS that is not out at this writing, but most of our information came from Sun's documentation and the Farrell and Schwartz short course mentioned above. PostScript is documented in its manual from Adobe systems. X is well described in a paper by Schiefler and Gettys and a short course by Jones and Hersh at SIGGRAPH, as well as other papers such as Rosenthal, Lee, and Leffler, and a book by Schiefler, Gettys, and Newman.

Our other window systems are curses and programmer-designed text windows. Like many Unix libraries, curses is poorly documented in manuals; our information came from a short course by Ken Arnold, the author of curses. There is a book by Rochkind that has some curses content, and Strang covers curses. Text windows involve simple data structures of strings and stacks and are rarely explicitly covered, but Comer and Fossum include text windows in detail.

Among UIMS's, again MacApp is well documented in Schmucker's book [1986], though we used Apple's MacApp manual as well. Open Look is described in a tutorial by Teitelman. All the others are documented only by vendors' or developers' documents: TIGER by Team Engineering, Actor by the Whitewater Group, Open Dialogue by Apollo Computer, and NewWave by Hewlett-Packard. Our information on iCpak 210 came by personal communication and promotional material, though Cox covers Objective-C, the basis for iCpak 201. A general book on User Interface Management Systems has been written by Pfaff.

Finally, in Chapter 9 we introduced the concept of object-oriented programming found so frequently in this chapter. We refer you to the Readings in Chapter 9 for sources on object-oriented programming.

## Chapter 11

HELPING THE USER
WORK WITH THE PROGRAM

A program may be used by persons with all levels of experience. They may have used your program before and be quite skilled with it; they may have used similar programs and have a general idea of its operation but need help on details; they may be complete novices on the application or on computers in general. You must provide a range of ways to assist the user. These must not get in the way of the experienced user, must give summary help to someone needing only details, and must give novices all the assistance they can get. Good programs provide a suitable level of assistance for every user.

An added aid to users is forgiveness in handling errors. Hands slip, people forget, and ill-designed programs can crash or freeze up when this happens, causing the user considerable distress. Making the program handle errors gracefully will make users accept it and use it much more readily. We have developed various techniques to detect and recover from errors in the earlier chapters, and we explore these techniques more thoroughly in this and later chapters.

In addition, some users may have physical disabilities that cause problems working with ill-designed programs, such as those which require multiple simultaneous keypresses. It is your obligation to design programs that can be used comfortably by everyone. A discussion of ways to make programs usable by persons with disabilities is in Chapter 14.

11.1   Providing Learning Aids

Software learning aids are traditionally paper oriented. Special tutorial sections in manuals have been, and continue to be, the main learning aids provided with software. The book industry in computer-related books is an indication that paper-based learning aids are widely used, and that manuals alone are not doing this job. Manuals are a critical part of any software project, but they often do not contain all the helpful information a user might want. More critically, they cannot give the user the information needed at a particular point in a program without digging through other, nonapplicable materials.

Online learning aids are an alternative to manuals and books. These go far beyond paper learning aids by working with the user as the user works with the software. The difference between learning aids and help facilities is that learning aids are used outside the actual program's operation, but help is used while working inside the program. Help facilities are discussed later in this chapter. Learning aids also differ from traditional computer-aided instruction or computer-based training in that they deal with using the program itself instead of using the computer to learn another subject.

Probably the simplest online learning aids are online manuals. These have been available on Unix for some time and are a major source of information on its commands. An example of a Unix manual page is given in Figure 12.6. However, the Unix online manual is written by and for Unix systems programmers and meets their needs for quick information. Online information for novices or casual users must be designed and written more carefully.

Online manuals are very expensive in terms of disk space but are remarkably flexible and easily updated as changes are made in the software. In some systems, such as Unix, users can even add their own manual pages to describe commands and applications they build. Thus, online manuals are more up-to-date than traditional printed manuals and are literally at the user's fingertips as he or she works with the system.

Another tool available on Berkeley versions of Unix is the *apropos* command. This gives a list of commands that apply to the general concept given by the user. Thus, the command *apropos files* would give a list of all commands dealing with files. This lets a user browse in the system and then use the online manual pages to obtain more information.

Tutorial programs are more informative for novice users. These are related to computer-aided instructional programs and teach the operations and principles of the main program. We recommend online tutorials as a useful way to introduce users to your software. Among tutorials, one of the most useful types is a guided tour of sample sessions. These take the user through typical uses of the program with descriptions of what is happening in suitably placed screen windows. Users become involved

```
Standard design:
    For each screen in the program
        Put up screen
        For each input in screen
            Get input
            Process input

Revised design:
    For each screen in the program
        Put up screen
        For each input in screen
            If the program is in standard mode
                Get input
                Process input
            Else {program is in tutorial or demo mode}
                Show sample input
                Give explanation in standard location {window?}
                Continue to next input when user says to
```

Figure 11.1   *Providing a tutorial function within a program*

with the program's operations but are only allowed to make appropriate selections, so that they can learn the program's details and also avoid errors due to unfamiliarity with its processes. Sample sessions can also be used for help if a request for help is set up to trigger the sample session for the current program operation.

This kind of tutorial is built from the actual application program by adding explanatory material and limiting the number of responses that are accepted. It can be built by extending the program's operation fairly simply, as the design sketch in Figure 11.1 illustrates. As we pointed out in Chapter 10, such a program extension is a specific part of the Hewlett-Packard NewWave system. Passive tutorials, where the user's involvement is limited to pressing the RETURN key after reading the screen, are much less valuable than active systems because the user quickly loses interest in them and retains little information.

Learning aids, whether online or on paper, have another valuable function in program building. If it is difficult to explain a program operation in the learning aid, it is probably also difficult for the user to understand that operation. If the learning aid is developed very early in the software development, it helps the programming team find difficult places early. This allows early redesign of such operations, resulting in an improved user interface at minimal cost. As always in software development, design changes made early are easy and inexpensive, while design changes made late are difficult, error-prone, and costly.

The principles of learning aids are based both on the wide range of experience a program's users will have and on the need to give users information with as little disturbance of their work as possible.

PRINCIPLE: Provide learning tools for your software.

PRINCIPLE: Provide a range of learning tools to accommodate people with different learning styles.

PRINCIPLE: Provide assistance for inexperienced users without requiring advanced users to use it.

PRINCIPLE: Design online learning aids to require no more than 20 to 30 minutes of a user's time.

11.2   Providing User Navigation Aids

With programs that have any real complexity, it is sometimes difficult for novice users to keep track of where they are in a program and what they can do at the current point. Navigation aids consist of information on current location, the path taken to this location, and the available options at this point. The availability and quality of navigation aids can make a significant difference in how well people can use the software.

Navigation aids are also tremendously important for support persons helping users with software. When a user has problems with a program, navigation information is a primary tool in recreating the problem and deciding whether it is a user error (and helping the user correct the error) or a software or system bug.

The basic functions of navigation aids are quite simple. They should give information on

- where the user is,
- how the user got here,
- what the user can do here (including mode information if applicable), and
- how the user can do it.

Navigation information can be maintained onscreen, as shown by the partial AppleWorks screen in Figure 11.2 and the Zenographics Mirage navigation information in Figure 11.3. Further information can be avail-

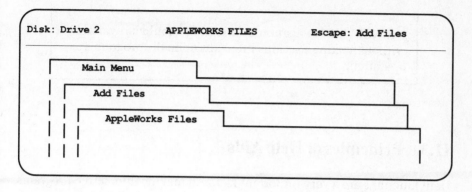

Figure 11.2 *How AppleWorks shows where the user is*

Copyright Claris Corporation, used by permission

```
CHART                    1: Who?              Curves 2
4: Axis Features         2: What?             Points 1-6
   5: Orientation        3: How?              Axes 2
                         4: Why?              Notes 1
                         5: When?
                         6: For example:      Create OFF
                         7: See Also:         Format... BAR
                         8: Where?            Help ON
                         9: Glossary          Record OFF
                                              Free Memory % 88
                        >4
---------------------   ---------------------   ------------------
```

Figure 11.3 *Mirage navigation information*

able on demand, as in the Mirage system where the user can ask "Who?," "What?," "When?," "How?,"or "An example?", for any menu item not understood, as shown in Figure 12.7. This latter design makes help aids a natural extension of the navigation system. Certainly three of the four basic navigation functions are often part of help information. The second basic function can be provided by a history file, a mechanism that is discussed in Chapter 13.

The principles of navigation aids are relatively simple.

> PRINCIPLE: At any point in a program users should be able to find out where they are, how they got here, and where they can go from here.

> PRINCIPLE: Navigation information should be available without making a serious interruption in the program's operation.

11.3   Principles of Help Aids

Help functions are a very important factor in making interactive programs usable. Novices rely on them heavily for assistance. Even after several years' experience with a particular piece of software, users still need the help function to refresh their memory on less frequently used operations. Chapter 12 is devoted to implementing help systems; here we simply put them in context as another tool to help the user work with the program.

The function of online help is to assist the user with the current operations. To do this, help should always deal with the specific program section from which it was called, and it should always provide genuinely helpful information. This latter may sound trivial, but it is not always easy to decide just what a user needs to know for a given operation. Providing the information the programmer thinks is needed is seldom a good idea.

When a program contains a help facility, it is important that help be available on all phases of a program. Users can come to depend on help for some operations and become confused and upset if none is available for others. As with all other aspects of your program, consistency counts.

For the general, nonexpert user, we offer the following principles for help systems.

> PRINCIPLE: Help should always be available by consistent means.

> PRINCIPLE: The user should know help is available and how to get it.

> PRINCIPLE: Help should be context sensitive; it should refer directly to the point from which it was called and tell the user what can be done there.

> PRINCIPLE: Help should speak in the user's language and in terms of the user's task.

> PRINCIPLE: Help should give examples and be dynamic, instead of giving manual-style descriptions.

> PRINCIPLE: Help should be presented in screen-formatted pages or in windows that leave the user's work showing.

> PRINCIPLE: Make the help system act as a learning aid by making it interactive.

If your program is intended for expert users as well as nonexperts, you should consider more than one level of help. In the case of the expert user you need to provide more expert discussions and more detailed description of the program's internal operations. Such multi-level help systems must, however, have a way to determine whether a user is an expert in order to set the help level. This is explicitly available in WordStar, for example, but could be inferred by the number of errors and/or amount of help requested by the user while the program is running.

11.4   Reducing and Controlling Program Errors

A user is working with your program, having no problems entering data and understanding the results—and then the program crashes or freezes up, causing your user to make a very sudden reevaluation of your program's value. You must insulate your users from program errors to have really usable software.

It would be wonderful to imagine that errors never occur while software is being used, but, in reality, we must build software that handles problems caused by users' control or input errors or by internal computation problems. Some errors are caused by careless design which makes it difficult for the user to control the program properly, and Chapter 1 discusses design issues. Chapter 5 describes how to avoid overflow problems in computations by checking the size of numbers before doing actual arithmetic, and in Chapter 13 we discuss additional error-handling techniques.

Some programs seem plagued with an unusual problem: spurious error messages. Experienced programmers may have met a compiler that gives error messages or (more commonly) warnings with no reason or effect, and for which the only response is to ignore the message. At least one major vendor has a number of meaningless messages in their system installation procedures. This points out the almost obvious need to ensure that any error or warning message presented by a program be genuinely necessary.

There are two main emphases in dealing with errors. The first is to ensure that errors neither crash nor freeze up the program. This requires careful programmer control of all aspects of the computer's operation, including proper device handling to ensure that your user can use any reasonable peripheral device. The second is to tell users about errors in a helpful way and allow them to correct or recover from any errors that may have been made. These are also covered in more detail in Chapter 13.

Chapter 13 covers techniques for error avoidance, handling, and reporting, as well as information on dealing with various internal hardware options and peripheral devices. However, this is the place to give general principles for dealing with program and system errors.

PRINCIPLE: Make sure your design does not contribute to errors by making it difficult for the user to remember proper controls.

PRINCIPLE: Include ways for data entry errors to be caught and corrected.

PRINCIPLE: Warn users when they perform an operation that can possibly cause irretrievable damage.

PRINCIPLE: Use environments that let the program field errors instead of using the computer's automatic error traps.

> PRINCIPLE: When an error occurs, give the user concrete information on what the error was and allow him or her to retreat from it.

> PRINCIPLE: When your program needs external devices, provide a wide range of device drivers.

> PRINCIPLE: When your program needs external devices, make it check for available devices automatically whenever possible.

11.5   Readings

This chapter covers several different topics with the common goal of increasing a program's usability outside the areas of routine input, output, and control. Help systems and error handling are covered in Chapters 12 and 13, respectively, and readings in these areas are included in these later chapters.

Learning aids are also covered in this chapter. There is a literature on computer-assisted instruction because of the interest in computers as general learning tools. However, most of this literature deals with stand-alone tutorials, instead of tutorials for using other programs. We refer the reader to that general literature. However, it seems to us that software learning aids are still in a very early state of development and a real literature in this area has not yet been developed. Brockmann includes some information on learning aids with his discussion of help.

## Chapter 12

PROGRAMMING HELP SYSTEMS

Help systems were not practical or even useful in the days of 24-hour turnaround times on batch FORTRAN compiles and end-user jobs. Manuals (sometimes) served the purpose of providing the users of these early computers with techniques and examples of computer use. In what seems now to be about the same point in the automotive industry, the fuel gauge was probably seen as a luxury by the designers of the Model T, since a driver could easily check a dipstick in the gas tank to see how much fuel was left. But now, all autos have fuel gauges (some even have gauges that give the estimated distance to empty with the currently-computed gas mileage) and the computer user of the late 1980's and beyond expects to have help available in almost every computer program. Moreover, users expect this help to tell them everything they need to know about a program, but nothing superfluous. This makes a help system a challenge for the program designer.

12.1 Examples of Help Systems

A number of common programs and systems have help facilities in them. These range from minimal to very helpful, and we consider examples along this whole spectrum. It is worth noting that few programs for the Macintosh computer seem to include help. Apparently it is felt that the other user interface features make it unnecessary. It will be interesting to see whether time proves this attitude to be valid.

AppleWorks

AppleWorks is an integrated package for the Apple II computer family (IIe, IIc, IIGS) offering a word processor, spreadsheet, and file system that can share information among its documents by using an internal buffer that it calls a clipboard. Its users are typical Apple II users: educators, students, and home users. Its help consists of a list of available OA-commands (OA stands for the open-Apple key, also called the command key). Help is requested by the OA-? key combination as shown in Figure 12.1 for the AppleWorks word processor subsystem. In this figure, just as on the Apple II screen, @ replaces the OA symbol.

This help serves mainly to jog the user's memory about the available functions but offers no added assistance. The overall help system includes help before any of the subsystems are chosen and a help screen similar to the one above for each of the spreadsheet and database subsystems. However, there is no additional help in AppleWorks beyond these screens. We would also prefer to see the use of serial key presses instead of two simultaneous keypresses. This causes potential problems for users with disabilities, as discussed in Chapter 14.

```
File: Example            HELP          Escape: Review/Add/Change
==:==:==:==:==:==:==:==:==:==:==:==:==:==:==:==:==:==:==:==:==

              @-C    Copy text (includes cut and paste)

              @-D    Delete text

              @-F    Find occurrences of....

              @-K    Calculate page numbers

              @-M    Move text (includes cut and paste)

              @-N    Change name of file

              @-O    Options for print formatting

              @-P    Print

              @-R    Replace occurrences of....

              @-T    Set and clear tab stops

Use arrows to see remainder of Help              55K Avail.
```

Figure 12.1 *AppleWorks OA-? word processing help screen.*

```
A1:
Fixed  Scientific  Currency  ,  General  +/-  Percent  Date  Text  Hidden
Fixed number of decimal places (x.xx)

/Worksheet Global Format — Sets default numeric format.

1. Select a numeric format.

2. (In some cases) Enter number of decimal places.  If you choose Date, select
   a date format or select Time and one of the four time formats.

Sets the numeric format for all cells not explicitly formatted with
/Range Format.  To return explicitly formatted cells to the default
format, use /Range Format Reset.

Numeric and label formats are independent, and have separate global settings.

The /Worksheet Global Label-Prefix command helps you control the way in
which label entries appear in their cells.
```

Next Step—Decimal Places	Next Step—Date Formats
Next Step—General, Text, Hidden Format	Numeric Formats
/Worksheet Global Commands	Label Formats
Global/Default Formats	Help Index

Figure 12.2 *Lotus help screen*

Copyright 1985, Lotus Development Corporation

Lotus 1-2-3

As illustrated in Chapter 1, Lotus 1-2-3 operates from a wide range of nested menus. The help system is built on this same concept. For each menu option there is a separate help screen that gives assistance with further available options. The help function is uniquely associated with the F1 function key, so there is never any confusion about how to get help. While AppleWorks has only one help screen for each subsystem, Lotus 1-2-3 has a much more extensive set of help screens, each associated with a separate option menu. An example of a Lotus help screen is shown in Figure 12.2. This is the screen for a /Worksheet Global Format operation and tells the user what the operation does. It is terse, and assumes some familiarity with the concepts of spreadsheets. It has the cursor in the area at the bottom of the screen, and the user can choose various options for additional help information by moving the cursor in this area.

dBASE IV

dBASE IV was described in Chapters 2, 3, and 4. It has a much more extensive help system than dBASE III had, in keeping with its increased emphasis on interactive database definition and operations. The help feature is always available by pressing function key F1; the command help or help <command> is also available from the dot command prompt, and a help button is available from any error box.

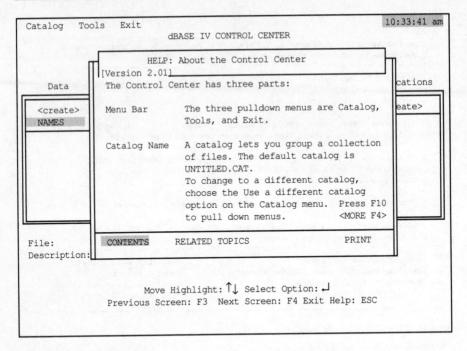

```
Catalog   Tools   Exit                                         10:33:41 am
                        dBASE IV CONTROL CENTER
                  ┌──────────────────────────────────────────┐
                  │      HELP: About the Control Center        │
                  │ [Version 2.01]                             │ cations
     Data         │   The Control Center has three parts:      │
   ┌──────────────│                                            │──────┐
   │  <create>    │   Menu Bar      The three pulldown menus are Catalog, eate>
   │  NAMES       │                 Tools, and Exit.           │
   │              │                                            │
   │              │   Catalog Name  A catalog lets you group a collection
   │              │                 of files. The default catalog is
   │              │                 UNTITLED.CAT.              │
   │              │                 To change to a different catalog,
   │              │                 choose the Use a different catalog
   │              │                 option on the Catalog menu.   Press F10
   │              │                 to pull down menus.        <MORE F4>
   └──────────────│                                            │
     File:        │  CONTENTS       RELATED TOPICS               PRINT
     Description:  └──────────────────────────────────────────┘


                    Move Highlight: ↑↓ Select Option: ↵
              Previous Screen: F3  Next Screen: F4 Exit Help: ESC
```

Figure 12.3 *A dBASE IV screen with a help box*

Courtesy of Ashton-Tate Corporation

This help system is context-sensitive; from the Control Center or an error box, help presents a sequence of screens directly relating to the current displayed choice or error term. An example of a screen with a help box is shown in Figure 12.3, although the effective use of color and boldfaced text actually used is not shown. Stepping through the help with the F4 function key or choosing CONTENTS or RELATED TOPICS from the help box are also good ways to learn about the dBASE IV system. However, while the help system knows contexts, it simply presents information from a help file with no attempt to understand or guide the user's actions.

An interesting aspect of this help system is its PRINT option. This prints the contents of the current help box with emphasized text, similar to the onscreen help, but without all the extraneous material given by a PrtSc printout. This provides additional learning support for the user.

It is interesting to note the evolution of the dBASE product from dBASE II to dBASE IV. The dBASE II system had only the command line input described in Chapter 4, and required quite a lot of expertise to use it effectively. For dBASE III Plus, an ASSISTANT facility was provided; this was an onscreen aid that allowed the user to build commands interactively. The system was still basically command-oriented: the ASSISTANT did not give the user access to all the system functionality and had the flavor of a help or learning aid. The dBASE IV system has the Command

Center, which may have evolved from the ASSISTANT, but it has a completely different interface and gives the user access to the full function of the system. This makes dBASE IV a fully interactive database system, retaining the dot command prompt as a separate mode for persons who want to write database programs. dBASE IV also adds the standard SQL query language. The price for this more mature interface and more advanced system is that dBASE IV cannot be run from diskettes and needs at least 640K of internal memory.

Prime's PRIMOS

PRIMOS is the operating system for the range of Prime computers, and supports general time-shared operation of many applications and terminals. PRIMOS offers a built-in HELP command, given by simply entering the command HELP. This command may be given by itself, or it may be given with the command on which help is desired, as in HELP *command*. The results are quite different. By itself, HELP simply lists all the PRIMOS commands the user can issue—and the list is 13 screens long and can only be interrupted with a BREAK. Part of the list is shown as Figure 12.4. At the University of Iowa, where the major educational work is done with Prime computers, users do not see this awkward interface because the systems programmers have improved the information and formatting of

LIST_QUOTA	Lists disk quota information
LIST_RBF	Describes the attributes of a ROAM file
LIST_REMOTE_ID	List's user's remote IDs
LIST_SEARCH_RULES	Lists contents of user's entrypoint search list
LIST_SEGMENT	Displays information about private segments
LIST_TAPE	List contents of an ARCHIVE, TRANSPORT, or BACKUP tape
LIST_VAR	Lists contents of global variable file
LOAD	Loading commands (R-mode)
LOGIN	Gains access to system
LOGOUT	Ends terminal session
LOGPRT	Displays system event log
LON	Controls Phantom Logout Notification
LOOK	(Operator command)
MAGNET	Magnetic Tape Interchange Subsystem
MAGRST	Writes files from Prime-format tapes to disk
MAGSAV	Writes disk file(s) to tape
MAGTAPE	(PRIMOS Magnetic Tape Subsystems)
MAKE	(Operator command)
MAXSCH	(Operator command)
MAXUSR	(Operator command)
MDUMP	Dumps a MIDASPLUS file
MEDUSA	Brings up PRIME MEDUSA workstation
MESSAGE	Sends message to users or operator

Figure 12.4 *A screen from the general PRIMOS HELP output*

```
HELP                                          Prints information at terminal

    HELP [command-name]
         [topic-name]

If HELP is invoked with a command name, information about that command
is printed at the terminal.  If HELP is invoked without a command name,
it prints a list of commands for which information is available.

The format of command description is:

COMMAND NAME                                           Brief description

[Abbreviation - if any]

    Command line syntax

Text describing command, options, etc. At the end of the listing are
any references to further information and the date the HELP
information was created or updated.

Information is also available for certain categories or groupings of
commands, such as compilers, loaders, Prime documents, etc.

October 1982
```

Figure 12.5   *The PRIMOS command* help help

HELP. When used with a command, HELP gives generally sound and useful information, as shown in Figure 12.5. The content of the help, however, is clearly oriented to the technical user, meaning that any applications on this system must provide their own help which is oriented to their users. Thus, we must give this HELP facility mixed reviews.

Unix man

The Unix on-line manual system, *man*, is described in Chapter 11. At the command level, a user may give the command *man command* to get the manual page(s) for the command indicated. As we indicated above, this is partly a learning aid, since novice users can browse across the system directly with *man* or can use the *apropos* command to find out what is possible and then use *man* to get detailed information. The manual pages are displayed using screen highlighting and other terminal-handling tools to make them as usable as possible. One tool used with *man* is named *more*; it displays a file one screen at a time. A sample manual page from *man* is shown as Figure 12.6.

The *man* system is sufficiently standard that people adding new tools or software on a local Unix system usually write manual pages to go online and describe the additions, and manual pages are routinely distributed along with new software. However, *man* is scarcely an extensive help system; it is only an online manual and is directed at the person who is knowledgeable in Unix.

PR(1)   **UNIX Programmer's Manual**   PR(1)

NAME

    pr — print file

SYNOPSIS

    pr [option] ... [file] ...

DESCRIPTION

    Pr produces a printed listing of one or more *files*. The output is separated into pages headed by a date, the name of the file or a specified header, and the page number. If there are no file arguments, *pr* prints its standard input.

    Options apply to all following files but may be reset between files:

    -*n*   Produce *n*-column output.

    +*n*   Begin printing with page *n*.

    -**h**   Take the next argument as a page header.

    -**w***n*   For purposes of multi-column output, take the width of the page to be *n* characters instead of the default 72.

    -**f**   Use formfeeds instead of newlines to separate pages. A formfeed is assumed to use up two blank lines at the top of a page. (Thus this option does not affect the effective page length.)

    -**l***n*   Take the length of the page to be *n* lines instead of the default 66.

    -**t**   Do not print the 5-line header or the 5-line trailer normally supplied for each page.

    -**s***c*   Separate the columns by the single character *c* instead of by the appropriate amount of white space. A missing *c* is taken to be a tab.

    -**m**   Print all *files* simultaneously, each in one column.

    Inter-terminal messages via *write*(1) are forbidden during a *pr*.

FILES

    /dev/tty? to suspend messages.

SEE ALSO

    cat(1)

DIAGNOSTICS

    There are no diagnostics when *pr* is printing on a terminal.

Figure 12.6   *Unix manual page from man pr*

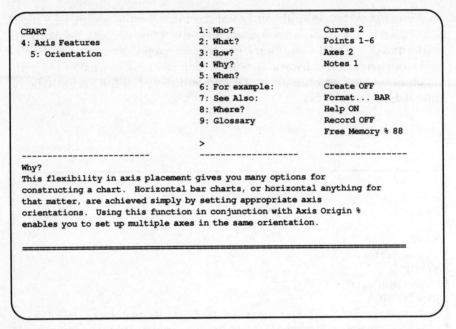

```
CHART                       1: Who?              Curves 2
4: Axis Features            2: What?             Points 1-6
   5: Orientation           3: How?              Axes 2
                            4: Why?              Notes 1
                            5: When?
                            6: For example:      Create OFF
                            7: See Also:         Format... BAR
                            8: Where?            Help ON
                            9: Glossary          Record OFF
                                                 Free Memory % 88

                            >
------------------------    --------------------    ----------------
Why?
This flexibility in axis placement gives you many options for
constructing a chart.  Horizontal bar charts, or horizontal anything for
that matter, are achieved simply by setting appropriate axis
orientations.  Using this function in conjunction with Axis Origin %
enables you to set up multiple axes in the same orientation.
```

Figure 12.7   *Mirage screen showing "Why?" one would use the "Orientation"*

Zenographics Mirage

We saw the Mirage formatted screen examples of navigation aids and screen layout in Figure 11.3. Mirage also includes a help function that describes several aspects of each choice in the graphics system. The range of aspects is very broad (Who? What? How? Why? When? Where? Examples? Others? Glossary), almost acting as a tutorial on graphics concepts as well as providing help on the immediate command. An example of Mirage's help screen with a descriptive text is given in Figure 12.7.

12.2   Make Help Work

In a help system, your first job is to communicate to your user. The six principles of Section 11.3 are really communications principles and can be summed up by:

- Communicate to your user exactly what is happening and what can be done now.

- Present that information in the user's language so that he or she can turn the help information into actual program operations as easily as possible.

Normal help systems impose no real programming difficulty. In a command system (see Chapter 4) a "help" command can always be recognized and acted upon at the exact point of the command. In a menu system (see Chapter 3) a "help" option may be an actual menu item or may be raised by a suitable choice, such as '?' instead of an option's letter. In either case, one of the special screen areas described in Chapter 7 may contain a message saying how to get help. It is not difficult to have help refer directly to the place from which it is called. We need only have any node in a state transition graph, or any screen in a menu system, or any blank in a form-fillout system, call its own help procedure. This procedure is then designed to have whatever kind of information is needed at that point in the program.

The real challenge in a help system is making the help really assist the user in the current task. To do this, the designer needs a deep understanding of the user, the task, and the language the user has to describe the task. This is in the area of interface design, not programming, and other references go into this in more detail. However, there is one technique you might consider to get started. Choose some individuals with the background you are trying to reach and have them go through a mockup of your program; this should be a very early version of the design, probably even before any serious programming is begun, and might just use paper and pencil. Ask them to talk as they do so, and record their comments. You will learn their language, their habits, and find out where they have difficulties. Program out the difficulties, design the interface to work the way they expect the job to be done, and incorporate their language into the help system.

In fact, help can have another important benefit to you as you design your program. Keep track of the help users request in your prototype and alpha versions through history files or other mechanisms and look for places where help is frequently requested. These are the trouble spots in your program; rework them carefully to reduce the amount of help that is requested.

The mechanics of programming help systems should be eased by advances in system software. As we noted in Chapter 10, Hewlett-Packard's NewWave system offers built-in help trapping and context-sensitive selection of help scripts. In addition, Apple is looking at adding help support to the Macintosh toolbox. Help is sufficiently critical that we expect such facilities to be relatively common in the future.

12.3   Options for Help Systems

As shown in the examples above, a help system can offer many kinds of information to the user. It can even offer different kinds of information at different times, depending on the environment from which it was called.

When help is called from the "waiting" state in a command system, the most useful help is probably an annotated list of the basic commands that are available. If, as with the Prime computer, there are too many to list, you can provide a list of general groups of commands. A group, say FILES, could be chosen with the command "help FILES" and the individual file commands could be listed; another help request would provide appropriate information on an individual command, such as an example of the command's use. However, a simple list of commands or options is often enough for the experienced (though infrequent) user who only needs to have a reminder of the command names. A novice user needs details and examples on each command.

A request for help from a partly completed command needs a different kind of response. This help might tell what the command under construction is intended to do, what its options are, and give examples of its completion. This could be "canned" text (possibly from a help file with suitable indexing to allow direct access) or output hardcoded into the program. Again, the amount of description given can depend on the user's help level.

With a menu system, a help request never needs to respond with the large-scale information of all possible commands. In this case, the help system only needs to respond to the particular menu from which it is called, which limits the scope of the necessary help information to the choices which are on the current screen. This is very much like the partial command type of help information.

While we usually think of help as being available only on request, the dBASE III Plus ASSISTANT treated a pause as a request for help, which can be appropriate for a novice user. To implement this you need a timing mechanism on input; once a certain amount of time has passed, a general help request is assumed, and the help is presented. The amount of time can be determined from user habits or help level settings. Such unrequested help can surprise the user but may be a real support to the novice ("The program really *wants* to help me!") Unrequested help should be tried out in the design phases before it is included, and if it isused, it must be used everywhere.

12.4 Pitfalls

The real problems with help usually stem from a thoughtless or hurried approach to the help system. You should be careful to avoid a few obvious traps that are always waiting for the unwary:

- Help that is obscure: "Syntax Error", "Invalid Command",
- Help that is expert-oriented or uses technical jargon: "Function must be invertible over the chosen domain",
- Help that doesn't really help: "SET allows you to set a variable's value",
- Help that is overwhelming: listing 200 commands in a scroll that cannot be stopped before it is complete, and
- Help that only refers to printed documentation or otherwise makes the user leave the job at hand to get information: "ERROR #275".

These problems can be avoided by sensitivity to your program's users. Thinking carefully about their experience, language, and needs is very important. Even more, careful prototyping and testing with the projected audience will give you very good feedback on this kind of mistake.

12.5   Example

In Chapter 3, we discuss menu-driven systems and note that it is possible to develop a help facility for each menu or even for each choice in each menu. This is not difficult. For this discussion let us assume that we want to build a help system for which each menu screen will have its own help information. To do this, we outline the purpose of the menu and describe briefly what each of the choices will do.

The first problem is to decide just how to invoke the help option. This can be an explicit item in the menu (simply expand the menu to include a help line), or it can be implicit when a particular key is pressed or when the user chooses a number or letter item which is not in the menu. Of course, this means that any typo could invoke the help, but this may not be a bad idea. In either case, you then call the help routine.

This routine may be one of two types: a simple procedure that includes its own specific help text, or a more general procedure that gets a parameter indicating which help text is needed and that then retrieves that text from a larger help file. Both routines require a large amount of storage for the help information. Individual help procedures lead to large code files and added complexity in code flow. The external help file is more flexible, might allow the help information to be customized if the user wants to do this, keeps the program code simpler, and can allow the help file to be removed if the user does not have enough disk space or wants to save the disk space for other files. We recommend the external help file.

In Chapter 4, we developed an example of a very small command-oriented system that included a minimal help facility. In Figure 12.8, we reprint the diagram of Figure 4.13 for your reference. Note particularly the help nodes DoCmdHelp, DoPrintHelp, VarHelp, and DoSetHelp in this diagram.

These nodes are called from particular points where commands are partially developed, and so allow us to give good, context-sensitive assistance to the user. Thus we can have the following kinds of designs:

DoCmdHelp:

Issue text that tells the user that the allowable options are SET and PRINT and gives the syntax of each command.

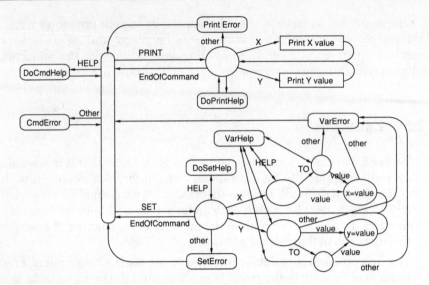

Figure 12.8   *The diagram of a simple command system*

DoPrintHelp:

Issue text that tells the user that the PRINT command allows him or her to print the value of the variables X and/or Y and that gives the syntax of the command.

VarHelp:

Issue text that tells the user what kind of values can be given to the variables X and/or Y and that gives the syntax of the SET command.

DoSetHelp:

Issue text that tells the user that the SET command allows him or her to set the value of the variables X and/or Y, indicates what the allowable values of the variables are, and gives the syntax of the command.

12.6   Readings

Kearsley is specifically about online help systems, but there are few other books on the subject. However, many of the principles of manuals and standard documentation do apply to help systems. The processes of testing help systems are particularly close to those for testing manuals. Several books describe manual preparation; for example, see Kelly. Brockmann's book on documentation, in particular, includes a discussion of online help, and Apple's Human Interface Design Guidelines give explicit guidelines for help systems. Many of the general books on user interfaces in our bibliography include sections on help systems.

Chapter 13

HANDLING AND AVOIDING ERRORS

It is critically important that a user have confidence in a program if he or she is to use it. A user without confidence who must save his or her work every few minutes, maintain a large set of backup files, or start over routinely, is a user who will not buy your program, will not recommend your program, and will find another program to use as quickly as possible.

There are several aspects to errors that we explore in this chapter. Primarily, we try to find ways to avoid errors whenever possible. This includes user errors, such as miskeying and data entry errors, as well as errors coming from within the program or computer system. When (inevitably) errors do occur, we look for recovery techniques. Techniques that work from within the program are our first goal. As a last resort we consider a technique that allows the user to reissue all the input that was made during a program's run and edit out the input that caused the error.

We divide errors into several groups for this chapter. The first class is user input errors. This can be faulty control input (mistaken choices or errors in commands), or it can be errors in data input. The second is computation errors, caused by attempts to do impossible arithmetic. The third class of errors is illegal file operations, and the fourth is improper use of the computer's devices.

This chapter deals with *some* techniques for handling *some* errors. Your own applications may require new techniques or may contain possibilities for errors we do not cover. Use this chapter to help you see the possibilities for error handling within your own programs.

13.1 Input Errors

Input errors stem from many sources: keyboard or screen design, careless user operations, or user confusion over exactly what command to enter or how to enter it. Your job as a designer or programmer is to anticipate these bad inputs and either prevent them or allow a graceful recovery from them.

Poor communication design is sometimes hard for a programmer to avoid. The original Apple II keyboard was notorious for its poorly placed RESET key. It was far too easy for a user to hit this key during normal typing, thus causing the computer to reboot and lose all the work that was done. This key was moved off the actual keyboard when the Apple IIe was introduced. Sometimes, however, poor design is the fault of the programmer or program designer. A program might have a QUIT menu line, icon, or function key too close to a common command, or might design an icon to look too much like a QUIT icon. Thus the user might make a careless choice without getting feedback or being required to confirm the QUIT. The designers might choose poor commands, meaningless icons, or random function keys, preventing the user from forming a good, consistent model of how the program is to work. Simple testing with normal users should catch such flaws, but testing only with programmers or others who know what the communication is *supposed* to do is not enough.

Data entry is a well-known weak point in all computer programs. Large data-processing shops realize this and set up a number of procedures to control bad data. We can use some of their techniques.

- Echo the user's input so that he or she can read (and edit) an entire logical set of input before it disappears from the screen; forms input is very useful for this.

- Check all input for "reasonableness." Set up templates for various kinds of inputs and make sure input fits them. Some examples include numeric or text input, name or address pattern fit, or an extended form of dictionary checking.

- For a program having intensive data input, allow the user to review a block of input data (say, a couple of hours' worth) against the original data and make editing corrections.

While this may not seem like a user interface concept, if your program helps its users ensure accurate data, it is helping them do their job. This is what applications are really for.

Control entry errors differ, depending on which control style you use. We have already mentioned one error-avoidance technique for text menus: highlighting the menu choice before it is selected by RETURN. This is also available for graphic menus via cursor, mouse, or tablet; simply highlight items as the selector moves over them, and the selection process will

```
Usage cat [-u][-n][-b][-s][-v][-e][-t][filename...]
```

Figure 13.1 *An error message for improper command arguments*

choose the one that is highlighted when the choice is made. Both graphic and text menus rely on recognition memory, so highlighting is a sound way of verifying to the user what he or she is choosing.

Unfortunately, command-line control does not offer the possibility of any simple mechanism like highlighting to work with the user. Here the user must rely on memorized commands, and there is no easy way to verify that a command is correct before it is issued. It is, however, possible, and recommended, to require that the user confirm any command that can cause damage, including the following:

- saving a file with a given name when a file already exists with that name,
- exiting a program without saving the work you've been doing, and
- on programs that expect standard stopping points, quitting at any other point.

When a user gives a command that is not recognized, the program response might be a simple "command - - - - not found." A more helpful approach, however, would be to act like a spelling checker, treating the list of possible valid commands like a spelling dictionary and suggesting possible alternatives. This allows recognition memory to supplement the user's memorized commands. The program can also summarize the usage of the command that is chosen, as in the example of the Unix cat command in Figure 13.1, which copies the contents of files (catenate) to other files or devices.

In Figure 13.1, the notation [. . .] means that this element is optional, and the other elements, such as [-u], are reminders of various options that can be checked in the online manual. Besides presenting this information, the program can allow the user to edit the original command and reissue the edited command.

13.2   Computation Errors

Mathematics is not always an ally in computation. While most computations work well for most values, there are exceptions:

- invalid operations (division by 0, the power 0^0, etc.) and
- invalid operands for functions (square roots of negative numbers, invalid arguments of inverse trigonometric functions, etc.).

```
Enter data
Save copies of all data
Set VALID to FALSE
While not VALID do
    Set VALID to TRUE
    { break down the computation into single steps }
    For each step in the computation do
        Check values to see if the computational step is OK
        If OK then
            Carry out the computation step
        Else
            Set VALID to FALSE and note the error type
    If not VALID then
        Display information describing the errors present
        If user wants to continue the computation
            Permit re-entry of user's choice of data
        Else
            Restore the original data values
            Allow user's choice of alternate operation
            Exit loop
End-While
```

Figure 13.2   *Design for an arithmetic error checker*

Operations can also result in underflow (values smaller than the smallest number the computer can represent) or overflow (numbers larger than the largest number the computer can represent). These are also serious errors.

Standard programming environments usually treat any of these as fatal errors and crash the program when they occur. In these environments, the programmer must do extra work to cope with these error situations. We suggest using a design like that of Figure 13.2 to ensure that these errors do not occur.

Note that this design is very generic and would not directly apply in some software. For example, a spreadsheet would stop the computation and simply place a diagnostic error message in the cell being computed, as is shown by the Microsoft Excel example in Figure 13.3, where the actual error messages are shown in column A, and our comments on how they were generated are to the right.

	A	B	C	D
1	Examples of Excel's error handling.			
2				
3	#DIV/0!	Error: division by 0		
4				
5	#NUM!	Error: ACOS(2)		
6				
7	#DIV/0!	Error: average of empty cells		
8				
9	#NUM!	Error: square root of -1		
10				
11	#NUM!	Error: logarithm of 0		

Figure 13.3   *An Excel spreadsheet with cells showing errors*

Courtesy of Microsoft Corporation

Not all errors in Excel are caught with such precision. Others result in a generic error box, as shown in Figure 13.4 below.

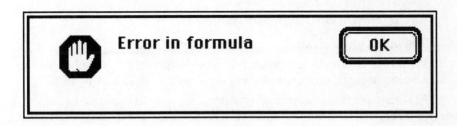

Figure 13.4   *Generic Excel error box*

Courtesy of Microsoft Corporation

Many newer systems such as the Apple Macintosh implement the IEEE 754 and 854 arithmetic standards. Here, the arithmetic errors discussed above are explicitly designated as exceptions that can be ignored, queried, or allowed to halt the program as the programmer wishes. The IEEE standards specify that the halts for all exceptions are initially off (that is, the program will not halt if any of the exceptions occur) and must be set on before a program will crash on such an error. The functions that deal with exceptions in the Macintosh Programmer's Workshop Pascal development system are typical of those you might find in this environment; they are as follows:

SetException(e:Exception; b:boolean)

sets or clears the exception e depending on whether the boolean is true or false, respectively. This lets the program clear exceptions that have been set elsewhere or set exceptions to accomplish other control.

TestException(e:Exception):boolean

returns true if the exception e has been raised, otherwise returns false.

TestHalt(e:Exception):boolean

returns true if the exception e has been raised, otherwise returns false.

SetHalt(e:Exception; b:boolean)

sets or removes the halt on exception e depending on whether the boolean is true or false, respectively.

Beyond this, the entire arithmetic environment can be saved and restored to make quick changes in the way arithmetic, such as exceptions and halts, is handled. Again, in MPW Pascal, two procedures are available for this:

GetEnvironment(VAR e:Environment)

saves a copy of the current environment in e.

SetEnvironment(e:Environment)

sets the current environment to the values in e.

The initial and default environment is named IEEEDefaultEnv.

With this information, we can redo the design we suggested earlier in this section using the concept of exceptions, as shown in Figure 13.5.

In some special cases it might be possible to know values that would cause errors in computation and catch them in the actual data input, but this seems to be so unusual that we cannot see it as a generally useful technique.

```
Enter data
Save copies of all data
GetEnvironment( e )
SetEnvironment( IEEEDefaultEnv ) {disable halts}
Repeat
    {AllExceptions is set to include all arithmetic exceptions}
    SetExceptions( AllExceptions, false )
    DoCalculations
    If TestException( AllExceptions ) then
        Use TestException for each separate exception to
            determine exactly what exceptions were raised
        Display message describing results
        If user wants to continue the computation
            Permit re-entry of user's choice of data
        Else
            Restore the original data values
            Allow user's choice of alternate operation
            Exit loop
Until not TestException( AllExceptions )
SetEnvironment( e )
```

Figure 13.5   *Design of arithmetic error checker via exceptions*

13.3   File and Device Errors

Files and devices are complicating factors on applications programs; devices are particularly problematic for personal computers where the CPU, keyboard, display controller, display, disks, modem, and an accelerator card may all come from different vendors. This section gives fundamental ways of avoiding file and device errors.

Besides actual disk hardware errors, there are three primary problems with files: nonexistent files, files with the wrong ownership or other properties, and insufficient file space. These can be handled with relative ease. Many computer systems and languages allow you to issue a system call to query a file with a number of access-control parameters. This call returns a value indicating whether the file has been opened with the attributes desired. If the file cannot be opened for any reason, such as wrong access mode, invalid permissions, or incorrect blocking factor, the value allows the program to detect the error. You must look at the details of this kind of operation for your particular computer system, but we give a couple of examples.

Hewlett-Packard 3000 with the MPE operating system: use the system intrinsic call

FOPEN(Name,FileOptions,AccessOptions,RecSize,Device,...)

where Name is the formal file name, FileOptions and AccessOptions are words whose individual bits and bit fields describe the file's properties and access modes, RecSize and Device are the record size and the name of the device on which the file resides, and there are a number of additional optional parameters. This call returns a file number and condition codes. These are standard HP information and are easily accessible: CCE (equal) means the open was successful, while CCL (less) means it was not. In addition, the system intrinsic FGETINFO can be used on an open file to return further information on file properties.

BSD 4.2 Unix: use the system call access(path,mode) to determine the accessibility of the file whose full path name is given. This tests for read access, write access, execute access, and/or the presence of the file, depending on the exact value of the mode variable. However, this tests only for the file's access mode, not the rest of the file information. Additional information is available by actually opening the file via fopen(filename,type) where filename is self-explanatory and type is a character string indicating what file access (read, write, read/write, append, etc.) is desired.

On the other hand, some systems are not so tractable. With Turbo Pascal for the IBM PC, the RESET procedure produces IORESULT whose value is 0 if the file has been opened. However, if the file is a read-only file or a hidden file, RESET cannot open it. To check for such files it is necessary to open the file with the DOS function call $30 (30 hexadecimal) issued by the system software interrupt call INTR as noted in *PC Magazine*. This kind of detail may be needed in the system you are using, but the information you need should be available in your operating system manual or from the technical side of a user group.

The problem of inadequate file system space for your work is more complex. If your program builds internal files and saves them only on command or on termination, suitable operating system calls can determine the space left in the file system, even if it means querying and summing the size of all free blocks. If insufficient space remains for your file(s), you must provide a way for the user to make space in the file system (say, by removing some files or compacting the file space) or to provide new media for storing the file. On the other hand, if the program works with external files and can increase their size, you should check for available space as the program begins and warn the user if there is little space left. You should also be prepared to halt gracefully when the file system is full and make it possible for the user to continue from that point when more space is available.

Three other points should be made about file use, although they are more routine and should be familiar to most programmers. First, and most trivial, beware of operations that could try to work beyond the end of the file. Standard end-of-file logic should be part of all file accesses; do not take shortcuts here. Second, beware of losing information by overwriting and destroying files. Whenever a user saves a file, check the name; if it is different from the file's original name (if any), and there is already a file by that name, be sure to warn the user and get a confirmation before the old file is overwritten. An example of this is shown in Figure 13.6. Finally, if there is a danger of file corruption or loss during program operations, make judicious backups of the original files; this might be an option the user could choose or reject, depending on his or her feelings of security.

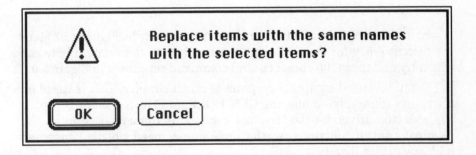

Figure 13.6   *A file warning*

Devices pose a unique problem for computer systems. As you use a richer computing environment for your programs, you run into the problem of large numbers of somewhat incompatible devices. Time-shared systems may have different terminals, but personal computers, especially IBM PC's and their compatibles, sport a remarkable range of devices. Since there are many different possible devices for each of your program's device functions, you must be prepared to cope with this variety.

Many timeshared computers have followed Unix's lead and deal with terminals' text dependencies indirectly. Programs need to know what kind of terminal is in use; Unix stores this in the user-settable system variable $TERM. When a program needs to use a special text attribute, it calls a library function which queries a file of terminal information (the file is named /etc/termcap in bsd Unix and /etc/terminfo in AT&T Unix). This information is retrieved, and the appropriate control sequence

```
vt100|dec vt100:\
    :do=^J:co#80:li#24:cl=50\E[;H\E[2J:sf=5\ED:\
    :le=^H:bs:am:cm=5\E[%i%d;%dH:nd=2\E[C:up=2\E[A:\
    :ce=3\E[K:cd=50\E[J:so=2\E[7m:se=2\E[m:us=2\E[4m:ue=2\E[m:\
    :md=2\E[1m:mr=2\E[7m:mb=2\E[5m:me=2\E[m:is=\e{1;24r\E[24;1H:\
    :rf=/usr/lib/tabset/vt100:\
    :rs=\E>\E[?31\E[?41/E[?51\E[?7h\E[?8h:ks=\E[?1h\E=:ke=\E[?11\E>:\
    :ku=\EOA:kd=\EOB:kr=\EOC:kl=\EOD:kb=^H:\
    :ho=\E[H:k1=\EOP:k2=\EOQ:k3=\EOR:k4=\EOS:pt:sr=5\EM:vt#3:xn:\
    :sc=\E7:rc=\E8:cs=\E[%i%d;%dr:
```

Figure 13.7   *bsd 2.10* termcap *for vt100 terminal*

is sent to the terminal to set the attribute. As an example, Figure 13.7 gives a termcap entry for the DEC vt100 terminal; note the relation between this entry and the vt100 cursor control command set shown in Figure 3.9.

Terminal-based computer graphics is much simpler. This is based on a graphics library, often meeting GKS, CORE, or PHIGS standards, which has a device driver for the terminal used. This library takes on all the terminal control functions, so the programmer need not be concerned with any device details.

Personal computers are an entirely different matter. To make your program usable by as many people as possible, you need to make your program work with the whole range of devices that might be used for its functions. For example, if you need graphics on an IBM PC or compatible, you should consider supporting the following displays: PC monochrome, Hercules monochrome, CGA, EGA, PGA, and maybe VGA if you are thinking of moving your product to the IBM PS/2. Printing is similar; your program should support either serial or parallel printers through any port and should be able to drive any of a dozen or more printers with varying ways of controlling text attributes, possibly supporting PostScript for laser printers.

There are two aspects to this range of functions and devices. The first is that you must write your program with a rather high level of functionality and then translate these functions to the actual devices with separate device-dependent operations. This is described quite well for computer graphics by Harrington. The second is that you must write the actual device drivers for each of the devices you will support. Writing device drivers is a book in itself and presents interesting challenges to the programmer. Their success depends largely on the quality of the design of the interface between the main program functions and the capabilities of the devices. In the areas of error handling, however, the primary concern of device drivers is handshaking and buffer management. The device driver must be prepared to control the device by whatever handshaking is needed (DC1/DC3, ENQ/ACK, etc.), and the program must be prevented from sending more information to the device than it can handle.

Having provided the range of device functions, you must now decide how to have your program know which device driver(s) to use. Your program can include a "setup" section allowing the user to state his or her device configuration; this configuration data can be saved in a .CONFIG file or in the program file itself. Alternately, and more clearly from the user's point of view, your program can be self-initializing. That is, it can query its host for information on the device(s) present. This information is more common than it may seem. Every kind of card in the internal slots of a Macintosh II is required to have an individual identification number. On the Apple II, there are certain addresses that can be read to identify which version of the machine it is, as shown in Figure 13.8 for monitor bytes and Figure 13.9 for ProDOS bytes. On the IBM PC, the DOS function call $10 returns BIOS video information via the INTR software interrupt as shown in Figure 13.10, courtesy of Hubert C. Callihan, University of Pittsburgh at Johnstown. More details on device identification can often be found in technical documentation, in higher-level technical magazines and journals, or from user groups.

Machine	$FBB3	$FB1E	$FBC0	$FBBF
Apple II	$38			
Apple II+	$EA	$AD		
Apple III	$EA	$8A		
Apple IIe (old)	$06			$EA
Apple IIe (new)	$06			$E0
Apple IIc (old)	$06		$FF	$00
Apple IIc (new)	$06		$00	$00

Figure 13.8 *Monitor bytes for various Apple II's*

Byte value	Meaning
00-- 0--	is an Apple II
01-- 0--	is an Apple II+
10-- 0--	is an Apple IIe
10-- 1--	is an Apple IIc
--01 ----	has 48K
--10 ----	has 64K
--11 ----	has 128K
---- --0-	has no 80-column card
---- --1-	has an 80-column card
---- ---0	has no compatible clock
---- ---1	has a compatible clock

Figure 13.9   *The Apple ProDOS $BF98 byte*

Value	Video Mode
0	40x25 monochrome
1	40x25 color
2	80x25 monochrome
3	30x25 color
4	320x200 color graphics
5	320x200 monochrome graphics
6	640x200 monochrome high-resolution graphics

Figure 13.10   *Results of the low byte of register ax when INTR($10,regs) is called*

13.4   Error Messages

As your user works with your program, the way you tell him or her that something is going wrong has a very large effect on his perception of the program. Both the content and the tone of these messages are critical. You must be extremely careful to keep the user from becoming confused and frustrated by error messages. The classical MS-DOS device or file error message: Abort, Retry, Ignore? may not be as bad as some, notably the Macintosh fatal error bomb box, but we should try to do better. Examples of better error messages are the following messages from Microsoft Word on the Macintosh. When you try to print without a printer present, you get the message shown in Figure 13.11.

When you try to save a file onto a disk which contains too little room, the message of Figure 13.12 is presented. When the computer cannot save a file because of a disk error, you get the error message in Figure 13.13. When you have too many documents open in Microsoft Word, the program presents the message in Figure 13.14. When you run out of working memory for your application, you get the message in Figure 13.15. Finally, from AppleWorks on the Apple II, when a file cannot be read from a disk drive, the screen of Figure 13.16 is presented.

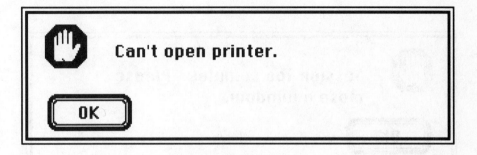

Figure 13.11 *Error: printer is not on line*

Courtesy of Microsoft Corporation

Figure 13.12 *Error: disk is full*

Courtesy of Microsoft Corporation

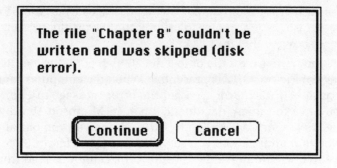

Figure 13.13 *Error: file write failure*
Courtesy of Microsoft Corporation

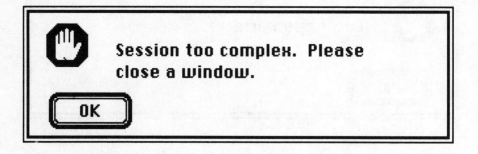

Figure 13.14 *Error: too many documents are open*
Courtesy of Microsoft Corporation

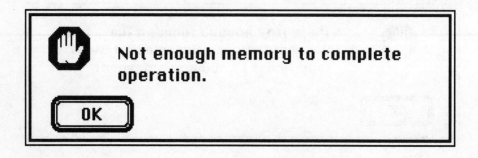

Figure 13.15 *Error: insufficient memory*
Courtesy of Microsoft Corporation

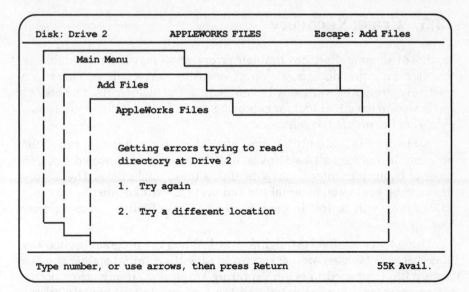

Figure 13.16 *AppleWorks error: bad disk read*

Copyright Claris Corporation, used by permission

A few general principles apply here.

> PRINCIPLE: Tell the user as specifically as you can what the error or problem is.

> PRINCIPLE: Tell the user as specifically as you can what might fix the problem.

> PRINCIPLE: Do both of the above in simple language with clear action verbs that emphasize the user's control of the program.

13.5   Crash Recovery

In spite of all your efforts to eliminate errors, some may be unavoidable, or the user may not do a good job of ensuring correct data. There is a relatively straightforward way to handle this: the history file. The history file is also an excellent tool for capturing errors at all development levels, even after the program is released.

A history file is simply a record of all the activity during a run of the program. It includes all keystrokes, even erasures and canceled lines, in order to capture unintentional side effects these might have. The history file must be kept as an external file and every keystroke must be sent to it so that none will be lost in the case of any kind of failure, even a power loss.

Using a history file is straightforward. When the program begins, any files that will be used are backed up to save their initial status, and the history file is opened to begin capturing keystrokes. If any errors occur, the program can be terminated and the history file will contain all the program activity; this file can be edited as needed to clean up anything that caused the error, and the program is rerun with the backed-up files and the history file replacing the standard input. When the end of the history file is reached, control can return to the standard input.

Besides its role in recovering from errors, the history file gives you the kind of documentation you need to trace error situations. Building it in from the beginning of program development gives you a valuable debugging tool. If you find that the file backups and history file take up too much file space on the completed program's host, or if the program is stable enough to make this kind of recovery generally unnecessary, it can be disabled for released versions. However, the history file mechanism adds very little code to the program, so we suggest leaving the code in place and allowing a user to enable it as desired.

13.6   Readings

The best sources of information on the details of implementing many of the error-handling features of this chapter are the manuals for your particular computer system. This may need to be augmented by additional technical manuals or detailed books on your system; this is particularly true for personal computers, which typically do not come with sufficient technical documentation. Good relations with users' groups can also be very helpful, particularly if the group is technically oriented. Some computer manufacturers maintain special developers' groups or information, which are excellent sources of technical data.

If your system, like the Apple Macintosh, supports the IEEE standards for numeric data, you should get the IEEE Standards Documents 754 and 854 from IEEE directly. These are often quite technical and give a wealth of detail that you will find helpful.

The resources we used to write this chapter are quite varied. The Macintosh information came from the Apple MPW Pascal manual, while technical information on the IBM PC came from the PC Lab Notes section of *PC Magazine*, and from some development work by Hubert Callihan of the University of Pittsburgh, Johnstown. Information on device drivers came from our experience in writing such drivers for several graphics systems. Harrington gives a very good description of designing a device-independent system and interfacing it with device drivers.

## Chapter 14

SPECIAL CONCERNS: MAKING PROGRAMS USABLE BY PERSONS WITH DISABILITIES

A s you design your programs, you must keep in mind special needs of users. Not everyone is able to type with ten fingers. Not everyone has good vision, or good hearing, or good physical control for working with computers. In our experience, people with disabilities tend to adapt to the hardware and software available and make it work somehow. However, there is no reason they should have to deal with unnecessarily clumsy software. In this age of information technology, *everyone* needs to be able to use computers. Writing computer programs that people with disabilities cannot use is as wrong as building a doorway less than 32 inches wide to an information resource such as a public library, thereby denying wheelchair access.

In many cases, the person really needs a special input device to allow use of all software. There are many such devices, but since they all fill the role the keyboard serves for most people, they are frequently called "special keyboards," even if they have no keys. Some special keyboards can track eye movement or detect eye blinking or any minute movement a person may be able to control. Other users may be served best by a voice recognition system. This chapter is intended to help you make your programs usable by persons with less severe disabilities, but the principles we discuss should also ease the use of your program with special keyboards.

You may design a program to be used primarily by persons with specific disabilities, or you may design a program to be used by a general audience (which you can be assured will include persons with disabilities). The important thing is to ask what your program's users need and want. As good as your intentions may be, you cannot assume that you know what someone else needs. A few years ago, a man's co-workers decided to surprise him by chipping in to buy a computer for him. This man did not have the use of his hands, but he could do virtually anything, including typing, with his feet. His colleagues looked at various systems and selected one with the keyboard and monitor as a single, inseparable unit. Hence, with the keyboard on the floor where it needed to be, the monitor was not within viewing range at all. Of course, his friends very sheepishly exchanged it for a system that could have the keyboard on the floor and the display at eye level.

PRINCIPLE: Ask users what they need.

You can get feedback on what your program might need by sending an electronic mail inquiry to the distribution list of *The Handicap Digest* on Bitnet, L-HCAP@NDSUVM1. (Bitnet is a network of colleges and other institutions that is used to transfer electronic mail and to distribute information to various special interest groups.) The Columbia University Center for Computing Activities recently used this forum to ask specific questions so they could make the next version of Kermit, a terminal emulator and file transfer program, as useful as possible. We used it to ask for advice on this chapter. Another good information source is the Special Interest Group on Computers and the Physically Handicapped of the Association for Computing Machinery (ACM SIGCAPH). Both IBM and Apple have shown a concern for users with disabilities. IBM created a National Support Center for Persons with Disabilities, headquartered in Atlanta, in 1985. It serves as a clearing- house for information on adaptive aids, programs, and resources. Apple Computer's Office of Special Education provides information about products that work with Apple computers that could benefit users with disabilities.

14.1   Considerations for Users with Manual Disabilities

Typing is a tedious process for many people. Many simply do not know how to type well, or perhaps have difficulty spelling. Others may have physical disabilities that affect their typing ability. You can decrease your program's difficulty for these people by requiring less typing. One way to minimize typing is to provide reasonable default values when the user must enter information. Another way is to allow the user to skip to a different field or a different page with a single keystroke.

> PRINCIPLE: Provide reasonable default values for user supplied information.

> PRINCIPLE: Allow the user to skip to other information or pages with a single keystroke.

Many people have difficulty pressing more than one key at a time. They may only be able to type with one hand, or they may be typing with a mouthstick or headstick. Many programs and systems require the user to press two or three keys simultaneously. The use of the Control, Alt, and Delete keys pressed simultaneously to reboot the IBM PC is not an isolated instance. This is partly a problem with keyboards that require the Control key to generate the lower part of the ASCII character set or to perform system functions. It can also be a problem with the software design. For example, AppleWorks requires the OpenApple key to be pressed with other keys for many of its functions.

There are utilities available that allow multiple keys to be pressed sequentially instead of simultaneously; it would be worthwhile to include such an option in your own software to support persons who have this difficulty. We can think of no reason why it should *ever* be necessary for users to press two or more keys simultaneously. Many systems and terminals have function keys that can be programmed to be equivalent to several key strokes pressed either simultaneously or serially. Other systems allow the keyboard to be reprogrammed. At the very least, you can write your program so that any combination of key strokes you need can be pressed one at a time.

> PRINCIPLE: Design programs so the user need never press two or more keys simultaneously.

Special Input Devices

Persons with visual or physical restrictions often cannot use the full range of input devices available to most users. Those with disabilities may have difficulties using ordinary keyboards and software. Such special input devices may be as simple as having a key that holds down several keys at once or as complex as being able to detect eye movement. Voice recognition systems can be very useful, although the most flexible of these are expensive and require extensive programming and user voice training.

Figure 14.1 *A one-handed keyboard, the NewO Writehander*

Software designers can do a lot to ease the use of their software by keeping these special needs in mind. A program's design should include ways of managing input from a range of sources so users can have special devices. Simply allowing input to come from a communications port instead of the keyboard will handle some of this.

In Figure 14.1, we show a one-handed keyboard, the NewO Writehander from the NewO Company. The four fingers each use one key on the unit's spherical surface, and the thumb operates the four pairs of keys. It comes in two sizes each for the right hand or the left hand.

In Figure 14.2, we show a Versabraille II+ from Telesensory Systems, Inc. This system, which is a microcomputer itself, can serve as both an input and output device to other computers. The six keys, three for each hand, allow braille input, while the one line display above the keys is a

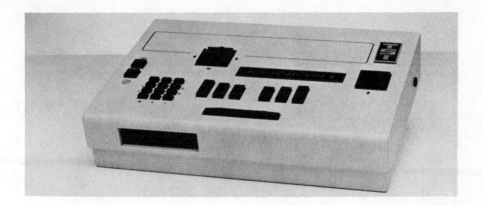

Figure 14.2 *A braille input and output system, the Versabraille II+*

20-character braille display. A blind student at The University of Iowa was able to do all his computer work with this device as long as the software let him send output to the parallel and serial ports. Since the Basic language on his IBM PC Jr. would not allow this, he had to have a special cable made in order to do some of his course work.

In Figure 14.3, we show a special input device which was developed for the Macintosh, the Headmaster from Personics Corporation. The Headmaster replaces the mouse with an ultrasound reflector which can be strapped on the head, and selections can then be made through the

Figure 14.3 *The Headmaster ultrasound input device for the Macintosh*

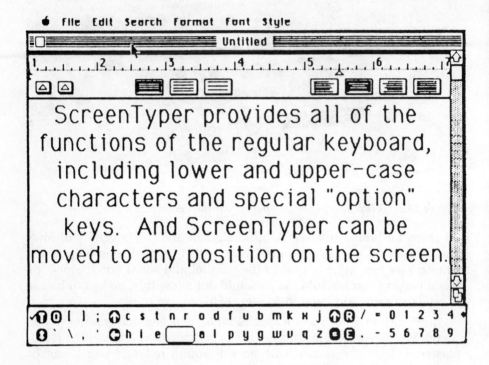

Figure 14.4   *A screen showing the Screen Typer keyboard substitution*

attached sip switch, a strawlike device that takes input from the user sipping on it. The accompanying Screen Typer software allows keyboard functions, as shown in Figure 14.4.

Menu Considerations

In our discussion of flexible menus, we describe several techniques for choosing a menu item. Of all the possible ways to handle such a menu, a user only needs two keys to have complete control: one arrow key and the RETURN key. (Remember that a single arrow key is enough if the menu selection wraps around after it goes off the top or bottom, as illustrated in Chapter 3.)

This elementary control can be achieved by someone with very limited physical abilities. If a user can make any two distinguishable actions, these can be interpreted by a suitable mechanism such as a pressure pad to be the two key presses. In fact, a single action can control both key options with the action performed once being the arrow key and the action repeated quickly being the return key.

Managing Commands

User-defined command files are a great benefit to users. If the user has a physical disability that makes typing difficult, command files can make computers much more easily used by allowing the user to execute a large number of commands with a few simple keystrokes or by simple input from some other input device.

Some users may need a voice recognition system. The most powerful of these require extensive user training so the computer will recognize their words. They also require programming of "scripts" for each software application. Intelligent voice recognition systems use command files. The choice of computer equipment may be influenced by the availability of specialized software, as well as input and output devices. At the time of this writing,voice recognition is not yet in widespread use on the Apple Macintosh, but many voice recognition systems can be used with the IBM PC and compatibles.

Other Ways to Get Interactive Input

There are many other possible interactive input devices besides keyboards for both disabled and nondisabled persons. This section introduces some of these devices and techniques but does not attempt to give an exhaustive description of devices or to mention brand names.

Characters can be selected by moving a graphic cursor across a set of keys onscreen. This movement can be accomplished through a pressure plate, eye tracking device, mouse, or any other input device. This technique is easily implemented by treating each character as a separate item in a graphics menu.

Characters can be selected by counting events such as a mechanical switch closure. This is easier for numbers than characters and could be used either for an entire real number or for digit input. One could use a timeout to detect end of input, or the user could take advantage of more careful timing to send a Morse-like code.

All of these are straightforward to program. Routines to implement them could readily replace the keyboard input routines we describe in Chapter 5 with no significant change in any program design. Other interesting environments such as those offered by the DataGlove, VIDEO-PLACE, and "Noobie" the New Beast use nonstandard techniques and are discussed in Chapter 9.

14.2   Considerations for Visually Impaired Users

People with visual impairments use a variety of input and output devices to assist them in using computers. They use large print systems, voice output, braille input and output systems, or a combination of these. Their selections depend on the degree of vision loss, the advantages of each type of hardware and supporting software, and personal preferences.

Commonly used braille output devices either produce 40-column by 24-row hardcopy or a dynamic braille display of 20 characters at a time, as shown in Figure 14.2. In either case, display area is at a premium, so compressed menus should be used to ensure that only important information is provided to the user. Further, since a screen erase results in a page feed for many printers, making it necessary to reinsert the paper in the less expensive single sheet printers, form feeds should be kept to a minimum.

There are programs that enlarge the print on most popular personal computers. Also, there is special equipment, used in conjunction with a

Figure 14.5 *Magnified display from Lyon Large Print program*

personal computer, that will allow anything that appears on the screen to be enlarged. Some of this equipment is not readily affordable, with a complete system costing up to $11,000. A screen enlarger function, CloseView, is a standard part of the Macintosh system in Release 6.0.1. It blows up the pixels for a "fat bits" version of whatever is being viewed, and may be useful in some instances and not in others, as shown in Figure 6.1. The Lyon Large Print software from VTEK generates a smooth magnified font, as shown in Figure 14.5. It includes the software and a color video adapter card. In addition, visually impaired users may also find a voice synthesizer useful. A blind user may choose to use input from a regular or braille keyboard and have either braille or voice output.

Much of the recent software emphasis on graphics, icons, and color renders this software unusable by those who rely on speech or braille output and difficult to use by those who have a lesser degree of visual impairment. Some software may demand the use of color or graphics to be effective; an air traffic monitoring system is one such example. However, graphics is sometimes added superficially and can be a distraction to those who are sighted and a barrier to those who are not.

The usual technique for managing text menus for the blind is to have output sent to a voice-output or braille device. With voice devices, the entire menu is spoken as it would be printed, and the "emphasis" on each new menu choice, mentioned in Chapter 3, is to speak the new choice. This works rather well. However, some common menu techniques cause users of spoken menus endless grief. Many software packages and newsletters on electronic bulletin boards and distribution lists make heavy use of character graphics, logos and boxes made of asterisks or hyphens. Have you ever thought how it sounds to have a voice say "asterisk asterisk asterisk..." 80 times? Since people who use your program may be visually impaired, use some technique to create screen regions that will not give endless repetitions of separator characters. There is software for a number of personal computers that will check for such repetition of characters and say something like "asterisk repeats 80 times." A person using a terminal connected to a mainframe to run software or read bulletin boards has no such option.

A few such character graphics may be useful and even necessary to separate information groups. Perhaps three to five asterisks at the beginning of a line could indicate the start of a new block of information. Even sighted users do not need more than that. You need not eliminate the use of all graphics, but you should be sure they are warranted and not excessive.

PRINCIPLE: Think about whether the graphics you are using are necessary.

> PRINCIPLE: Minimize repetitive character graphics.

If you are designing information retrieval system software to make important information available electronically, be sure that you do not incorporate unnecessary barriers. The computer has opened up many doors to persons with disabilities so that they can communicate better and pursue many new careers. The *Handicap Digest* recently had a note about a prospective computerized dictionary. A blind English professor was very excited to learn that there were plans to make the Oxford English Dictionary available in electronic form. Since this would certainly be a real boon to a blind writer, you can imagine his disappointment when he heard that they planned to use color to display different types of information. His speech synthesizer cannot tell him the color of selected text. Such a use of color can be a real benefit to sighted users. However, for such an important information resource, which must be accessible to everyone, alternative means to access the information must be available.

> PRINCIPLE: Provide alternatives to color and graphics, especially in information retrieval systems.

A major problem with using Braille or voice output devices, especially with MS-DOS machines, is that software frequently sends text output directly to screen memory. Currently available speech software usually works better if the software with which it is used writes to the Basic Input Output System (BIOS), so it can be redirected to the device. This use of the BIOS is not always best for the standard software; for example, word processors may write output to screen memory directly to save time. However, the program should allow the user to control this in order to get to DOS and BIOS-level commands and drivers. Since many special devices require serial data, the user should also be able to set serial output.

> PRINCIPLE: Allow output to be directed to the BIOS or other system component where it can be redirected to special devices.

Another problem faced by blind users is software documentation. The key here, as above, is to provide alternatives and let the user decide what works best. Documentation delivered as an ASCII text file permits this flexibility. With this format, an online document can be printed in Braille or in large print, or it can be directed to a voice synthesizer and put onto a cassette tape. The same text file can be read on the screen or printed on a regular printer, allowing a sighted person to read the instructions and assist a blind user in that manner, if that were desirable. If screen formatting is desired, the file can include special characters that are interpreted by the screen display system to do the formatting and are skipped by the spoken or braille output.

> PRINCIPLE: Allow the user to select the most useful form of documentation by providing it as an ASCII text file.

14.3   Color "Blindness" and Age

As mentioned above, the use of color, as well as other visually effective graphs and icons, makes a program less usable and possibly totally unusable by blind people. These users would need additional software which tells them each item's color to be able to use programs which rely on color to get the user's attention. In addition, straightforward guidelines can allow software to help those with color deficiencies, unfortunately referred to as "color blind." Only a very small percentage of the color deficient have a true blindness for color. About 8% of males and 0.5% of females have some color deficiency that renders them unable to distinguish small color differences, especially with low brightness levels. Since color deficient viewers frequently have reduced sensitivity to brightness, the problems of differentiation may be increased with a monochromatic display if subtle differences in gray level are used. People also need higher brightness levels to distinguish colors as they grow older, and blue is especially difficult for elderly users to see.

Earlier guidelines are not only applicable here, but are more important. Redundant coding of font, shape, or brightness, in addition to color, makes objects more easily distinguishable. Since color deficient persons make fewer errors with large areas, color coding the background instead of the text is helpful.

> PRINCIPLE: For color deficient viewers, color code background rather than text.

People who have difficulties detecting differences between reds and greens can differentiate colors if you combine red with cyan or combine blue with yellow. In general, when mixing colors, if you change at least two of the three primaries, instead of varying only one of the hues, problems of detection are reduced.

PRINCIPLE: Avoid subtle differences in color or gray scale.

14.4   Considerations for Hearing Impaired Users and Those with Reading Disabilities

Programmers are frequently unaware of the difficulties that hearing impaired persons may have using computers. Besides the fact that audible signals are useless for these users, persons with hearing impairments frequently have reading difficulties. If you are designing a program for these users, you want to use graphics to augment the textual information. Graphics are encouraged for this audience, but you must be sure they are appropriate and convey the information you intend. Consult with a graphic design artist, and test your designs on prospective users. In addition, all text must be made as clear as possible. This, of course, is true for all programs but is even more vital for this group of users. This includes both onscreen text and documentation.

PRINCIPLE: Make use of appropriate graphics for users with hearing impairments or reading disabilities.

PRINCIPLE: Be sure all text is clear and understandable.

At the National Technical Institute for the Deaf (NTID) at the Rochester Institute of Technology, information is presented in a visual format, principally through the Macintosh and the IBM PC/AT Windows environments. Students in the School of Visual Communications use mostly Macintosh-based software because the graphic/text software can be used by faculty to prepare mediated course materials, especially for those students entering with low reading levels, and can be used by students in

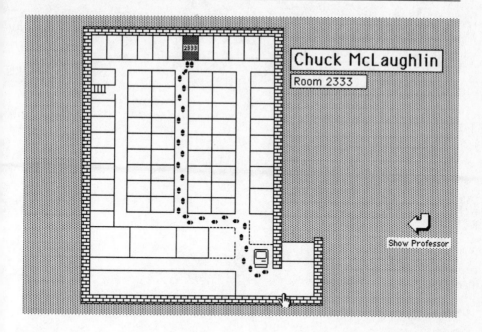

Figure 14.6   *A HyperCard map for deaf users*

preparation for careers in the graphic arts. HyperCard has become a very valuable tool for these students.

Figure 14.6 illustrates a HyperCard screen used in an orientation program for the NTID Data Processing Department. This HyperCard stack, provided by Michael Voelke presents catalog and faculty information to students. The figure shows a map of the building and a faculty office location and conveys this information much more clearly than text would.

14.5   Readings

There is not always one answer for either software or hardware for users with disabilities. So much depends on the disability and user preference. Most of the information in this chapter came from the electronic *Handicap Digest* mentioned at the beginning of the chapter and from asking people with disabilities. We cannot emphasize too strongly the necessity to ask your users what they need and want.

The information on color "blindness" came primarily from research by Murch [1984a] at Tektronix, by Smith [1987a] and Smith and Farrell [1984a] at Hewlett-Packard.

Appendix I

LIST OF PRINCIPLES

W̲e stated a number of principles of user interfaces as we presented the various user interface topics in this book. We think it is worthwhile to present these principles again here to provide a summary of the concepts we have found important in user interfaces. These principles are organized by chapter and are in the order they are found in the text. This allows you to use this appendix as a quick reference for the book as well as a summary of a number of user interface concepts.

Chapter 1   PRINCIPLES

PRINCIPLE: The main function of the user interface is communication.

PRINCIPLE: The interface must keep the computer from coming between the user and the work.

PRINCIPLE: The interface must be consistent throughout the program.

PRINCIPLE: The interface must be flexible to work with a wide range of users.

PRINCIPLE: The interface must keep the user aware of what is going on in the task.

PRINCIPLE: The interface must include access to help.

PRINCIPLE: The program must not crash.

PRINCIPLE: The program should work hard so the user does not have to.

PRINCIPLE: Make your program work like others similar to it.

PRINCIPLE: Make all parts of your program work alike.

Chapter 2 PRINCIPLES

PRINCIPLE: Use menu techniques for a program intended for casual or infrequent users.

PRINCIPLE: Use command techniques for a program whose users will become skilled in its operation.

PRINCIPLE: Make data input fit consistently with the control input and information output phases of your program.

PRINCIPLE: Always provide the user with information on what is happening with the program.

Chapter 3 PRINCIPLES

PRINCIPLE: Keep menus short and clear.

PRINCIPLE: Keep nested menus as simple as possible, and do not nest them deeply.

PRINCIPLE: Design your programs to give the user access to the most natural and powerful devices available for program interaction.

PRINCIPLE: Be sure your graphic menu items are easily selectable by the system's graphic devices.

PRINCIPLE: Be sure your graphic representations are immediately distinguishable from each other.

PRINCIPLE: Use grouping to give a first level of discrimination in graphic menus.

PRINCIPLE: Be sure your graphic items carry the meaning you intend.

PRINCIPLE: In any graphic or text menu, highlight the currently selected item.

PRINCIPLE: Use toolkits whenever possible to make your job easier and to be consistent with the user's expectations.

Chapter 4 PRINCIPLES

PRINCIPLE: Design your commands to fit the level of expertise of your audience

PRINCIPLE: Make your commands use action-oriented words that fit the actions of the program.

PRINCIPLE: Wherever possible allow the use of filler words to make the commands more natural.

PRINCIPLE: Choose your command words so they have unique abbreviations, and allow the user to enter the abbreviations instead of the entire command word.

PRINCIPLE: Allow your users to write command scripts to simplify complex operations with your program.

Chapter 5 PRINCIPLES

PRINCIPLE: All input must be managed a character at a time.

PRINCIPLE: Numeric input must be flexible in handling various numeric formats.

PRINCIPLE: Implement input-editing operations in your own software.

PRINCIPLE: Treat text as whole words for input, allowing operations such as word-wrap and cancellation of the most recent word.

PRINCIPLE: Allow your program to accept expressions anywhere a number would be entered.

Chapter 6 PRINCIPLES

PRINCIPLE: Plan screen design from the beginning.

PRINCIPLE: Present information consistently.

PRINCIPLE: Present information so that it can be read quickly and correctly.

PRINCIPLE: Make the program phrase all action in words that emphasize the user's control, describe positive actions, and reflect the user's normal usage.

PRINCIPLE: Use vocabulary and techniques consistent with traditional working methods.

PRINCIPLE: Use the computer capabilities to full advantage.

PRINCIPLE: Present information in a similar fashion as popular existing programs.

PRINCIPLE: Make screens simple and legible.

PRINCIPLE: Present only one major idea on a display.

PRINCIPLE: Indicate when there is more information than is currently displayed.

PRINCIPLE: All information necessary to perform a given task must be on the screen.

PRINCIPLE: Use a graph to display information if it conveys information more effectively.

Chapter 7   PRINCIPLES

PRINCIPLE: If you want to build a window-based program, use a window system and appropriate toolkit.

Chapter 8   PRINCIPLES

PRINCIPLE: Be consistent in the use of colors.

PRINCIPLE: Seek advice of professional artists in the use of color.

PRINCIPLE: Use no more than five to seven colors in a display.

PRINCIPLE: If you use red and green, place them in the center of the display, not in the periphery.

PRINCIPLE: Use blue for background or large areas.

PRINCIPLE: Avoid adjacent use of two colors that differ only in the brightness of blue.

PRINCIPLE: Do not rely on color coding alone to distinguish small areas.

PRINCIPLE: Do not use intense combinations of blue/yellow, red/green, red/blue or green/blue.

PRINCIPLE: Use warm colors for objects that are closer to the viewer.

PRINCIPLE: Use familiar color codings appropriately.

PRINCIPLE: Put light colors next to dark colors to remain black and white compatible.

Chapter 11 PRINCIPLES

PRINCIPLE: Provide learning tools for your software.

PRINCIPLE: Provide a range of learning tools to accommodate people with different learning styles.

PRINCIPLE: Provide assistance for inexperienced users without requiring advanced users to use it.

PRINCIPLE: Design online learning aids to require no more than 20 to 30 minutes of a user's time.

PRINCIPLE: At any point in a program users should be able to find out where they are, how they he got here, and where they can go from here.

PRINCIPLE: Navigation information should be available without making a serious interruption in the program's operation.

PRINCIPLE: Help should always be available by consistent means.

PRINCIPLE: The user should know help is available and how to get it.

PRINCIPLE: Help should be context-sensitive; it should refer directly to the point from which it was called and tell the user what can be done there.

PRINCIPLE: Help should speak in the user's language and in terms of the user's task.

PRINCIPLE: Help should give examples and be dynamic, instead of giving manual-style descriptions.

PRINCIPLE: Help should be presented in screen-formatted pages or in windows that leave the user's work showing.

PRINCIPLE: Make the help system act as a learning aid by making it interactive.

PRINCIPLE: Made sure your design does not contribute to errors by making it difficult for the user to remember proper controls.

PRINCIPLE: Include ways for data entry errors to be caught and corrected.

PRINCIPLE: Warn users when they perform an operation that can possibly cause irretrievable damage.

PRINCIPLE: Use environments that let the program field errors instead of using the computer's automatic error traps.

PRINCIPLE: When an error occurs, give the user concrete information on what the error was, and allow him or her to retreat from it.

PRINCIPLE: When your program needs external devices, provide a wide range of device drivers.

PRINCIPLE: When your program needs external devices, make it check for available devices automatically whenever possible.

Chapter 13   PRINCIPLES

PRINCIPLE: Tell the user as specifically as you can what the error or problem is.

PRINCIPLE: Tell the user as specifically as you can what might fix the problem.

PRINCIPLE: Do both of the above in simple language with clear action verbs that emphasize the user's control of the program.

Chapter 14   PRINCIPLES

PRINCIPLE: Ask users what they need.

PRINCIPLE: Provide reasonable default values for user supplied information.

PRINCIPLE: Allow the user to skip to other information or pages with a single keystroke.

PRINCIPLE: Design programs so the user need never press two or more keys simultaneously.

PRINCIPLE: Think about whether the graphics you are using are necessary.

PRINCIPLE: Minimize repetitive character graphics.

PRINCIPLE: Provide alternatives to color and graphics, especially in information retrieval systems.

PRINCIPLE: Allow output to be directed to the BIOS or other system component where it can be redirected to special devices.

PRINCIPLE: Allow the user to select the most useful form of documentation by providing it as an ASCII text file.

PRINCIPLE: For color deficient viewers, color code background rather than text.

PRINCIPLE: Avoid subtle differences in color or gray scale.

PRINCIPLE: Make use of appropriate graphics for users with hearing impairments or reading disabilities.

PRINCIPLE: Be sure all text is clear and understandable.

Appendix II

Projects

It is one thing to read about techniques for constructing user interfaces, but it is quite another to have actual experience with implementing them. In order to suggest some ways to get experience, especially for students who may use this book as an introduction to user interface work, we have included several projects in this Appendix. These projects are divided by chapter, and most of the projects involve programming to implement some topic covered in the chapter. Some of these projects may not be appropriate for any one reader's environment. However, a careful selection of projects should help a reader get started with user interface development.

Chapter 2 Projects

1. Take a (standard, with rolling ball) mouse and turn it around, so the cord is facing you. Now move it around, and note that all motion is backwards. Why? Now turn it upside down, and repeat the experiment, moving your hand over the mouse ball; note the results.

2. It is very interesting to look at the use of scroll controllers in various programs. Sometimes (as on the Macintosh) you scroll the window indicator down to move down through the document (and thus to move the document up on the screen), while sometimes (as in Smalltalk) you scroll the window indicator down to move the document down on the screen (and thus move the window indicator up on the document). Discuss these two options; which seems more natural to you? Did it seem natural when you started to use software with these features?

3. In Chapter 2, we showed how a locator device can be simulated with cursor control keys, and how a pick can be simulated with a locator. Design other device simulations as follows:

    (a) simulate a valuator with an onscreen scale and a locator device,

    (b) simulate a locator with two valuator devices, such as game paddles,

    (c) simulate a pick with two valuators built as in (a).

4. Experiment with proportion-finished indicators to give activity feedback. Try different kinds of indicators and variations in their size, screen position, and color. Have several users or friends look over your experiments to see how well your indicators give them information.

Chapter 3   PROJECTS

1. We used inverse video techniques to highlight selections in the text menu example above. Modify this example to use the following kinds of highlighting if they are available on your computer:

    (a) brightened text

    (b) colored text

    (c) underlined text

    (d) an arrow such as —> to the left of or replacing the selection's number.

2. Write a menu prototype for your personal computer which allows three options for choices as in our example: numbers, letters, and arrow keys. Have friends of yours who are novice computer users try it out, and note their comments. Which techniques do they prefer?

3. If you have access to a vt100-class terminal, implement the GotoXY routine we outlined above and use it as in project 2. Try to put in as many of the optimizing features as possible so it will be a useful addition to your user-interface toolkit. For other terminals with similar screen-control operations (though different codes), write a similar GotoXY.

4. Implement the generic menu approach of Section 3.2 with your own choice of data structures. Include a resource compiler to build a binary version of the menu resource.

5. Build a graphical menu of shapes for your personal computer. Put these shapes in a rectangular region at the right-hand side of your screen and have one selected; then draw the shape larger in the square left-hand part of the screen. How many shapes can you put in the small right-hand part before it becomes too hard to choose one? Draw the shapes in one color and use another to show the highlighted shape that has been picked before the final choice. What standard and highlight color choices make shapes easy to see while still having a highlighted shape stand out?

6. Find a set of icons, such as a set of airline terminal indicators, and show them to your friends out of context. Note which ones are identified and which ones are not. Try to find a pattern as to why some icons are identifiable and some are not.

7. (a) Design a set of icons using the tools available on your personal computer; these can include shape tables or sprites. Make these icons describe familiar household items as if they were to give a home inventory; some such shapes might be lamps, chairs, tables, bookcases, beds, etc. Display a menu of these icons in rectangles of the size you discovered to be comfortable in exercise 2, and ask other persons to identify them. Were they successful? Were they easy to distinguish?

   (b) Do as above where the icons are to represent non-concrete ideas associated with the processes of file management (for example, saving a file, retrieving a file, copying a file, and deleting a file.) See if they are more difficult to identify than the icons in (a).

Chapter 4   Projects

1. Find a command driven system in an area you are familiar with.

   (a) Catalog its commands as fully as you can.

   (b) For each important command with parameters, catalog the parameters and how they are used with the command.

(c) Identify its users, and discuss how well it fits those users and how it might be improved to serve its audience better.

2. Implement wildcard matches to match a word with wildcard characters against a word list. Since these matches involve so many partial matches, look carefully at the problem of making partial word matches efficient.

3. Experiment with the UNDO operation by saving the state of affected data before an input or other operation is carried out. How can you undo UNDO?

4. Implement a user-defined command system using a file, in which the command processor looks in the file if it is unable to find the command in the standard command set. Extend this to capturing commands from the standard command input and placing them in the user-defined command file.

5. Use the more complex definition of "word" to rewrite the GetWord procedure in the text.

Chapter 5   PROJECTS

1. Implement a procedure to give text input with simple editing and word wrap. Add other features, including input cancel (cancel whole string), word cancel, and abbreviation expansion.

2. Tighten up the input checking for commas in numbers by allowing commas to appear only at genuine thousands-group break points. Use either the compute-as-you-go or the prescan technique.

3. Adapt input checking to non-U.S. environments by allowing any currency symbol (pounds, yen, ...) and any suitable separator and decimal point symbols. Consider determining such constants from a switch setting (in C, suitable #define and #ifdef.....#endif settings or resource file) in order to adapt software readily for a range of local conditions.

4. Reverse Polish expressions are expressions in postfix notation (the operator follows the operator) with no operator precedence, such as

x y + instead of x + y. They can be handled readily with nonrecursive techniques. This is done by omitting the operator stack completely; whenever an operator is read by NextToken, it is applied immediately to the operand stack. Implement the evaluation of reverse Polish expressions.

5. Design an input screen and implement its programming. Use special background colors for alphabetic and numeric fields if you have colors available. Provide default values for the screen's data, and display them before screen input begins.

6. Design and implement a virtual device for direct manipulation data input. Extend this by adding other virtual devices to a full virtual control panel for a control program, as described in Chapter 6.

Chapter 6 PROJECTS

1. Define the following special screen areas and implement procedures to put text passed as a parameter into the screen area:

   (a) screen title area,

   (b) error/warning message area,

   (c) status line.

2. Design and implement one or more of the following special-purpose screens discussed in Chapter 6:

   (a) menu,

   (b) formatted data entry,

   (c) question and answer,

   (d) inquiry,

   (e) information,

   (f) control.

3. Extend either project 1 or 2 above to add highlighting to specific fields. Experiment with several kinds of highlighting available on your system, such as high intensity, underlining, blinking, colored text, or colored background to find a style that gets attention but is not intrusive.

Chapter 8   Projects

1. Create a display with a bright red circle on a bright blue background. Notice the edges where the colors meet. Do the same with the colors reversed. Which part of the image seems closer?

2. Put red and green squares or circles in the middle of your display and on the periphery. Notice the difference in appearance of color. Do the same with green/blue and blue/yellow color pairs.

3. Place small blue objects in the middle and the periphery of the display. Are the objects in the periphery distinguishable?

Chapter 9   Projects

1. Define a custom cursor and find a way to replace your standard cursor with the custom cursor in a program.

2. Extend project 3 from Chapter 2 to provide more extensive on-screen controls for data input. Implement pushbuttons or dials for input, or extend the scale and locator of Chapter 2 to a real data slider.

3. Take a program you now have and modify it to show the structure of its data on the screen, similarly to Figure 9.4. For some programs, it may take some effort to discover a displayable structure in the data; if so, this is clearly the first job in this project.

Chapter 10 Projects

1. Define a resource file format for various kinds of windows on character-mapped screens and, as in Chapter 3, adapt simple window-handling procedures to read the file and put up the windows appropriately. Extend the resource file concept to handle various kinds of windows.

2. Implement the alternate approach to text windows: handle a list of windows that are interpreted to provide the final display. Include the operations of displaying the windows, reordering them, resizing and moving them, and removing them.

3. Extend the curses string-input window program to handle input with your own input editing as described in Chapter 4.

4. Implement a curses window that incorporates a menu as discussed in Chapter 3.

5. Do as in project 4 for Microsoft Windows.

6. Do as in project 4 for the Macintosh toolbox.

7. Implement a dialog box in MacApp for the Macintosh with the following communication options:

   (a) Radio buttons

   (b) Check boxes

8. Choose a User Interface Management System and do as in projects 4 and 7 for this system.

Chapter 11 Projects

1. Scan several commercial software products to see what assistance they provide to the user. Make tables that list the following information:

- Manuals and other off-line aids, such as templates and pocket references,

- online learning aids,

- commercial books available to help the user,

- online learning tools,

- online help facilities.

Be especially careful to note what help is available at each point of the program. Typically, different helps are available at different points; what is the relation between the program function and the help information?

2. Again, with several commercial software products, what happens when you mis-type data or commands? What happens when you try to do file or printer operations when the device is not available? What do you find that you never want to see on your own products?

3. Take a small program and make it into a tutorial by providing predefined input and a window-type explanation of that input at each point where input is required.

Chapter 12 PROJECTS

1. Evaluate a given help system on a software product for the following users:

   (a) the audience you think the software was designed for.

   (b) a person who writes such software (for example, yourself).

   If the software is business-oriented:

   (c) an office worker who is relatively new on the job and has no real computer background,

   (d) an office worker who has several years' experience and has used a computer successfully before.

If the software is education-oriented:

(e) a student who is doing satisfactory but not outstanding work in the software's subject,

(f) a student who is doing very well in the subject.

2. Write a help file and a procedure to read a given piece of help from the file. Try several different approaches to the system:

   (a) Identify the help information with a keyword, and read the file for the keyword at the beginning of a line of the file.

   (b) Make the file with variable-length records, each containing a binary (and compressed) image of the text for a single help message. This would be produced by a program—a resource compiler. The help identifier is to be the integer index of the record.

3. Attempt to write help information for starting a balky car in the winter. Remember that help does not tell everything that must be done, but responds to particular points where someone may have problems. Assume that your audience is fluent in English but has no experience in the area; for example, a Californian might be caught in an Iowa snowstorm. In fact, you might think of your audience as someone from early in this century. Test your help on someone with a literal mind.

4. In Section 12.5 we limited our discussion of help systems for menus to providing a help screen for each menu. Using the menu systems developed in Chapter 3, build a help system that allows the user to highlight a menu item and, before actually selecting it, get help on the highlighted function by pressing a certain key (say, 'H'). Do this by having the help selection use the currently-selected value and branch to an appropriate help selection based on this value.

Chapter 13 PROJECTS

1. Implement "reasonableness checkers" as follows:

   (a) Check input for numeric-only entries, each of which is to have exactly two decimal places.

(b) Have a user input a name (first and last names), and match the input name against standard lists of first and last names. If the name does not match, allow the user to override the lists and say that a name is entered correctly.

(c) Check an address against three possible patterns:

A business pattern:
Department, Company, Street Address, City, State, Zip

An apartment pattern:
Street Address, Apt. No., Street Address, City, State, Zip

A home pattern:
Street Address, City, State, Zip

2. Add a feature to a command handler: when a command is not recognized, a list of all available commands with the same first letter is presented as a menu. If one of these is chosen, put up a one-line summary of the command's usage in a line at the bottom of the screen. Of course, more sophisticated choices of the commands to be listed can be substituted to make this more useful.

3. Investigate whether exceptions and exception handling are available on your system. If not, is there some way to redirect an error to an error-handler you write yourself instead of allowing a general halt? Is there anything like the BASIC statement ON ERROR ....?

4. Take two error situations you have encountered and write error handlers for them. Include at least the text of improved error messages; try to determine also what internal information the computer generates to handle the message and how to override the standard error handler so you can handle the error yourself.

5. Investigate the way you can get file size and access information from your operating system.

6. Investigate the way your system provides internal information on the kinds of devices that are on it. How can you get access to this information from within a program?

7. Write a device driver for a device one of your programs might use, and design an interface for the program so it could use this device or others to do its work.

Chapter 14 Projects

1. Adapt a small program of your own to be able to accept input from a range of devices, and write a configuration routine and configuration file to set up the program for a particular device.

2. If your system uses simultaneous keypresses to generate particular characters, write a replacement section in your input to allow users to enter sequential keystrokes, such as escape sequences, and return these particular characters to your system's input register.

3. Talk to your system vendor(s) to find out what kind of alternate devices are available for users with disabilities. Be sure to have them find out about third-party devices that will work with your system.

List of Color Plates and Illustrations

Color Plates

Color Plate 1: The same color appears different against different backgrounds. Albers, Plate IV-1, copyright 1963, Yale University Press, courtesy of the Josef Albers Foundation.

Color Plate 2: The same color appears different in different sized areas. Albers, Plate XVI-4, copyright 1963, Yale University Press, courtesy of the Josef Albers Foundation.

Color Plate 3: Two colors look the same. Albers, Plate VII-5, copyright 1963, Yale University Press, courtesy of the Josef Albers Foundation.

Color Plate 4: Compliments of Munsell Color, 2441 N. Calvert St., Baltimore, MD 21218.

Color Plate 5: Courtesy of Tektronix, Inc.

Color Plate 6: Courtesy of Tektronix, Inc.

Color Plate 7: Neutron star collision. Courtesy of the National Center for Supercomputing Applications.

Color Plate 8:   An Interactive Image installation. Courtesy of the Electronic Visualization Laboratory.

Color Plate 9:   An Interactive Image educational screen. Copyright 1987 Debra Weisblum Herschmann, courtesy of the Electronic Visualization Laboratory.

Color Plate 10: Noobie with a child. Courtesy of Allison Druin.

Color Plate 11: VIDEOPLACE user controlling the shape of a B-spline curve. Courtesy of Myron W. Kreuger, Artificial Reality Corporation.

Color Plate 12: A VIDEOPLACE image combined from two sources. Courtesy of Myron W. Kreuger, Artificial Reality Corporation.

Cover Slide: ICARE: Interactive Computer-Aided RGB Editor. Courtesy of Donna Cox, National Center for Supercomputing Applications, University of Illinois, Urbana-Champaign.

Illustrations

BIBLIOGRAPHY

Adobe Systems [1985]. *PostScript Language Reference Manual*. Reading, MA: Addison-Wesley.

Aho, Alfred and Jeffrey Ullman [1977]. *Principles of Compiler Design*. Reading, MA: Addison-Wesley.

Albers, Josef [1963]. *Interaction of Color*. New Haven: Yale University Press.

Apollo Computer [1988]. *Creating User Interfaces with Open Dialogue*. Chelmsford, MA: Apollo Computer.

Apple Computer [1985-87]. *Inside Macintosh: volumes 1-5*. Reading, MA: Addison-Wesley.

Apple Computer [1986]. *MacApp Reference Manual*. Cupertino, CA: Apple Computer.

Apple Computer [1987a]. *MPW Pascal 2.0.1 Reference Manual*. Cupertino, CA: Apple Computer.

Apple Computer [1987b]. *User Interface Guidelines: The Apple Desktop Interface*. Reading, MA: Addison-Wesley.

Apple Computer [1988]. *Design Principles for On-line Help*. Human Interface Design Guidelines Update #12, September, 1988.

Arden, Michelle, James Gosling, and David Rosenthal [1989]. *The NeWS Book*. New York: Springer-Verlag.

Arnold, Ken [1983]. *Using Curses Effectively.* Tutorial Notes. San Francisco: International Technical Seminars.

Baecker, Ronald A. and William A. S. Buxton, eds. [1987]. *Readings in Human-Computer Interaction.* Los Altos, CA: Morgan Kaufmann.

Badre, Albert and Ben Shneiderman (eds) [1982]. *Directions in Human/Computer Interaction.* Norwood, NJ: Ablex.

Beech, D. (ed) [1986]. *Concepts in User Interfaces.* Lecture Notes in Computer Science, New York: Springer-Verlag.

Bly, Sara A. and William R. Mallgren [1988]. "Cycling Softkeys". *IEEE Computer Graphics and Applications.* September, 1988.

Bly, Sara A. and Jarrett K. Rosenberg [1986]. "A Comparison of Tiled and Overlapped Windows". *Proceedings,* CHI '86 Conference. New York: ACM.

Brockmann, R. John [1986]. *Writing Better Computer User Documentation.* New York: Wiley.

Brown, C. Marlin [1988]. *Human-Computer Interface Design Guidelines.* Norwood, NJ: Ablex.

Brown, Maxine D. [1987]. "ICARE: Interactive Computer-Aided RGB Editor". *Access,* National Center for Supercomputing Applications, September-October, 1987.

Brown, Maxine D. [1988]. "Displays on Display: The Interactive Image". *IEEE Computer Graphics and Applications,* June, 1988.

Buxton, William and Ronald Baecker [1986]. *Human Computer Interaction: Selected Theories, Technologies, Techniques and Tools: Tutorial Notes.* New York: ACM/SIGGRAPH.

Calude, C. and S. Marcus [1985]. "Introduction to the Semiotics of Man-Computer Interaction". In M. Nadin (ed), *New Elements in the Semiotics of Communication.* Tübingen: Gunter Narr Verlag.

Card, Stuart K., Thomas P. Moran, and Allen Newell [1983]. *The Psychology of Human-Computer Interaction.* Hillsdale, NJ: Lawrence Erlbaum Associates.

Carey, Jane M. [1988]. *Human Factors in Management Information Systems.* Norwood, NJ: Ablex.

Carroll, John M., ed. [1987]. *Interfacing Human Thought: Cognitive Aspects of Human-Computer Interaction.* Cambridge, MA: MIT Press.

Comer, Douglas and Timothy Fossum [1988]. *Operating System Design: Volume I, The XINU Approach, PC Version*. Englewood Cliffs, NJ: Prentice-Hall.

Coats, R. B. and I. Vlaeminke [1987]. *Man-Computer Interfaces: An Introduction to Design and Implementation*. Palo Alto, CA: Blackwell Scientific Publications.

Cox, Brad J. [1986]. *Object-Oriented Programming: An Evolutionary Approach*. Reading, MA: Addison-Wesley.

DeFanti, Charles [1988]. "Hands-on Video: The Coming 'Interactive' Age". *Children's Video*, June, 1988.

Densmore, Owen M. and David S. H. Rosenthal [1987]. "A User Interface in Object Oriented PostScript". *Computer Graphics Forum*, September 1987, 171-179.

Dreyfuss, Henry [1955]. *Designing for People*. New York: Viking.

Druin, Allison [1988]. "NOOBIE: The Animal Design Playstation". *SIGCHI Bulletin*, October, 1988.

Dumas, Joseph [1988]. *Designing User Interfaces for Software*. Englewood Cliffs, NJ: Prentice-Hall.

Ehrich, R. W. and R. C. Williges [1986]. *Human-Computer Dialogue Design*. New York: Elsevier.

Enderle, G., K. Kansy, and G. Pfaff [1987]. *Computer Graphics Programming: GKS - The Graphics Standard*, 2nd revised edition. New York: Springer-Verlag.

Farrell, Jerry and Mike Schwartz [1988]. *User Interfaces in Window Systems: Architecture and Implementation: Tutorial Notes*. New York: ACM/SIGCHI.

Foley, James D. [1987]. "Interfaces for Advanced Computing". *Scientific American*. October, 1987.

Foley, James D. and John L. Sibert [1986]. *How to Design User-Computer Interfaces: Tutorial Notes*. New York: ACM/SIGGRAPH.

Foley, James D. and Andries van Dam [1982]. *Fundamentals of Interactive Computer Graphics*. Reading, MA: Addison-Wesley.

Galitz, Wilbert O. [1985]. *Handbook of Screen Format Design*, revised edition. Wellesley, MA: QED.

Goldberg, Adele [1984]. *Smalltalk-80: The Interactive Programming Environment*. Reading, MA: Addison-Wesley.

Goodman, Danny [1987]. *The Complete HyperCard Handbook.* New York: Bantam.

Grimes, Jack and Michael E. Atwood [1986]. *Advanced Topics — Human Factors in Computing Systems: Tutorial Notes.* New York: ACM/SIGGRAPH.

Greenberg, Donald, Aaron Marcus, Allan H. Schmidt and Vernon Gorter [1982]. *The Computer Image.* Reading, MA: Addison-Wesley.

Hartson, H. Rex and Deborah Hix (eds) [1985, 88]. *Advances in Human/Computer Interaction, Volume I; Volume II.* Norwood, NJ: Ablex.

Harrington, Steven [1987]. *Computer Graphics: A Programming Approach*, 2nd edition. New York: McGraw-Hill.

Heckel, Paul [1984]. *The Elements of Friendly Software Design.* New York: Warner Books.

Heines, Jesse M. [1984]. *Screen Design Strategies for Computer-Assisted Instruction.* Maynard, MA: Digital Press.

Hewlett-Packard [1988]. *HP NewWave General Information Manual for Software Developers.* Palo Alto, CA: Hewlett-Packard.

Hopgood, F. R. A. et.al. [1986a]. *Advances in Computer Graphics II.* New York: Springer-Verlag.

Hopgood, F. R. A. et. al. (eds) [1986b]. *Methodology of Window Management.* New York: Springer-Verlag.

Horowitz, Ellis and Sartaj Sahni [1976]. *Fundamentals of Data Structures.* Rockville, MD: Computer Science Press.

Jamsa, Kris [1987]. *Windows Programming Secrets.* New York: Osborne McGraw-Hill.

Jones, Oliver and Harry Hersh [1988]. *Introduction to Programming the X Window System, Version 11: Tutorial Notes.* New York: ACM/SIGGRAPH.

Kearsley, Greg [1988]. *Online Helps: Design and Implementation.* Norwood, NJ: Ablex.

Kearsley, Greg and Robin Halley [1986]. *Designing Interactive Software.* La Jolla, CA: Park Row Press.

Kelly, Derek A. [1983]. *Documenting Computer Application Systems: Concepts and Techniques.* New York: Petrocelli.

Kernighan, Brian and P. L. Plauger [1980]. *Software Tools*. Reading, MA: Addison-Wesley.

Kreuger, Myron W. [1983]. *Artificial Reality*. Reading, MA: Addison-Wesley.

Kreuger, Myron W. [1985]. "VIDEOPLACE: A Report from the ARTIFICIAL REALITY Laboratory". *Leonardo*, Vol. 1, No. 3, 1985.

Lee, Ed [1987]. "Window of Opportunity". *Unix Review*, June 1987, 47-61.

Leffler, Samuel J. [1987]. "A Window on the Future". *Unix Review*, June 1987.

Marcus, Aaron [1985]. "Tutorial: Users Must Establish Own Rules for Color". *Computer Graphics Today*, September, 1985.

Marcus, Aaron [1986]. "Tutorial: The Ten Commandments of Color". *Computer Graphics Today*, November, 1986.

Mathias, Henry and Patterson, Richard [1985]. *Electronic Cinematography*. Belmont, CA: Wadsworth.

Meads, Jon [1988]. "The Future of User Interface Management Systems". *Proceedings*, 1988 NCGA Conference. Fairfax, VA: NCGA.

Meyer, Bertrand [1988]. *Object-Oriented Software Construction*. Englewood Cliffs, NJ: Prentice-Hall.

Minsky, Margaret R. [1984]. "Manipulating Simulated Objects with Real-world Gestures Using a Force and Position Sensitive Screen". *Computer Graphics* (Proceedings of SIGGRAPH '84), July, 1984.

Monk, Andrew (ed) [1984]. *Fundamentals of Human-Computer Interaction*. New York: Academic Press.

Murch, Gerald [1984a]. "The Effective Use of Color: Physiological Principles". *Tekniques*, Tektronix, Inc., Volume 7, No. 4.

Murch, Gerald [1984b]. "The Effective Use of Color: Perceptual Principles". *Tekniques*, Tektronix, Inc., Volume 8, No. 1.

Murch, Gerald [1984c]. "The Effective Use of Color: Cognitive Principles". *Tekniques*, Tektronix, Inc., Volume 8, No. 2.

Murch, Gerald [1985]. "Effectuve Use of Color in Graphics Displays". *Handshake*, Volume 9, No. 2.

Murch, Gerald [1987]. "Human Factors of Color Displays". In *Color in Computer Graphics: Tutorial Notes*. New York: ACM/ SIGGRAPH.

Myers, Brad A. [1988]. "A Taxonomy of Window Manager User Interfaces". *IEEE Computer Graphics and Applications*, September, 1988.

Nickerson, Raymond S. [1986]. *Using Computers — Human Factors in Information Systems*. Springfield, OH: Bradford Books.

Norman, Donald A. and Stephen Draper (eds) [1986]. *User Centered System Design*. Hillsdale, NJ: Lawrence Erlbaum.

Norman, Donald A. [1988]. *The Psychology of Everyday Things*. New York: Basic Books.

Patterson, Gerald [1988]. *Tutorial: Object-Oriented Programming, Volume 1: Concepts, Volume 2: Implementations*. Washington, DC: Computer Society Press, 1988.

PC Magazine [1987]. "Internal Error Handling in PC-DOS". *PC Magazine*, PC Lab Notes, November 10, 1987.

Peterson, Ivars [1985]. "Artificial Reality". *Science News*, Vol. 127, 1985.

Petzold, Charles [1988]. *Programming Windows*. Redmond, WA: Microsoft Press.

Pfaff, G. E. (ed) [1985]. *User Interface Management Systems*. New York: Springer-Verlag.

Rasmussen, Jens [1986]. *Information Processing and Human-Machine Interaction*. New York: Elsevier.

Rochkind, Marc J. [1988]. *Advanced C Programming for Displays*. Englewood Cliffs, NJ: Prentice-Hall.

Rosenthal, David S. H. [1988]. "A Simple X11 Client Program, or How Hard Can it Really Be to Write 'Hello, World'?". *Proceedings*, Winter 1988 USENIX Conference.

Rubenstein, Richard and Harry Hersh [1984]. *The Human Factor*. Maynard, MA: Digital Press.

Schwartz, Michael, William Cowan and John Beatty [1987]. "An Experimental Comparison of RGB, YIQ, LAB, HSV, and Opponent Color Models". ACM *Transactions on Graphics*, April, 1987.

Schiefler, Robert W. and Jim Gettys [1986]. "The X Window System". ACM *Transactions on Graphics*, April, 1986.

Schiefler, Robert W., James Gettys, and Ron Newman [1989]. *X Window System: C Library and Protocol Reference*. Maynard, MA: Digital Press.

Schmid, Calvin F and Stanton E. Schmid [1979]. *Handbook of Graphics Presentation*, 2nd edition. New York: Wiley.

Schmucker, Kurt J. [1986]. *Object-Oriented Programming for the Macintosh*. Hasbrouck Heights, NJ: Hayden.

Schmucker, Kurt [1988]. "Using Objects to Package User Interface Functionality". *Journal of Object-Oriented Programming*, April/May, 1988.

Shneiderman, Ben [1980]. *Software Psychology*. Cambridge, MA: Winthrop.

Shneiderman, Ben [1987]. *Designing the User Interface*. Reading, MA: Addison-Wesley.

Shu, Nan C. [1988]. *Visual Programming*. New York: Van Nostrand Reinhold.

Sime, M. E. and M. J. Coombs (eds) [1983]. *Designing for Human-Computer Communication*. New York: Academic Press.

Simpson, Henry [1985a]. *Programming the Macintosh User Interface*. New York: Byte/McGraw-Hill.

Simpson, Henry [1985b]. *Programming the IBM PC User Interface*. New York: Byte/McGraw-Hill.

Smith, Randall B. [1986]. "The Alternate Reality Kit: An Animated Environment for Creating Interactive Simulations". *Proceedings*, 1986 IEEE Computer Society Workshop on Visual Languages. Washington, DC: Computer Society Press.

Smith, Randall B. [1987]. "Experiences with the Alternate Reality Kit: An Example of the Tension Between Literalism and Magic". *IEEE Computer Graphics and Applications*, September, 1987.

Smith, Wanda and Joyce Farrell [1987]. "The Ergonomics of Enhancing user Performance with Color Displays". In *Color in Computer Graphics: Tutorial Notes*. ACM/SIGGRAPH.

Smith, Wanda [1987a]. "Multicolor Displays for Office Environments". In *Color in Computer Graphics: Tutorial Notes*. New York: ACM/SIGGRAPH.

Smith, Wanda [1987b]. "Computer Color and Psychophysics: Task Application and Aesthetics". In *Color in Computer Graphics: Tutorial Notes*. New York: ACM/SIGGRAPH.

Steinhart, Jonathon E. [1988]. *Introduction to Window Management: Tutorial Notes*. New York: ACM/SIGGRAPH.

Stoustrop, Bjarne [1986]. *The C++ Programming Language*. Reading, MA: Addison-Wesley.

Strang, John [1985]. *Programming with Curses*. Newton, MA: O'Reilly and Associates.

Sun Microsystems [1986]. *NeWS Preliminary Technical Overview*. Mountain View, CA: Sun Microsystems.

Taylor, Joanne M., Gerald M. Murch, and Paul A. McManus [1988]. "Tektronix HVC: A Uniform Perceptual Color System for Display Users". *Proceedings*, Society for Information Display, Vol. 29.

Taylor, Joanne and Jerry Murch [1988]. "The User Interface of Color: A New Model for Computer Color Graphics". *Tekniques*, Tektronix, Inc., Volume 11, Number 1.

Team Engineering [1988]. *TIGER User Interface ToolKit Technical Summary*. Santa Cruz, CA: Team Engineering.

Teitelman, Warren [1988]. "OPEN LOOK: A User Interface". In Grimes, Jack. *User Interface Considerations of Windowing Systems: Tutorial Notes*, New York:ACM/SIGGRAPH.

Thomas, John and Michael L. Schneider (eds) [1984]. *Human Factors in Computer Systems*. Norwood, NJ: Ablex.

Townsend, Carl [1988]. *C Programmer's Guide to Microsoft Windows 2.0*. Indianapolis, IN: Howard W. Sams.

Tufte, Edward R. [1983]. *The Visual Display of Quantitative Information*. Cheshire, CT: Graphics Press.

Utz, Peter [1985]. "Color Aesthetics". *AV Video*, November, 1985.

Varley, Helen (ed.) [1980]. *Color*. Los Angeles: Marshall Editions Limited, The Knapp Press.

Vassiliou, Yannis (ed) [1984]. *Human Factors and Interactive Computer Systems*. Norwood, NJ: Ablex.

Verriest, G., I. Andrew, and A. Urichjla [1985]. *Multicolor Visual Display Unit of Color-Defective and Normal Trichromatic Subjects*. IBM Technical Report 12.241. Armonk, NY: IBM.

Whitewater Group [1987]. *Introducing Actor*. Evanston, IL: The Whitewater Group.

Williams, Tom [1988]. "Input Technologies Extend the Scope of User Involvement". *Computer Design*, March 1, 1988.

INDEX

Abaton, 19
ACM SIGCAPH, 314
ACM SIGCHI, 13
ACM SIGGRAPH, 13
Actor, 259
  objects in, 259
alarm, 128
Albers, Josef, 162
alerts, 10, 153, 213, 226
algebraic notation, 98
Alternate Reality Kit, 186, 192
  objects in, 195
anarchist, 207
Andrew, 241
ANSI X3.64, 44
Apollo, 263
Apple Computer, 19, 314
Apple II, 22, 296, 305
AppleWorks, 27, 39, 41, 276, 284, 307, 315
apropos command, 274
ARK, 186, 192
arrow key, 41, 108, 318
artificial reality, 193
Artificial Reality Corporation, 201
ASCII, 322
AT&T, 255
attention focus, 151
audible signal, 324
AutoCAD, 37
Bezold effect, 163
BIOS, 322

bitmap, 222, 239
  display, 152, 236
  screen, 222
blank space, 118, 120
body, used to control computer, 201
Borland International, 106, 138
Bourne shell, 62
Bowers, Steve, 130, 142
braille, 319, 321
Burns, Fran, 132
button, 191, 215
C shell, 62
C++, 190, 263
calculated fields, 83
Callihan, Hubert, 305
case, upper/lower, 117
category heading, 124
CH Products, 20
charts, color in, 159
client, 190, 210
CloseView, 320
color, 116, 128, 157, 321
  adjacent colors, 162
  background, 158, 162
  "blindness", 323
  charts and graphs, in, 159
  chroma, 165, 167
  CIE, 167
  CMY model, 166
  CNS model, 168
  coding, 158, 181, 323